From Harvard
to the
Ranks of Labor

Robert Bussel

From Harvard to the Ranks of Labor

Powers Hapgood and the American Working Class

The Pennsylvania State University Press
University Park, Pennsylvania

Library of Congress Cataloging-in-Publication Data

Bussel, Robert, 1951–
    From Harvard to the ranks of labor : Powers Hapgood and the
American working class / Robert Bussel.
        p.   cm.
    Includes bibliographical references and index.
    ISBN 0-271-01897-6 (cloth : alk. paper)
    ISBN 0-271-01898-4 (pbk. : alk. paper)
    1. Hapgood, Powers, 1899–1949.   2. Labor leaders—United States—
Biography.   3. Social reformers—United States—Biography.
    4. Labor movement—United States—History.   5. Trade-unions—United
States—History.   6. Working class—United States—History.   I. Title.
HD8073.H27B87   1999
331.88′092—dc21
[B]   98-41426
                                                                         CIP

Copyright © 1999 The Pennsylvania State University
All rights reserved
Printed in the United States of America
Published by The Pennsylvania State University Press,
University Park, PA 16802-1003

It is the policy of The Pennsylvania State University Press to use acid-free
paper for the first printing of all clothbound books. Publications on uncoated
stock satisfy the minimum requirements of American National Standard for
Information Sciences—Permanence of Paper for Printed Library Materials,
ANSI Z39.48-1992.

Frontispiece. Powers Hapgood during his Harvard years. (Courtesy of Lilly
Library, Indiana University)

To the memory of my father-in-law,
Albert Nelson

Contents

Illustrations

Acknowledgments

During the research and writing of this book, I have received support and encouragement from many sources. It is my pleasure to thank both old friends and new benefactors for their interest and assistance.

Several institutions provided funding for the archival research that became the foundation of this book. During graduate school I benefited from a McVoy Fellowship at Cornell University and a Mellon Foundation Fellowship that enabled me to complete the dissertation stage of the project. A grant from the Indiana Historical Society funded my initial trip to Lilly Library at Indiana University where the Powers Hapgood Papers are located. Additional research was supported by a Kaiser Travel Grant from the Walter P. Reuther Library at Wayne State University and funding from the Research and Graduate Studies Office of the College of Liberal Arts at Penn State University.

I am deeply indebted to a group of archivists, teachers, and history buffs who were unfailingly generous with their time and astute in their guidance. I am especially grateful to Saundra Taylor and the staff at Lilly Library for helping me navigate the Powers Hapgood and Columbia Conserve Company collections. They handled my many requests with kindness and professionalism and provided a supportive environment in which to work. At Indiana University of Pennsylvania, Eileen Cooper was a wise and reliable guide to the District 2 United Mine Workers of America collection. I also received invaluable assistance and warm hospitality during my stay from Irwin Marcus and Elizabeth Ricketts, who allowed me to tap their vast knowledge of mine workers' history and politics in District 2. Bob Branham of Bates College

graciously shared interviews and documents compiled during his research for a film on the 1937 shoe workers' strike in Maine that enabled
me to recreate Powers Hapgood's role in that important event. Denise
Conklin shepherded me through the United Mine Workers' archives at
Penn State University, while Richard Strassburg and his staff at
Cornell University's Labor-Management Documentation Center ably
assisted my examination of Rose Pesotta's papers.

Powers Hapgood's daughter, Barta Monro, shared memories of her
father that deepened my appreciation of the meaning of family in his
life. Steve Hendrickson at the Indiana AFL-CIO granted me access to
files on the Indiana CIO that helped me to understand the latter years
of Hapgood's career. Through Alice Mills, I was introduced to Alan
Bassett, whose father, Edgar, became one of Powers Hapgood's friends
during his trip to Wales in 1925. Mr. Bassett offered much useful
information on Welsh coal miners and their culture. Most important, in
exposing me to a group of people who have devotedly honored the
achievements and struggles of their parents' generation, he provided a
sense of historical memory and cultural transmission that gave my
work new meaning.

Peter Potter at Penn State Press believed in this project from the
beginning and led a first-time author through the publication process
with the utmost capability and courtesy. Irwin Marcus and Alan Singer
served as readers for the manuscript and offered many valuable suggestions that have found their way into the final version of this book. I
am also grateful to Daniel Leab at *Labor History* and Thomas McCraw
at *Business History Review* for permitting me to use materials contained in articles that appeared in their publications.

Colleagues and coworkers at Penn State University have been generous with their assistance. Alan Derickson gave the manuscript a
careful reading, and his sound advice sharpened both my prose and my
argument. At the Labor History Workshop coordinated by Daniel
Letwin, I received many useful suggestions on improving the early
chapters of the manuscript. I owe Howard Harris, my fellow labor
educator, an enormous debt. He not only encouraged me to sustain my
effort but unselfishly volunteered to lighten my workload, thereby
providing me with much-needed time to reflect and write. My former
administrative assistant, Donna Woodruff, cheerfully tolerated my
obsession with Powers Hapgood and skillfully proofread earlier ver-
sions of the manuscript. My current assistant, Peggy Wright, provided
consistent support during the hectic final weeks of revision and rewrit-
ing. Finally, the library staff at Penn State Great Valley processed my
many interlibrary loan requests with efficiency and patience.

During my graduate years at Cornell University, Yong Chen, John Fousek, Lorena Oropeza, Jim Siekmeier, and Sayuri Shimizu, enriched my perspective and functioned as true friends and colleagues. My teachers at Cornell were also instrumental in aiding my personal and professional development. Michael Kammen convinced an uncertain graduate student returning to school after a thirteen-year hiatus that he would be able to learn the craft of writing history. Richard Polenberg and Larry Moore first kindled my interest in American history some thirty years ago and provided me with wise counsel throughout the research and writing of my dissertation. I am especially indebted to Nick Salvatore for his friendship, loyalty, and insight. He has watched this project develop through its various incarnations, critically read innumerable drafts, and held me to high standards. He knew when to give me rope and when to rein me in. Above all, he has taught me that it is possible to combine personal commitment with scholarly integrity, a sensibility that I have attempted to incorporate in this book.

Bruce Smith has been my closest friend for nearly thirty years. He helped me make the transition from activism to the academy and has permitted me time and again to draw on his keen insights into politics and history. As a result of our many conversations, I began to rethink old assumptions and arrive at new understandings. From him, I have learned much about fraternity and democracy, not as abstract concepts but as living ideals forged in the shared experience of friendship and political commitment.

My family has been integrally involved in this project from the outset. My father and stepmother, Norman and Melanie Bussel, and my aunt, Fay Marker, are all writers, and I am grateful for both their encouragement and editorial suggestions. My mother, Ricky Bussel, has also offered staunch support and sound advice throughout.

My daughter Lily's often-asked dinner table question—"Daddy, is your book done yet?"—was both a welcome expression of interest and a not-so-subtle admonition to keep working! My wife, Jewel Nelson, has been both my strongest booster and toughest critic. With her artist's eye, she has helped me understand the importance of the small detail, and her passionate insistence on "getting it right" has inspired this work at every turn. Her companionship, wit, and love have enriched both my work and my life.

My father-in-law, Albert Nelson, took a profound interest in the progress of my work. A true intellectual and a man of conviction, he taught me much about the meaning of character, craftsmanship, and principle. It is to his memory and spirit that I dedicate this book.

Introduction

After ten years as a labor union organizer, I began the study of history in order to examine the assumptions that had inspired me to become a political activist and to place my experiences within a larger context. Having witnessed firsthand the reluctance of workers to organize, the hostile environment in which unions were forced to operate, and labor's difficulties in formulating a strategic response, I felt the need to step back from the field of battle and gain some perspective on these troubling developments.

My reflections coincided with the labor movement's struggles during the 1980s as it contended with the decline of liberalism and the resurgence of conservatism. As a result, I became particularly interested in understanding how an earlier generation of union activists and radicals had coped with similar circumstances. Conventional wisdom suggested that the fate of labor radicals was either involuntary displacement to the margins or reluctant absorption into the mainstream. I wondered, though, if the experience of these activists might have been more complex and revealing than this simple dichotomy suggested. My search for an answer to this question led me to Powers Hapgood.

I first encountered Powers Hapgood in Irving Howe's essay collection, *Socialism and America*. One of the key figures in Howe's discussion of socialism during the 1930s, Hapgood was described as a Harvard graduate from a distinguished liberal family who went on to devote his life to the labor movement and radical politics. Intrigued by Howe's description of an activist who struggled to reconcile his loyalties to both socialism and trade unionism, I recognized tensions that in a different context had surfaced during my own tenure in the labor movement. As I delved into the extensive archival record that Powers Hapgood left behind, I uncovered a fascinating political odyssey that spanned the Progressive era, the New Deal, and the beginnings of the cold war. Hapgood participated in some of the most stirring historical events of his time—an epic 1922 coal miners' strike in western Pennsylvania, an insurgent attempt to oust John L. Lewis as president of the United Mine Workers of America (UMWA), the defense of Nicola Sacco and Bartolomeo Vanzetti, and the electrifying victories of sit-down strikers in Akron, Ohio, and Flint, Michigan. His circle of friends and acquaintances included some of America's best-known reformers and activists as well as working people whom he had encountered in a variety of venues. Hapgood faithfully recorded his experiences, leaving behind a rich chronicle of the American working class, the labor movement, and the practice of radical politics. Moreover, Hapgood did not simply narrate his impressions of what he saw. His journals were a continuing reflection on his interactions with intellectuals, workers, labor leaders, and managers as he attempted to make sense of his experience and adapt to the changing cultural and political circumstances that occurred during his career.

Nonetheless, Powers Hapgood has been regarded primarily as a historical footnote. He was neither the architect of policy, the leader of a recognized constituency, nor a political thinker of discernible influence. Most often, he appears in connection with a chorus of critics who unsuccessfully challenged John L. Lewis's rule of the UMWA and later reconciled with him to help build the industrial union movement. Hapgood has also received attention for his role in the Socialist Party, but his stature certainly did not match that of a Eugene Debs or a Norman Thomas. Why, then, devote a biography to a man who was a bit player or at best a supporting actor in a historical drama where others played much more prominent roles?

Powers Hapgood's greatest significance derives from his ability to illuminate the experience of an important social group: middle-class liberals, reformers, and intellectuals who embraced the working class and the labor movement. This relationship has a long and complex history. Throughout the nineteenth century, middle-class reformers often supported and participated in workers' efforts to preserve republican values, limit special privilege, and ensure equal opportunity. Inspired by images of the "cooperative commonwealth" and solidarity among producers that countered the dominant cultural ideology of laissez-faire and social Darwinism, reformers perceived the labor movement as an indispensable defender of the nation's democratic, egalitarian traditions. This alliance grew closer during the Progressive era, as many liberals saw a strong labor movement as the best hope for offsetting the power wielded by large corporations. Later, those influenced by Marxism envisioned an even greater role for the working class as an agent of revolutionary change and sought more direct participation in the struggles of workers. Especially during the 1930s with the rise of the New Deal and industrial unionism, it was possible for both liberals and radicals to regard the labor movement as the conscience of America and a powerful voice for industrial and political democracy. Although the ties among liberals, the labor movement, and the working class have grown less intimate since World War II, recent attempts to revive the relationship attest to its continuing importance and potential.

This relationship mattered deeply to a small but visible segment of Powers Hapgood's generation. The conduct of corporate capitalism disturbed this group of young people from middle- and upper-middleclass backgrounds. They deplored the human cost of industrialism and the social disruption that accompanied increasing concentrations of wealth and power. Whether influenced by the prophetic tradition of liberal Protestantism, the visionary aspirations of Jewish socialism, reform-minded college professors, or reports of social injustice that they encountered in liberal journals, these young people were outraged by the company town, the sweatshop, and the tenement. Their willingness to act on these convictions varied and is impossible to quantify. Nonetheless, whether out of guilt, humanitarianism, religious conviction, or political commitment, a generational group emerged during the first half of the twentieth century that avidly supported the struggles of working people and extended its loyalty to the labor movement. This group played a crucial role in helping the twentieth-century American labor movement to shape public opinion, influence policy makers, and gain acceptance as a legitimate social actor.

Powers Hapgood provides important insights into this generational experience. His impeccable credentials—a Harvard education, membership in a family of muckraking journalists and advocates of industrial democracy, work as a coal miner and involvement in the United Mine Workers of America, participation in dramatic campaigns for workers' rights and civil liberties—won him widespread admiration and respect as an emblem of courage and social commitment. To be sure, few of Hapgood's contemporaries committed themselves to the working class with his fervor and intensity. Nonetheless, his career reflected both the expectations and the qualms that liberals brought to their encounters with workers and unions. Like many of his cohorts, Hapgood was both inspired and confounded by the working class, and his conflicting attitudes were inseparable from the profound personal needs that attracted him to the labor movement. His attempts to resolve these conflicts broaden our understanding of not only his contemporaries but also succeeding generations of intellectuals and activists who have looked to the working class and the labor movement as a source of personal inspiration and political fulfillment.

Powers Hapgood's career must also be considered in the context of changing historiography on the New Deal, American liberalism, and industrial unionism. Until the last decade, historians tended either to celebrate the ability of the New Deal to create alternatives to radicalism or criticize New Deal reformers for coopting popular militancy and thwarting the possibilities for more far-reaching change. Recent scholarship has rejected these views as too confining and taken a more nuanced approach. By examining how different segments of the working class (women, African-Americans, ethnic workers, local unionists) and their leaders interpreted and attempted to shape both New Deal liberalism and the industrial union movement, we are gaining a clearer picture of this crucial historical engagement. Working-class mobilization during this period encompassed an array of complex interactions: defining the relation between a resurgent labor movement and the Democratic Party; approaching the new state apparatus that emerged to govern labor relations; determining how power and authority would be allocated between leaders and the rank and file in the new industrial unions; and dealing with issues of race, gender, and ethnicity that conflicted with the CIO's attempt to create a class-based political coalition. In subjecting these intricate transactions to closer scrutiny, scholars have deepened our understanding of how workers and their allies negotiated a new American social contract.

My study of Powers Hapgood both reflects and attempts to enlarge upon this historiography. Although recent scholarship has astutely identified the complexities and tensions that accompanied the forging of a new social contract, it still appears that most liberals and radicals made their peace with the New Deal, accommodated the industrial order that was crafted during World War II, and accepted a limited role for trade unions. Powers Hapgood resisted this scenario. Part of his historical significance derives from his status as a rare public voice who questioned the direction of the industrial union movement and New

Deal liberalism. Expressing his reservations regarding labor's course, Hapgood attempted to articulate a more ambitious labor strategy that incorporated the legacy of an older dissent tradition. He sought to develop alternatives to centralized union governance, cautioned against too entangling an alliance between labor and the state, foresaw the consequences of cold war attacks on civil liberties, and recognized racism as the issue that would determine the fate of both American labor and the American polity. As an eloquent exponent of the road not taken, Hapgood offers key insights into the character of labor radicalism, the prospects for union democracy, and the possibilities for political independence during the formative years of industrial unionism.

Powers Hapgood's lengthy and unusual relationship with working people also affirms the significance of his career. Over the course of two decades, he encountered the American working class in all its diversity—Eastern European coal miners in western Pennsylvania, native-born clothing workers in Kentucky, Irish textile workers in Massachusetts, French-Canadian shoe workers in Maine. In Indiana, he spent three years alongside rank-and-file employees at his father's experiment in workers' management and ownership. Nor were his encounters confined to American soil. During the 1920s, Hapgood's travels took him to England, Germany, France, and the Soviet Union, where he worked in coal mines, lived in mining towns, and observed the operation of the European labor movement.

Hapgood's experiences provide an unusual glimpse into the relationship between the union organizer and the worker. He saw how workers labored and how they lived. He met their children and their families. In tavern, worksite, front-porch, and parlor conversations, he learned about their hopes and frustrations. These encounters revealed broad fluctuations in attitude between fraternity and individualism, loyalty to the working class and the desire to escape it, transcendent visions of worker solidarity and parochial attachments to ethnicity, community, and faith. Confronting these tensions, Hapgood searched for language, imagery, and symbolism that would inspire workers to mobilize and develop alternatives to the dominant culture of individualism and acquisitiveness. Because Hapgood reflected on his interactions with working people in rich detail, we are able learn much about how individual workers reacted to his attempts at persuasion and made decisions regarding their participation in the labor movement, their role in the employment relationship, and their involvement in community life. For Hapgood, the working class was not an abstraction, and it is the insights gained from his close encounters with working people that make his career both personally and historically compelling.

In addition to his relationships with working people, his attempts to reshape industrial unionism, and his role as an emissary to the working class, Powers Hapgood's life exemplifies important aspects of the American middle-class experience. The middle class has alternately been praised as the bulwark of a stable American democracy and criticized as complacent, distant, and self-absorbed. These criticisms accelerated during the late nineteenth century as American society turned more corporate, bureaucratic, and consumer-oriented, and middle-class Americans began to feel overwhelmed by the advent of mass society. Although the extent of its anxiety should not be exaggerated, it is clear that the American middle class has often suffered from uncertainty and questioned its purported attainment of "the good life."

Powers Hapgood spent much of his life grappling with the dilemmas that faced the American middle class. Born at the dawn of the twentieth century, he was imbued with the moral and ethical values that guided much of the nineteenth-century middle class in its behavior. Hapgood remained loyal to these values and to an unusual degree persisted in attempting to inject them into public settings. Rebelling against what he regarded as the shortcomings of middle-class life, his efforts assumed many forms: the quest for meaningful work, the search for attachment and fraternity, the assertion of his masculinity, and the attempt to align private need and public commitment. Although few in the middle class attempted to resolve these issues as publicly as Hapgood, they certainly recognized the dissatisfactions that drove his restless searching. Indeed, explaining the interplay between the public and private spheres, a tension that was familiar to both Powers Hapgood and the American middle class, has led me to enter and speculate about his interior world. Although I have resisted the temptation to psychologize, I have attempted to understand the complex ways in which personal imperatives influenced his political choices and his public career.

The appeal of Powers Hapgood is perhaps best conveyed, however, by the vehicle of personal reminiscence. The writer Kurt Vonnegut once met Hapgood in Indianapolis following World War II and was fascinated by the wonderful stories that the labor activist told about his experiences. He recalled the impact of this encounter years later in the introduction to his book *Jailbird:* "I have always been enchanted by brave veterans like Powers Hapgood, and some others, who were still eager for information of what was really going on, who were still full of ideas of how victory might yet be snatched from the jaws of defeat." Vonnegut concluded, "If I am going to go on living, I had better follow them."[1]

Of necessity, the historian's judgments must be more critical than those of the novelist. Nonetheless, at a time when the labor movement is showing signs of resurgence and liberals are expressing renewed interest in labor as an agent of social change, Kurt Vonnegut's recollection captures well the passionate spirit of Powers Hapgood's personal odyssey and the relevance of his story for our times.

Chapter One

"A Sincere Consuming Quest for a Faith"

College bred men should be agitators to tear a
question open and riddle it with light and to
educate the moral sense of the masses.
—Wendell Phillips

Powers Hapgood had deep roots in the American past. His ancestors'
lives both paralleled and reflected important developments in the
evolution of the young republic, leaving him a rich legacy that would
profoundly shape his identity and influence his political choices.

When Powers Hapgood's uncle and aunt set out to trace the genealogy of the Hapgood family, they entitled their volume *The History of an
American Family*. Their decision to write a family history was not
unusual. Tracing and even publishing family genealogy was a widespread practice among upper-middle-class Americans who felt threatened by the late nineteenth- and early twentieth-century influx of
European immigrants from unfamiliar points of origin. For Hutchins
Hapgood and Neith Boyce, however, their enterprise was neither a
defensive attempt to affirm family status nor an elitist assertion of
superiority. Rather, they sought to document the Hapgoods' enduring
connections to the American past, perhaps aiming to legitimize the
family's iconoclasm as firmly rooted in American soil.

The first family member to arrive in the New World was Shadrach
Hapgood, a Puritan who left England for Massachusetts in 1656 and

was killed by Indians in Brookfield, Massachusetts, in 1675. Other relatives fought in the Revolutionary War and against Shays's Rebellion, while Jonathan Grout, the grandfather of Powers Hapgood's great-grandfather Seth Hapgood, was a member of the first Federal and Continental congresses. The family moved from farming into business during the nineteenth century, with Seth becoming a state legislator and the respected president of a local bank in Petersham, Massachusetts. His 1864 obituary lauded his "useful and virtuous life" and also cited his "patriotism and loyalty" on behalf of the Union cause during the Civil War. At the time of his death, Seth Hapgood was reportedly advising a widow about her business affairs and was praised as a "counselor of the entire community" whose services were readily available and freely dispensed. Seth and his ancestors epitomized Alexis de Tocqueville's concept of American citizenship with their abiding commitments to public life, civic participation, and face-to-face relationships among social equals. The identities of citizen and patriot, embodying notions of public service and personal sacrifice, became an integral feature of the family's legacy and were faithfully passed from one generation of Hapgoods to the next. A willingness to stand alone against the crowd was also a Hapgood trait: Jonathan Grout had been the only northern legislator to vote against Alexander Hamilton's banking plan, and another ancestor had been one of the few Democrats in his Massachusetts town during the Civil War.[1]

Seth's son Charles was Powers Hapgood's grandfather. After graduating from Brown University with a law degree, he became one of the first Hapgoods to move west, making his way to Chicago in 1860 and establishing himself as a successful businessman. In 1871, after the Chicago fire destroyed his dry goods business, Charles went to St. Louis, only to be victimized again by a blaze that leveled his thriving farm equipment company. Subsequently, he relocated to Alton, Illinois, where he was able to reestablish his business and gain a measure of economic security. In his autobiography, Charles's son Hutchins described his parents as exiles set adrift by nature's fickle hand and deprived of a secure sense of social place. Whereas the family occupied a prominent position in their community in Massachusetts, Hutchins portrayed Alton as a small town devoid of culture and public spiritedness where Charles Hapgood had become, against his will, a mere "economic man." In response to his misfortunes, Charles embraced a stern Victorian morality anchored in "honesty, industry, exactness, and punctuality."[2]

As a disciple of the noted American agnostic and social critic Robert

Ingersoll, Charles was skeptical of religious faith. Hutchins Hapgood later complained of receiving no "spiritual support" from his father, who adopted the secular, Protestant virtues of the nineteenth-century middle class—self-discipline, self-improvement, service to others—in constructing the moral code that guided his life. Despite his own business success, Charles disdained inordinate or ostentatious wealth and exhorted his children to prove their moral worth through social service. Late in his life, he lamented that the hard circumstances of making a living had inhibited him from contributing to the public weal, regretfully characterizing himself as a "link between generations of merit" and one who had failed to uphold the exacting standards established by his forebears. Charles's dilemma presented itself as both an inspiration—the family's historic adherence to values of citizenship and service—and a test—whether or not the younger generation of Hapgoods could match or surpass the achievements of their predecessors. Both Charles's sons and later his grandson, Powers, would face the challenge of how to best maintain these values and defend the family's heritage in a changing social environment. By all accounts, Charles's three sons accepted this challenge, although each chose different vehicles through which to fulfill his father's high expectations.[3]

Charles's sons—Norman, Hutchins, and William—rose to prominence during the Progressive era. In addition to absorbing their father's strict morality, their education coincided with emerging Progressive criticism of the new corporate state's corrosive impact on older values of community, responsibility, and thrift. Between 1886 and 1894, at least one Hapgood was in attendance at Harvard, where they were exposed to a community of learning that questioned dominant cultural values and urged students to work for social betterment. Hutchins later extolled Harvard as the place where the Hapgoods reclaimed their heritage amid "men of real culture and power" after their unedifying sojourn in Alton. During their sons' matriculation, Charles and his wife, Fanny, actually moved from Alton to Cambridge, further testifying to the meaning of Harvard for a family separated from its past and mired in Midwestern exile.[4]

After college, Norman spurned his father's advice that he become a lawyer and along with Hutchins chose journalism as a career. He first assumed the editorship of *Collier's* and later *Harper's,* where he wrote muckraking exposés of corporate malfeasance and championed Louis Brandeis's ideas of restoring competition via government intervention and the encouragement of cooperative enterprises. Norman also joined other Progressives in endorsing scientific management as a guarantor of industrial efficiency and workplace harmony. In journeying from muckraking to Progressivism, he sensed the limits of public exposure and turned to politics and the application of technical expertise as the best means of preserving his father's values.[5]

In contrast to his more sober, respectable brother, Hutchins became "the personification of the bohemian intellectual." The most rebellious of Charles Hapgood's sons, he was attracted to the exotic outcasts of New York's Lower East Side and wrote popular books (*The Spirit of the Ghetto, The Spirit of Labor*) on Jewish immigrants, the labor movement, and anarchism. In his beloved outcasts, Hutchins found an authenticity that he saw as lacking within the comfortable middle class. The "spiritual and the sensual" fascinated Hutchins, who was cool to the political and technocratic side of Progressivism that his brother Norman found so appealing. Yet for all his attraction to outcasts and his close association with Mabel Dodge Luhan's Greenwich Village salons, Hutchins entitled his autobiography *A Victorian in the Modern World,* underscoring that he had by no means abandoned his father's rigorous conception of middle-class morality. Ultimately, the demanding requirements of being a Hapgood overwhelmed Hutchins, who opted for private pleasure and personal fulfillment in contrast to the public commitments that occupied his brothers.[6]

William, Powers Hapgood's father, was the youngest of Charles's children. With some disdain Hutchins recalled his younger brother as a sickly child who was pampered and overprotected. Like Theodore Roosevelt, William overcame his youthful infirmities through the pursuit of a strenuous life characterized by physically demanding outdoor activities. Unlike his brothers who remained in the East and pursued literary careers, William duplicated his father's course by returning to the Midwest and going into business. One acquaintance recalled that "Billy was always the practical man of the family. . . . Hutch and Norman liked to talk rather than live their ideas." Hutchins observed in his autobiography that his father looked to William to be the family success, since his other sons had opted for the uncertain fortunes of journalism. More robust and less introspective than his brothers, William worked for a wholesale grocery business in Chicago following his graduation from Harvard. After nearly a decade there, he found himself discomfited by Chicago's size and disorderliness and wanted the opportunity to run his own business. With the financial backing of his father, William purchased in 1903 a small cannery in Indianapolis that later became known as the Columbia Conserve Company.[7]

It was thirteen years before the company turned a profit, and William was forced to rely on his father's resources during this lean period. Then, buoyed by the business's new stability, he decided to turn Columbia into a worker-controlled enterprise, a venture that his family came to describe as "the experiment." Although the exact origins of William's decision remain uncertain, it appears he was influenced by several considerations. Like his brothers, he was imbued with his father's exhortation to render social service. Through Norman and Hutchins, William had been exposed to the innovative social thinking of the Progressive era, which sought to reduce conflict between labor and capital while retaining the benefits of industrial growth. But in contrast to his brothers, William was determined to implement democracy rather than merely publicize its shortcomings, a preference not lost upon his only son.[8]

Perhaps the most significant clue to William Hapgood's intentions can be gleaned from Columbia Conserve's statement of purpose. In explaining the company's rationale for equalizing pay between salaried and wage employees, William claimed that the policy was "essential to the development of that fraternity without which democracy is a creed, and not a manner of living." He attempted to recreate an older world where the worker would regain "a creative relationship to his work" akin to "what he had during the craftsmanship period." Echoing the artisan republicanism and free labor ideology of the nineteenth century, William Hapgood advocated a meritocracy where ability rather than seniority or social connection was the principal criterion for advancement. In contrast to the acquisitive, market-driven culture that had wounded his father, Columbia Conserve would stand as a clear alternative and reflect the values that the Hapgoods were struggling to sustain. Coinciding with the rise of welfare capitalism and broad public discussion regarding the need for industrial democracy, Columbia Conserve was widely regarded as an exemplary business. William Hapgood's "experiment" received substantial publicity, and he was hailed in liberal circles as one of the most articulate exponents of enlightened management during the 1920s and 1930s.[9]

In 1898, William married Eleanor Page, an Indianapolis resident whose well-to-do family had originally come from Chicago. Powers, their only child, was born in Chicago on December 28, 1899, and was named after the family surname of his paternal grandmother. He was raised in Indianapolis, where the family had moved so that his father could assume control of Columbia Conserve. Indianapolis at the turn of the century was undergoing an economic and social transition that was

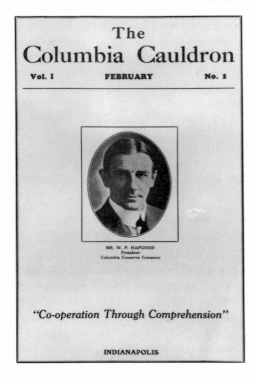

The

Columbia Cauldron

Vol. I   FEBRUARY   No. 1

MR. W. P. HAPGOOD
President
Columbia Conserve Company

"Co-operation Through Comprehension"

INDIANAPOLIS

William P. Hapgood, father of Powers Hapgood, on the cover of *Columbia Cauldron,* official publication of the Columbia Conserve Company, February 1927. William purchased the small Indianapolis-based cannery in 1903 and turned it into a worker-controlled enterprise. (Courtesy Lilly Library, Indiana University)

later referred to as its golden age. In spite of its industrial growth and expanding population, Indianapolis was described by one historian as a "provincial capital" that became "a city against its will." Even with the transition from farm to factory, Indianapolis's population was far less mobile than that of comparable American cities, held the highest percentage of single-family dwellings in the nation, and retained an intimacy and neighborliness that became a staple of Hoosier lore. Preserving this sense of neighborliness and social connection became integral to the identity of the archetypal Hoosier, who was allegedly not contaminated by the impersonal forces of change sweeping the rest of the nation.[10]

Although the Midwest may have appeared as "exile" to his older brother and his father, William Hapgood found Indianapolis a congenial location for his experiment. The forces of finance capitalism had not been as intrusive in Indiana as they had been elsewhere; the opportunities for indigenous industries to develop were more readily available. Indiana's remarkable homogeneity, distinguished by a population that was 95 percent native-born and 97 percent white, the majority Protestants, offered an atmosphere less susceptible to ethnic antagonism and possibly more conducive to a cooperative spirit. Yet Indiana's homogeneity and its history as an autonomous Western territory left it wary of outside influences and fostered a profound, even virulent conservatism. Although Eugene V. Debs was personally popular in his home state, he never won substantial electoral support during his repeated runs for the presidency on the Socialist ticket. The Ku Klux Klan exercised considerable authority during the 1920s, and its activities were condoned by many Hoosiers. Indianapolis was infamous as an open-shop town. Under the leadership of David A. Parry, a local auto magnate and an early president of the National Association of Manufacturers, the Employers' Association of Indianapolis prided itself on the city's imperviousness to union penetration.[11]

Nonetheless, Indiana was not entirely a conservative anti-union bastion. The state had witnessed frequent agitation among miners and railroad workers, and by the first decade of the twentieth century, Indianapolis was the headquarters for nine national unions. Still, establishing a worker-controlled business in an open-shop, Midwestern city must have appealed to William Hapgood's eagerness to take on new challenges. Unlike his brothers and his contemporaries safely ensconced in the more liberal political culture of the East, he was fighting for his values on less welcoming terrain. This missionary sense of purpose was passed on to his son, Powers, who would share many of his father's values and fight for them in arenas not usually associated with someone of his class and cultural origins.[12]

Growing up in a city that retained an aura of small-town intimacy and in a state which prided itself on its "Americanness," Powers Hapgood enjoyed an idyllic childhood. Encouraged by his parents to keep a diary, young Powers recorded experiences reminiscent of Norman Rockwell's paintings: milk shakes at the local pharmacy after school, moving pictures and vaudeville shows, a chauffeur-driven hunting trip with a friend, a ride in David Parry's racer, reading Zane Grey novels and the *American Boy* magazine, and summer trips to the family's vacation retreat at Rainy Lake along the Minnesota-Canadian border. Although his father's business struggled during much of Powers's childhood, the family had sufficient resources for a comfortable upper-middle-class life, including a maid to cook meals and a private tutor to coach Powers for entrance exams to prep school. Yet there was also palpable tension simmering just beneath the surface of this pleasant upbringing as Powers struggled to meet both his father's

Powers Hapgood held by his father, William, c. 1899. Growing up in Indianapolis, Powers enjoyed the resources of a comfortable upper-middle-class life, including a maid to cook meals and a private tutor to coach him for prep-school entrance exams. (Courtesy of Lilly Library, Indiana University)

expectations and his family's historical commitments. Throughout his childhood and adolescence, Powers often encountered William Hapgood's disapproval when he failed to measure up to these exacting standards.[13]

Powers's mother, Eleanor, was active in community affairs in Indianapolis, serving as president of the Public Health Nursing Association in 1915 and later working with the YWCA. John Brophy, a United Mine Workers leader who became Powers's mentor, noted that he inherited "his mother's sweetness" and nurturing qualities. The greater influence on Powers's development, however, appears to have been asserted by his father. Just as his own father had instructed him in the importance of self-discipline, productive work, and ethical behavior, William Hapgood sought to transmit these values to his only child. William's concerted efforts at instruction created considerable tension between himself and his son. In his diary Powers noted frequent arguments with his father over his failure to study hard and work efficiently. One dispute resulted in Powers throwing a book at his father; on another occasion, William refused to speak to his son for several days as punishment for his alleged indolence. "You have no idea of the mental torture I am in," Powers complained in his May 10, 1915, diary entry as he studied for exams. Since his father read his diary regularly, it was quite probable that "you" referred to William Hapgood. In all likelihood, this complaint represented Powers's plea for more moderate expectations and less intrusive paternal supervision.[14]

Autocratic in temper by his own admission, William Hapgood was once described by some of his employees as "sharp-tongued, nervous, and irritable" in addition to being "kind and considerate." His emotional volatility stemmed in part from a demanding work schedule that occasionally led him to the brink of collapse. Eleanor Hapgood, who worried about the well-being of both her husband and her only child, also suffered from brittle nerves and was subject to periodic bouts of anxiety. Although neither William nor Eleanor experienced the debilitating kind of neurasthenia that afflicted many members of the turn-of-the-century upper middle class, their anxieties and expectations clearly affected their son. Powers often alluded to "feeling rotten" and was examined for recurring outbreaks of rashes and boils, both maladies that could be linked to feelings of emotional stress. His parents' careful monitoring of his activities knew few boundaries. William was displeased, for example, that Powers once swam a long distance underwater, and he and Eleanor insisted that a doctor check Powers's heart after this aquatic exploit. Prodded on one hand and protected on the other, Powers would soon feel an overwhelming need to prove himself outside the cocoon of parental oversight and middle-class security.[15]

Powers's rebellion against his father's will was accompanied, however, by unabashed admiration for his prestige and integrity. Beyond his public stature, William's conception of character profoundly influenced his son. Powers would later recall family camping trips where he learned about working cooperatively, not consuming more than his share of available resources, and accepting responsibility for both himself and his fellow campers. His relations with his parents were invariably open and candid. Powers proudly recorded in a February 1917 diary entry a "confidential talk" with William, who told him "things not many boys are told by their fathers." He concluded, "It is one of the finest things in the world to have a father like mine," delighting in the fact that William was willing to trust his judgment and share confidences with him.[16]

Powers kept few if any secrets from his parents. He confided in his father about the "Hill Club," a loose organization of friends, which he hastened to explain was neither a secret society nor a fraternity, both of which were prohibited at Shortridge High School. William's disdain for privilege and advantage based on extrinsic rather than intrinsic qualities had clearly been communicated to Powers, who judged subsequent affiliations by strict egalitarian and democratic standards.[17]

Throughout his youth, Powers Hapgood regarded his family as a model for the cooperative, fraternal relations that he later sought to nurture in public life. Yet the Hapgoods were resisting important changes that had been eroding the intimacy of the family bond for well over half a century. The separation of home and work, the weakening of religious influence, and the increasing financial independence of middle-class children from their parents conspired to diminish the power of parental authority. The values of the market—competition, acquisitiveness, individualism—could no longer be kept from intruding upon the family's ability to act, in Christopher Lasch's words, as a "haven in a heartless world." While William Hapgood hoped to advance older values of cooperation and selflessness in both home and workplace, these ideals were being undermined by the dominant cultural ethos and viewed as obsolete by many in the increasingly affluent middle class. Moreover, Powers's idyllic family life was itself fraught with its share of tensions, most notably his parents' overprotectiveness, anxiety, and insistence that he measure up to both their standards and the family's heritage. His tendency to ignore these tensions and romanticize the warmth of family life underscored his profound dependence on his parents and his intense need to depict the Hapgood family as a repository of moral virtue.[18]

In spite of distancing himself from the intellectual environment of the East, William Hapgood insisted that his son follow the family tradition and gain his education there. In September 1915, Powers enrolled at Phillips Academy in Andover, Massachusetts, a prestigious boarding school that prepared upper-class boys for entry to Ivy League colleges. Describing his studies as "black and gloomy," he showed little enthusiasm for classroom activity. He displayed a much greater interest in sports, where he became captain of his class wrestling team and aspired to play football at Harvard. But Powers's attention was chiefly occupied by reports of the war in Europe, some of which he received firsthand from visitors to Andover. As the possibility for American involvement grew more likely, Powers decided he wanted to participate. Members of the Andover ambulance corps, he explained, would have the opportunity "to show the stuff they're made of." Powers became a cadet in the Andover Military Training Corps, and upon entering Harvard in fall 1917, he began pressuring his parents to allow him to enlist. Recuperating from jaundice in the school infirmary, he wished instead that he were in Europe recovering from battle wounds and enjoying the "satisfaction of duty well and faithfully done." As he wrote to his mother, "my age is a terrible one to be in at the present time. Too darn young to be in France acquiring manhood and a real education, not one of a bookworm."[19]

Powers endorsed the United States' decision to enter the war in April 1917 and applauded Woodrow Wilson's moral justification for American involvement. "My mind is never free of thoughts of the war," he wrote his parents in December 1917. While he was supposedly in college to "broaden his mind for service to [his] fellow man," he insisted that only in Europe could one learn about "passion" and "character." Urging his parents to allow him to become an aviator, Powers touted the "self-reliance" and "initiative" associated with piloting aircraft. Meanwhile, he did what he could individually to support the war effort at home, foregoing a "wasteful" train trip to visit his Uncle Hutch, asking his parents to spend less money on Christmas presents so they could send the savings to the troops, and voting to start Harvard classes earlier in the day in order to conserve fuel. Powers's commitment to the Allied cause reflected not only his deep desire to serve but also his burning personal need to prove himself and gain recognition for his efforts. Early in 1918, he summarized his feelings in a letter to his parents: "no matter at what age I go, I'll go happily if only I've completed or helped to complete some work which will permanently help the world. The tragedy of death, it seems to me, is not in the mere leaving of the earth and friends, but in the leaving of it before one has had a chance to do something of value."[20]

Powers Hapgood's desire to prove himself in battle was not an isolated case; rather, it epitomized the tensions often felt by young men of his generation and background. For many of Powers's contemporaries, World War I assumed special significance. Some like Gardner Jackson, later to become a prominent New Deal liberal and one of Hapgood's political acquaintances, were attracted to Woodrow Wilson's lofty rhetoric and the opportunity to extend democratic ideals throughout the world. Others, encouraged by "the beleaguered defenders of nineteenth-century tradition" and the romantic imagery of popular culture, saw the war as "a strenuous and virile antidote to the effete routine of modern life." Elite universities contributed scores of volunteers to the war effort, with Harvard supplying 375 drivers, including John Dos Passos, to the American Ambulance Field Service. To Dos Passos and his fellow volunteers, manhood was to be acquired on the battlefields of Europe, a far cry from the urbane gentility of Harvard Yard. As he subsequently recalled: "We had spent our boyhood in the peaceful afterglow of the nineteenth century. What was war like? We wanted to see with our own eyes."[21]

In the nineteenth century, however, manhood had not simply been a matter of proving moral worth or personal courage. It was rooted in a web of public understandings that contained important political implications. Especially for the working class, manhood was intimately linked to artisanship and productive labor, to property ownership and self-employment, all of which contributed to a sense of independence and self-reliance that formed the core of republican values. With the de-skilling of labor and the decline of opportunities for proprietorship or landholding, the very concept of manhood appeared imperiled. Accordingly, leaders of some of the nineteenth century's most powerful protest movements had explicitly cast their aims as a defense of manhood and an attempt to restore the conditions necessary for its sustenance.[22]

Powers Hapgood's quest for manhood, though by no means devoid of public meaning, was far more personal than that of his predecessors. His near obsession with demonstrating his manliness was driven by a set of intense needs—to prove his ability to withstand hardship, endure suffering, and behave heroically, qualities that seemed difficult to obtain in the cloistered world of the university and the comfortable parlors of the upper middle class. The linkage of manhood with passion, competitiveness, and ambition reflected a late nineteenth-century shift toward defining independence in terms of self-expression. As John Dos Passos had suggested, this quest for meaning and proof of manhood gripped not only Powers Hapgood but many of his upper-middle-class contemporaries. What distinguished Powers from his cohorts was his unwavering commitment to the values of personal restraint and frugality that had sustained nineteenth-century notions of manhood, his insistence that his private needs could only be fulfilled within a public context, and an almost desperate desire to demonstrate his personal courage. As he proclaimed in a March 1918 diary entry, quoting Ralph Waldo Emerson, "'Tis man's perdition to be safe/When for the truth he ought to die."[23]

Powers Hapgood's assertions of manhood were complicated by the powerful presence of his domineering father. William Hapgood, an engaged man and a respected reformer, was himself a harsh critic of middle-class complacency and detachment. While such young men as Gardner Jackson and John Dos Passos rebelled against the business ethics of their banker and lawyer fathers, Powers Hapgood saw his father as a role model. Having accepted William Hapgood's moral code of work, self-control, and service to others, Powers rejected the bohemianism that attracted some members of his generation. One influence that may have deterred any tendency toward bohemianism was the example of his Uncle Hutch, whose descent into a life of drinking and sexual infidelity offended both Powers and his parents. Instead of the usual form of adolescent rebellion, he chose other vehicles through which to challenge parental authority and establish his own identity.[24]

Rather than seeking to subvert his father, Powers endeavored to outdo him at his own game. His ambitions to be "one half the man Lincoln was," "to show the stuff [he was] made of," and experience "the satisfaction of duty well and faithfully done" reflected both his adolescent search for a heroic persona and the extent to which he had internalized his father's values. No sacrifice would be too great, no hardship too arduous, no form of selflessness too exacting for Powers as he sought to meet his father's expectations and fulfill the demands of his family's legacy. This conception of responsibility left Powers perpetually anxious over his ability to measure up and match his father in character and courage.[25]

Powers's zest for combat was dampened by his first exposure to modern weaponry. In January 1918, he marveled over the efficiency of a new machine gun but also noted that "it seems terrible to have such efficient methods for taking human life." Later, he deplored the killing associated with combat and proclaimed that he had "lost all desire to be talked about for my share in the war." Despite this revulsion, Powers did not relinquish his desire to distinguish himself in battle. After enlisting in the Student Army Training Corps and being inducted into the army in October 1918, he was bitterly disappointed to learn that the army would not accept enlistees for officer training school. Several days later, the war ended, leaving him without a definite goal and ambition and feeling "a little lost." Yet Powers assured his father that he was not "in a dangerously low stage of depression" and spoke again of his need for direct experience and adventure: "if I could only get into work where I could see myself and others helping in some cause, suffer hardship, and I'll admit frankly, see some unusual experiences, I'm sure that I would be very glad to get out after the work was finished and go into business . . . or study for a time."[26]

Even during his student years at Harvard, Powers had sought the hardship of a strenuous life. During a school break in February 1918, he chopped wood, citing the need of fuel for the war effort and expressing pride in his ability to perform demanding labor. He also purchased war bonds with his earnings as a further expression of sacrifice and solidarity. Two months later, Powers took a laborer's job at the Watertown Arsenal near Boston. Although he made no direct mention of it, Powers may have chosen Watertown because of its recent status as an industrial battleground. Three years earlier, molders in the arsenal's foundry had rebelled against Watertown's introduction of scientific management, protesting the institution of time studies as "un-American in principle." Their protest led to congressional restrictions on the use of Frederick Winslow Taylor's techniques in government facilities, thereby limiting the application of one of Progressivism's most vaunted initiatives.[27]

Exposed to unskilled ethnic laborers, Powers was disconcerted by his initial encounter with working people. He wrote his parents that he was repelled by their coarseness and the grimness of "the life they have to lead." The Italian workers "jabbered" incessantly and were often uncooperative and inefficient, prompting Powers to wish that they could learn to work more "scientifically." Despite his estrangement from his coworkers, he observed that their attitudes were understandable given the monotony of their jobs and the lack of alternative opportunities. Thoroughly imbued with Progressive notions of efficiency and an acute sense of noblesse oblige, Powers concluded that his stint at the arsenal would "enable [him] to help others more knowledgeably" now that he had shared their everyday experience. At this point he looked upon working people as needing the benefit of middle-class tutelage in order to lift themselves to higher levels of productivity and refinement.[28]

During the second semester of his junior year, Powers became involved in a heated competition to write for the Harvard *Crimson*. Among his assignments as a trainee, Powers interviewed such luminaries as former President William Howard Taft and Secretary of War Newton Baker. These experiences, coupled with winning a coveted spot on the *Crimson*, went to Powers's head, earning him a rebuke from his father. He vowed to write letters less "taken up with I" once the competition was over and felt "ashamed" for celebrating his own elevation at the expense of his rivals. As he wrote his parents, the *Crimson* competition helped him to realize the evils of "striving for more like the capitalists."[29]

In contrast to his uncles who fondly recalled the intellectual stimulation of their years at Harvard, the classroom held little allure for Powers. Although he studied with the famed historian Frederick Jackson Turner, economist F. W. Taussig, and William Z. Ripley, who had administered labor standards for army clothing production during the war, Powers was unimpressed by these men. Searching for knowledge gained via experience and applied in real-life settings, he did not look to his professors as role models or mentors. The more important influences on Powers's development emerged from people he met and activities he pursued outside the classroom. These contacts contributed significantly to his emerging social awareness, introducing him to the yeasty arena of left-wing and working-class politics.[30]

Post–World War I Cambridge and Boston were hotbeds of political and labor activity. Although Powers failed to note one epic event—Calvin Coolidge's suppression of the 1919 Boston police strike—he observed other local incidents that reflected important national developments. For example, in March 1920, he visited Frank Mack, a political prisoner jailed during the Palmer Raids, and learned that the detainees on Deer Island had established a "soviet" in order to protest their internment. Citing Oliver Wendell Holmes, Powers approved the jurist's endorsement of a marketplace of ideas and denounced the government's heavy-handed attempt to squash dissent. Through first-hand investigation, he was beginning to acquire insights into social problems and speak with greater confidence about public issues.[31]

Encouraged by his friend Mary Reed, a young communist sympathizer, Powers also went to "bohemian tea rooms" in Cambridge, where he heard such speakers as John Reed (no relation to Mary) and Louis Fraina of the nascent American communist movement. After each of these encounters, he would carefully assess the arguments made by each person or faction, praising those who relied on fact rather than emotion to persuade their audiences. Although he admired Mary Reed's "character" and "sincerity," he was disturbed by some of her radical friends, whom he described as "headstrong and often times unpoised." During spring 1920, Powers's search for political direction was rewarded. In several crucial encounters, he located individuals whose lives affirmed his conceptions of character and demonstrated the possibility of fruitful interaction between the middle and working classes.[32]

Attending a dinner addressed by Cornelia Stratton Parker, a writer and lecturer, he learned about the work of her late husband, Carleton, an economist who had investigated labor unrest firsthand. Cornelia Parker's biography of her husband, entitled *An American Idyll,* became a literary rage on its publication in 1920. Carleton Parker was an academic renegade who criticized university education as conventional and irrelevant, lauded the self-education of workers, and attributed their militancy to the "maladjustment between a fixed human nature and a carelessly ordered world." He then proceeded to adapt the insights of Freudian psychology toward Progressive solutions, declaring that class conflict could be stemmed by making civilization less "repressive," thereby permitting healthier instincts to develop among unruly workers.[33]

Powers Hapgood was largely uninterested in Parker's theoretical assumptions. What excited him about the Parkers were their democratic sensibilities, their advocacy of knowledge derived from direct experience, and their disdain for middle-class security. Unlike Powers's professors at Harvard, Carleton Parker had spoken with personal authority about working-class life. He knew hoboes and migrants not as abstractions but as real people. For many young intellectuals and rebels, Parker's "idyll," guided by its respect for instinct and its denunciation of repression, represented a refreshing alternative to the detachment of the academy. Powers Hapgood took the idea of an idyll even more seriously than others, finding support in Carleton Parker's example for the unusual journey that he was about to undertake.[34]

Addressing the same dinner group as Cornelia Parker was John "Red" Doran, a member of the Industrial Workers of the World (IWW), whose demeanor and presentation enchanted the young Harvard student. Well educated and from a middle-class background, Doran had become a Wobbly out of conviction rather than necessity. Following his speech, Powers mingled with Doran and some of his admirers, whom he referred to in his diary as the "more ignorant types" of radicals. In contrast, Red Doran was articulate and refined, projected a clear sense of honesty and sincerity, and in Powers's words, was a "real man." By electing to spend his life serving the working class, Doran had transcended his origins and found a sense of connection and meaning that eluded other members of the anxious middle class.[35]

When they had a few minutes alone, Powers confided with Doran about his future plans. He cited three possible options: heading a business and running it as an industrial democracy, entering politics, or joining the labor movement and striving to gain a position of influence. Doran discouraged Powers from the first two possibilities, arguing that business and politics were corrupting and antithetical to idealism. According to Doran, labor was a worthy arena, but he encouraged Powers to go to sea if he wanted to experience the worker's world directly. Mines and factories, he thought, were simply too debilitating to the spirit. While respectful of Doran's argument, Hapgood maintained that neither a business nor a political career would preclude idealism. Yet he insisted that regardless of his choice, only by sharing the plight of workers would he be fully qualified to understand their suffering, a view readily endorsed by Doran.[36]

Whereas the examples of Red Doran and Carleton Parker provided Powers with important role models, a series of encounters with liberal Protestantism furnished additional justification for his post-Harvard plans. During his youth in Indianapolis, Powers had received little religious instruction; his grandfather's agnosticism was a legacy bequeathed to subsequent generations of Hapgoods. Powers himself displayed little interest in the formal ceremonies of religious practice, complaining to his parents that mandatory chapel attendance at Andover was a nuisance. Nonetheless, he chaired the Harvard Mission at the Phillips Brooks House, the center for religious life at Harvard that had links to the settlement house movement and missionary work abroad. Powers attempted to recruit his classmates for these activities but to his disappointment received a cool reception. His work with the Brooks House did lead him to attend several student religious conferences in 1919, even as he deflected his parents' qualms about an open flirtation with the official church.[37]

To his surprise, Powers discovered that most of the church leaders present at the Minnesota conference he attended in June 1919 were not "hypocrites." As advocates of the social gospel, they preached passionately about the importance of service to others and insisted on the need to "apply the teachings of Christ to everyday life." J. Stitt Wilson, a prominent social gospel advocate who spoke at the conference, especially stirred him with his emphasis on identifying with the most lowly. Powers now expressed regret over his own "selfishness," declaring that he needed to "live closer to suffering" as a true demonstration of his social commitment.[38]

In spite of his warm praise for the participants at the summer conference, Powers avoided any official affiliation with the social gospel movement. He attended another meeting in Des Moines late in 1919 but bemoaned the dogmatism and prayer that permeated the rhetoric of the keynote speakers. Ultimately, Powers's attitude toward formal religion was best summarized by the title of a talk he gave at the Phillips Brooks House in March 1920: "The Fundamental Aims of Religion and the Church's Failure to Fulfill Them." In his view religion was valuable only to the extent that it spurred citizens to address social problems; otherwise it lacked intrinsic meaning or usefulness. Powers's audience apparently disagreed with this assessment, an indication that most of his contemporaries were unwilling to apply such stringent standards in their evaluation of the church's social role.[39]

For all his misgivings about the church, Powers was profoundly influenced by these religious conferences. Thirty years later he cited them as having inspired him to investigate the conditions of working-class life in America. Seeking to imbue his quest for self-actualization with transcendental meaning, Powers found the imagery of the social gospel indispensable. The Sermon on the Mount, a favored biblical reference for social gospel advocates, suggested that a life of commitment would ultimately be rewarded, and Jesus fascinated him as a perfectionist symbol of selflessness and sacrifice. The social gospel's "conviction that man was of such a nature that he could become ideal" made it possible to conceive of social transformation and the creation of "ideal business, ideal labor, [an] ideal church and ideal politics." Finally, the insistence by religious liberals that human agency would be essential in bringing the Kingdom of God to earth provided Powers with the loftiest of aims, ushering in the millennium. These powerful images appropriated from the social gospel allowed him to craft a noble, heroic persona that for all its secularity could scarcely conceal the quasi-religious fervor of his newfound commitment.[40]

Having made important strides toward satisfying what one observer later called his "sincere consuming quest for a faith," Powers decided to graduate a year early [June 1920] and seek his education in the "real world." School remained a burden for him. His grades were average, and he ruefully noted his "total lack of any brilliant qualities." Earlier, he had expressed his preference for "strenuous work abroad," combining activities that were "half brain and half manual." His parents reluctantly accepted his plan for early graduation, and in tacit recognition of their concession, Powers vowed to work more diligently in order to compensate for his lack of interest in his studies. "I will need hard work and persistence to succeed or accomplish anything," he wrote his parents, and his work during his final year at Harvard reflected this new sense of intellectual commitment.[41]

In 1917, William Hapgood had embarked on his experiment to convert the Columbia Conserve Company into a model of industrial democracy. His first steps were to institute profit-sharing and establish a workers' council that was granted the power to set salaries and advise the board of directors on company policy. Powers supported his father's actions and, in a series of papers written during his last two years at

Harvard, explored the possibilities of cooperative control of business enterprise. Noting what he termed "the confusion between public and private interests," he advocated public ownership of the railroads, both for reasons of efficiency and the enhancement of democracy, neither of which he felt would result from private control. Later, in a paper on "The Life and Times of Louis Blanc," Powers evaluated the French socialist's program of social workshops as a means of structuring the workplace. Blanc's workshops, he observed, were small and decentralized, accepted only workers of solid character, rejected competition, and curbed selfishness. The workshops failed, he argued, not due to any intrinsic shortcomings, but only because Blanc's opponents, who were devoid of "generosity, imagination, or courage," had purposely subverted his ideas. Powers demonstrated a tendency, which later became more pronounced, to question the character of his opponents rather than engage the substance of their arguments. Although his professor questioned the value of Blanc's work, Powers had succeeded in his principal objective—finding historical precedent to justify William Hapgood's bold undertaking.[42]

The young idealist's thoughts on industrial relations and social class emerged most clearly in his last two Harvard papers: a short essay called "Democratic Government in Industry" and his 145-page senior thesis entitled "The Works Council Movement in the United States." Both works reflected a keen awareness of varied approaches to industrial democracy inspired by World War I and the War Labor Board's ambitious attempts to manage relations between labor and capital. In part, Powers took his cues from Carleton Parker, noting that the works council movement sought to ease the psychological sources of working-class discontent by conducting labor-capital relations on a basis of mutual respect and reason rather than raw conflict. He went on to evaluate several companies, including Columbia Conserve, that offered workers a greater voice in shop floor governance.[43]

Powers examined employee representation plans in both union and nonunion settings. His research included interviews with company officials and workers at Dennison Manufacturing, International Harvester, and General Electric. Powers hailed these programs for granting workers some degree of independent authority, but his highest praise was reserved for Columbia Conserve. Under William Hapgood's leadership, the company had moved toward greater equalization of salaries between men and women, sought to limit layoffs during seasonal slowdowns, and welcomed worker participation in decision making. As a result, some Columbia employees had shown a "surprising rise in intelligence" and "in some cases, refinement," qualities that Powers assumed were not prevalent within the working class. Yet he was also critical of the experiment, observing that the workers' council at Columbia was limited to an advisory status and lacked real power. Works councils could only enhance democracy, he concluded, if they permitted employees to exercise genuine authority and influence fundamental managerial decisions.[44]

Powers's thinking at this point reflected important Progressive assumptions, especially the notion that class conflict could be eased by providing workers a formal outlet for their grievances. Viewing Columbia as a vital experiment, he suggested that employers take the lead and initiate similar programs in order to stimulate workplace democracy. Although he advocated cooperation over class conflict, Powers acknowledged that the state might have to intervene if employers were unwilling to embrace industrial democracy. Most important, he was beginning to question the paternalistic motives that had often prompted welfare capitalist programs, implying that even as enlightened an employer as his father had not fully embraced the concept of genuine workers' control. Despite the implicit condescension of his own aim to inculcate workers with intelligence and refinement, he insisted that a commitment to independence and democracy was the essential feature of a legitimate employee representation plan. In order to advance these visionary goals, he looked to enlightened employers like his father to extend the spirit of industrial democracy that had been planted by works councils during World War I.[45]

His thesis completed, Powers Hapgood graduated from Harvard in June 1920. Throughout their senior year he and some of his college friends had spoken of either going on a bumming trip or exploring the Canadian Falls in Labrador after their graduation. But Powers's classmates backed away from these plans and moved toward establishing their postcollege careers, leaving him to his own devices. Eager to gain firsthand knowledge and test his mettle in an arena more demanding than that of Harvard Yard, he developed his own plan of exploration. In fall 1920, twenty-one-year-old Powers Hapgood took to the open road, embarking on a journey that would irrevocably influence the course of his life. This journey marked the beginning of his lifelong engagement with the American working class, leading him "from college to the ranks of labor."

Chapter Two

From College
to the Ranks of Labor

> The terrible danger to explorers is that they will
> always find what they are looking for. . . . I
> want an expedition that will find what it's not
> looking for.
>
> —John Dos Passos

As Americans prepared to reject the reform spirit of Woodrow Wilson
and embrace Warren Harding's call for a return to "not heroism, but
healing, not nostrums, but normalcy," Powers Hapgood began his
earnest pursuit of a strenuous life. Eager to break free from his parents'
overprotectiveness and Harvard's gentility, he looked to mythic American symbols—the railroads and the West—to abet his escape. Travers-
ing the expanses of the northwestern Plains, he sought to fulfill his
need for adventure, his quest for identity, and his search for a calling.
The young Harvard graduate hopped freights, lived in boarding houses,
attended union meetings, and worked at a variety of jobs in his attempt
to feel the pulse of working-class life. His journey, which lasted from
September to December of 1920, took him to coal mines in Minnesota
and Montana, construction work in Wyoming, and a stint at the
Colorado Fuel and Iron Company in Denver, where the celebrated
employee representation plan of John D. Rockefeller Jr., had been
established. The romance of life on the road and the excitement of his
initial experience as a coal miner led Hapgood to further encounters
with the working class and a political mentor whose encouragement
affirmed his decision to join the labor movement.[1]

Although he gained grudging parental approval for his westward journey, Hapgood still felt compelled to justify his travels. He insisted that he was "only doing what 90 percent of the youth of this country do before they're of age." Throughout the trip he kept a journal of his daily experiences, citing it as proof of his discipline and confirmation of the education he was receiving. He sent copies of his journal entries to his parents, along with frequent letters assuring them of his safety. Carrying travelers' checks "to relieve Mother's mind," Hapgood sought to assert his self-sufficiency by declaring his determination to use them only in case of emergency. By living "wholeheartedly" rather than "hypocritically," he explained, he could better understand the lives of workers because he was sharing their experience directly.[2]

Among the first group of workers that Hapgood encountered in his travels were the Wobblies, members of the Industrial Workers of the World, who had paid dearly for their militant advocacy of syndicalism and their opposition to World War I. The IWW was attractive to many young Americans of Hapgood's generation. Several of his future friends, including American Civil Liberties Union (ACLU) director Roger Baldwin, Congress of Industrial Organizations (CIO) publicist Len DeCaux, and activist intellectual Frank Tannenbaum, were among those fascinated by the Wobblies' apparent freedom from bourgeois constraints and their transcendent vision of "One Big Union" encompassing all workers. Hapgood, however, did not fully share this romantic identification with the IWW. Unconvinced by the Wobbly argument that workers had the right to dispossess private owners, he was troubled by the bitterness and class hatred that often accompanied the IWW's uncompromising denunciation of capitalism. Hapgood deplored the IWW argument that labor and capital had nothing in common, citing his father's enlightened stewardship at Columbia Conserve as evidence that class conflict was not irreconcilable.[3]

To his surprise, Hapgood was impressed by the "intelligence" and "sincerity" of the Wobblies. Their reasoned arguments and astute critique of American capitalism jibed with his own misgivings regarding the troubled relations between labor and capital that followed World War I. Before these boxcar encounters, Hapgood had accepted Carleton Parker's view that the Wobblies' extremism stemmed from the transiency and harshness of their environment rather than a substantive social or economic analysis. Up close, however, the Wobblies appeared far more sympathetic than the crude, irrational disturbers of the peace depicted by their critics. Hapgood proclaimed to his parents that one of his Harvard professors, F. W. Taussig, who had denounced

the Wobblies, "may not know his subject." Based on personal observations, Hapgood was beginning to question the assumptions that
Progressive intellectuals held about the working class and to offer
alternative interpretations.[4]

The experience that had the most profound effect on the young
Harvard graduate was his exposure to coal mining. It was no accident
that when William James sought to boost the spirits of young Americans, he had suggested mining as a "moral equivalent of war." Mining
was an industry that required considerable skill and independent
judgment in order to extract coal. It possessed a unique work culture,
for scientific management had not yet made the inroads in mining that
it had in other industries. As late as the 1920s, mining was "very
far . . . from the regularity and regimentation of the time clock and
the factory whistle." Because of the decentralized layout of underground mining and difficulties in standardizing operations, miners
were loosely supervised and tended to be their own bosses. Mining was
also exceedingly dangerous work. The risk of cave-ins and gas explo-
sions was always present; of necessity, miners were sensitive to the
safety and well-being of their fellow workers. By all accounts, coal
miners exercised a degree of job control and esprit perhaps unsur-
passed within the American working class. They almost universally
perceived themselves as "useful" and "self-respecting," terms that by
this time had grown less applicable to most wage labor in the United
States.[5]

Through liberal magazines like the *New Republic* and *The Nation*,
the mystique of coal was well known to middle-class progressives who
sympathized with working people. A 1922 editorial in *The Nation* noted
that mining "invites men to invest their lives in darkness, ugliness, and
constant danger for an utterly inadequate annual wage and without
guaranty of steady employment." Although attracted to the bravery of
those who toiled underground, most liberals were nonetheless repelled
by the harsh conditions faced by miners and preferred to exhibit their
sympathies from afar. Upon entering his first mine, however, Powers
Hapgood was awestruck. Writing his parents, he described the physi-
cality of the United States Steel pit mine in Hibbing, Minnesota, as
"satisfying to one's soul." Here was an industry populated by "real men"
who worked hard and skillfully under dangerous conditions. As he later
noted, his choice of mining was by no means accidental. Coal was an
important basic industry with well-organized workers who possessed
what Hapgood described as "superior social intelligence." He was also
attracted to the self-reliance associated with mining and the sense of

responsibility that miners felt for each other, values that his family had traditionally honored. For a middle-class youth who had missed the opportunity to establish his manhood during World War I, the mines were a worthy proving ground, and Hapgood sought to demonstrate his ability to withstand the rigors of hard labor.[6]

In addition to finding satisfaction in the work, Hapgood was initiated into the United Mine Workers of America (UMWA) local in Bear Creek, Montana, on October 26, 1920. The miner's oath was known within the union as the "obligation," directing UMWA members to an ethic of mutual responsibility. Miners took the obligation seriously, often citing it when explaining the almost religious loyalty that they felt for their union. Reassuring a union leader during a 1923 strike in Pennsylvania, a local officer wrote that his fellow miners "have not forgot the obligation they took and they will stick to it." Another Pennsylvania miner described himself in a 1928 letter to union president John L. Lewis as "a Union Man with every pound of flesh and drop of blood." The ritual of the obligation underscored the miners' fierce sense of duty and commitment, affirming a sense of fraternity that pervaded the union and was consciously transmitted from one generation to another.[7]

Years later, Hapgood would recall taking the miner's obligation as a transforming experience, exulting "that a great change had come over me. I felt that I was no longer a student who had come to work for a few months to study labor problems at first-hand. I was now a member of the working class, a trade unionist." This identification was filled with romantic implications for a middle-class youth searching for commitment and authenticity. In addition to the call for solidarity contained in the obligation, the miner's oath also directed UMWA members to defend "freedom of thought whether expressed by tongue or by pen." Hapgood later remembered that these noble sentiments "first made me realize that the labor movement is the most idealistic movement in the world." Freedom of expression and tolerance were values that liberals held dear, and taking such an oath demanded the kind of personal commitment that Hapgood saw as essential to manhood and which he felt was insufficiently honored by the middle class.[8]

Hapgood's contact with the UMWA strengthened his faith in the labor movement. During his stay in Montana, he attended union meetings and was impressed by the level of participation, the spirited debates, and the "intelligence" of the miners. The work process itself, punctuated by frequent intermissions while miners waited for cars to arrive in which to load coal, encouraged conversation among workers that Hapgood found far more interesting than the parlor talk of the middle class. He likened the atmosphere of the mining camps to Andover, where people "say hello whether they know you or not." This attraction to the intimacy of community life, nurtured in Indianapolis and continued during his college years, inspired Hapgood's fervent search for connection and attachment. Underground, in local union halls and mining camps, he was witnessing, in his father's words, the elevation of democracy and fraternity beyond the status of a creed to a manner of living.[9]

Yet Hapgood conceded that for all their admirable qualities, the miners seemed to lack an "idealistic interest in their future." At the union meetings he attended, members tended to focus on immediate needs rather than visionary plans for social transformation. In characterizing labor as the "most idealistic movement in the world," Hapgood ignored the larger context of union politics within both the UMWA and the American Federation of Labor (AFL). Ironically, while the young activist was praising the obligation's charge to defend freedom of expression, UMWA president John L. Lewis was solidifying his hold on leadership by using constitutional technicalities in order to declare his rivals ineligible for office. Concurrently, AFL president Samuel Gompers condoned the suppression of radicals, advocated the maintenance of racial purity in labor's ranks, and continued to preach a pure and simple unionism based on economic interest. But such evidence suggesting a singular lack of idealism in the house of labor was far from Hapgood's mind during these heady days. As he would soon discover, the fraternal, democratic values that he saw displayed at the local level were not universally shared nor did they necessarily extend to the top ranks of labor leadership.[10]

To his further dismay, not all of Hapgood's contacts with working-class life were romantic or uplifting. The democratic spirit of union meetings was occasionally marred by violence, which he discovered in Montana when a union leader bloodied the nose of a member who disagreed with him. Appalled, Hapgood protested, but to his subsequent regret, retreated when the union leader challenged him to back up his words with his fists. His Victorian sensibilities were also offended during his journey, once when he insisted against derisive dissent that premarital sex would constitute unfaithfulness to his future bride, and later in a fight with a boss who had called him a son of a bitch. Interpreting the epithet literally as an insult to his mother, Hapgood fought back but refused to adopt the gouging and kicking tactics of his opponent, who was dumbfounded by "this bit of decency."[11]

Like his Uncle Hutch, Powers Hapgood was a "Victorian in the modern world." But in contrast to Hutchins Hapgood's attraction to the seamier side of working-class life, his nephew found himself at odds with workers regarding questions of sexual morality, drinking, profanity, and the pursuit of pleasure via such unproductive activities as gambling. These activities, which in his view reflected a lack of self-control, undercut his emerging contention that the working class could claim moral superiority over a corrupt and hypocritical middle class.

But the qualms Hapgood displayed toward working-class morality paled before his growing estrangement from the middle class. He frowned on the newly affluent middle class's embrace of manners over morals, leisure over work, and pleasure over sacrifice. America's turn-of-the-century shift from a producer to a consumer culture threatened what Warren Susman has called the "culture of character"—a commitment to the values of work, loyalty, duty, and honor that had defined manhood and citizenship throughout the nineteenth century. These values combined self-mastery with social obligation and appeared in both the republican rhetoric of artisans and the language of middle-class reformers, businessmen, and religious leaders. For young idealists like Powers Hapgood, the twentieth-century middle class dishonored the culture of character as it began to eschew productive labor, direct experience, and notions of sacrifice and social obligation. This inadequate fealty to older values smacked of hypocrisy, especially given the claims of the middle class to a higher morality. In order to sustain the culture of character, Hapgood became convinced that he would have to look beyond the middle class if he were to keep faith with the legacy of his ancestors.[12]

Among the workers he encountered, Powers Hapgood found an honesty, directness, and spontaneity that the academy, the professions, and Progressive reformers could not approximate. On the road people were willing to share food, money, campfires, and advice. The UMWA, with its idealistic oath, its combination of self-reliance coupled with an ethic of mutualism, and the staunch loyalty it evoked among miners, appeared more attuned to the values on which Hapgood had been weaned than a middle-class culture whose confidence in such values had plummeted. Yet in his zeal to distance himself from his class origins, Hapgood became, in John Dos Passos's words, an explorer who "found what he was looking for." The seeds of romanticism were already well planted in his thought, leading him to see virtue as residing almost exclusively within the working class, notwithstanding the presence of contradictory evidence and the limited scope of his contacts.[13]

Hapgood's western sojourn led to the publication of an article in *The*

Nation. Entitled "Paternalism vs. Unionism in Mining Camps," the article was based on his experiences at a Colorado Fuel and Iron mine, where he worked briefly near the end of his trip. Hapgood sought to compare the benefits offered under the Rockefeller Plan to those afforded members of the United Mine Workers. The Rockefeller Plan had been devised following a bitter miners' strike in 1914. It garnered widespread praise as a model of enlightened labor relations that offered workers a voice in decision making along with an array of social benefits designed to meet their personal needs. Hapgood conceded that the Rockefeller Plan granted workers superior facilities—company housing, recreation, reading rooms—but argued that the UMWA did much more to encourage self-help and independence among workers. Paternalism, he insisted, did little to enhance crucial notions of fraternity and self-respect. Instead it accentuated a corrosive sense of dependency between workers and owners.[14]

According to Hapgood, miners themselves demonstrated little interest in the plan, though workers of Spanish and Mexican descent seemed more amenable to paternalistic appeals than native-born miners, perhaps due to the hierarchical patron-client relationships embedded in their cultural heritage. This was an astute observation, acknowledging the influence that culture and ethnicity could have on working-class consciousness. Hapgood's conclusion, however, downplayed the appeal of paternalism and indicated the emerging thrust of his own thought. Quoting the famed columnist Mr. Dooley (Finley Peter Dunne), he asserted that rights were only meaningful when struggled for. Increasingly, Hapgood was beginning to question a major tenet of Progressivism—its belief that reforms promoted by disinterested experts could enable workers and immigrants to adjust to the demands of industrial life. Rather, he suggested that unions were essential institutions capable of providing workers with an independent, democratic voice free of paternalistic manipulation. Yet, despite an increasing estrangement from middle-class culture, Hapgood's eagerness to publish his findings in a leading Progressive publication reflected an ongoing desire to communicate with a liberal, educated audience. He was reporting to this audience that all was not well on the industrial front, despite the appearance of corporate programs designed to placate workers and remove the causes of class conflict.[15]

After a short Christmas visit to Indianapolis in 1920, Hapgood persisted in his "quest for a faith," seeking reassurance that casting his lot with the labor movement was the most appropriate choice for a career. Post–World War I America did not offer many inviting options for a young activist seeking a place in public life. Progressives like Hapgood's Uncle Norman had hoped that the war might serve to further social reform; instead, it "nearly drained the last reserves of utopianism from American social thought." The political left was in shambles, with the IWW and the Socialist Party discredited because of their antiwar stances and much of the newly formed American Communist Party driven underground by the postwar red scare. Strikes led by resurgent unions were crushed. Employers began their own offensive seeking to roll back labor's wartime gains, combining paternalistic welfare capitalist schemes with the tougher medicine of the American Plan, which sought to establish the open shop in workplaces throughout the country. Most intellectuals "lost faith in the possibility of faith;" Powers Hapgood's Uncle Hutch was just one of many who left America for Europe in order to assuage his disillusionment. American culture itself was on the verge of profound shifts with the growth of advertising, mass communications, popular entertainment, and looser sexual mores, developments that offered citizens private alternatives to public involvement and further eroded the producer awareness that had given nineteenth-century radicalism much of its moral appeal.[16]

But the decade of the 1920s was not wholly characterized by tired radicals, hedonism, or political reaction. There were pockets of resistance against the return to normalcy undertaken by Republican administrations during the 1920s; Progressivism and cultural radicalism did not entirely perish as the world was "made safe for democracy." The "labor question" in particular occupied many Progressives, intellectuals, and religious and civic leaders who continued to debate the possibilities of achieving industrial democracy following the bitter wave of strikes after World War I. It was to these remaining citadels of faith and vision that Powers Hapgood turned for advice as he assessed his options for leading a socially useful life.[17]

Hapgood moved to a New York apartment in January 1921 and from there continued to research possible careers. His wide range of contacts suggested that he had by no means decided to join the labor movement and still regarded enlightened capitalists with some measure of respect. Journeying to Chicago, he met with officials at Hart, Schafner, and Marx and International Harvester. On the same trip, he consulted the utility industrialist Samuel Insull on the operation of employee representation plans. A month later, he attended a meeting of the Cooperative Congress where he heard the veteran reformer Frederick Howe, a friend of his uncles, speak on the virtues of small, cooperative banks that made credit available to workers and farmers. Hapgood was impressed by Howe's assertion that these banks made loans on the basis of character, not personal resources. After hearing Howe's speech, he concluded that cooperatives were "one of the most hopeful methods of achieving a better world."[18]

Cooperatives demanded that citizens demonstrate the principles of fraternity and the virtues of productive labor, a far more demanding approach than that of simply seeking legislative reform or intervention by the state. They also provided a socially harmonious alternative to the IWW's vision of unremitting class struggle. Potentially, Hapgood reasoned, producers and consumers could find common ground in an arrangement that valued older notions of work and character. What he did not address, however, was the applicability of this nineteenth-century vision to the twentieth century, where corporate consolidation had driven many from farms to factories and converted most independent craftsmen into wage earners. In a social structure that valued centralization and bureaucratic control, the fate of small, cooperative institutions based on personal relationships appeared precarious. Nonetheless, his father's experiment gave Hapgood hope, as did the continuing efforts of reformers like Howe, that alternatives to large-scale corporate capitalism could be sustained.[19]

In addition to encountering advocates of the cooperative movement, Hapgood also met with a wide array of liberal contacts provided by his Uncle Norman. In seeking confirmation for his attraction to the labor movement, he received little encouragement from Norman Hapgood's friends. Imbued with a Progressive faith in education, expertise, and moral exhortation, most of them looked askance at the young Harvard graduate's infatuation with the working class.

The muckraker Ray Stannard Baker urged Hapgood to take up engineering as the best means of gaining influence, whereas Louis Brandeis advised him to work with cooperatives. Whiting Williams, a personnel director who had spent several months as a white-collar hobo in order to better understand the plight of workers, suggested that he act as an interpreter who would explain labor-management conflict to a middle-class audience. An official at the U.S. Department of Labor's conciliation service urged him to work for the Bureau of Labor Statistics, perhaps seeing research as a natural progression for a Harvard graduate from a distinguished family of journalists. Although Hapgood did not record the advice offered by editors of such journals as *Survey,* the *New Republic,* and the *New York Post,* all of whom he visited, each presumably encouraged him to pursue the writing life. All these suggestions were too removed from direct contact with workers and the demands of a strenuous life to suit Hapgood. Instead, he drew inspiration from other sources who sympathized with his budding commitment to the working class.[20]

Frank Tannenbaum was one activist intellectual who warmly endorsed Hapgood's attraction to the labor movement. Tannenbaum had won notoriety for joining the IWW and leading groups of homeless New Yorkers into churches where they agitated for food and shelter. His repeated breaches of the sanctity of the church led to a year's prison sentence in 1914. Tannenbaum later turned to scholarly pursuits, publishing a pioneering work, *The Labor Movement: Its Conservative Function and Social Consequences,* just as Hapgood met him in 1921. Although Hapgood tended to disparage intellectuals as disconnected from the social problems they chronicled, he lauded Tannenbaum's immigrant roots, his activist past, and his use of firsthand experience as a foundation for his research.[21]

Tannenbaum saw the social consequences of unions as both radical and conservative. As he would later write, "the values implicit in trade unionism are those of an older day . . . security, justice, freedom, and faith." By presenting a moral critique of America's affinity for individualism and the pursuit of self-interest, unions offered an alternative ethic that stressed mutual responsibility and group solidarity. Simultaneously, labor met the needs of workers for a sense of security and acceptance, thereby enhancing the potential for social stability.[22]

This analysis, which Powers Hapgood hailed as not just an "intellectual tract," suggested that class conflict could be waged without class hatred and countered the IWW's argument denying any commonality between workers and owners. Tannenbaum also inferred that labor was capable of adapting older values to combat the atomistic, dehumanizing impact of modern industrialism, a claim that William Hapgood was testing with his experiment at Columbia Conserve. Tannenbaum's vision of the role of trade unions opened the possibility for constructive relations between labor and capital and allowed Hapgood to cast unions as defenders of the cooperative ethic favored by his family. When Hapgood told Tannenbaum of his aspirations, the veteran activist encouraged him to spend at least ten years in the labor movement to help "guide it intelligently" and learn if "a college man" could rise through the ranks to a position of leadership. Tannenbaum's advice reflected his awareness of a burgeoning connection between segments of the middle class and the labor movement. As writer Joseph Freeman later observed with only slight exaggeration, no one thought it incongruous that the college-educated middle class should serve the labor movement, either as organizers, educators, or chroniclers of working-class exploits.[23]

Further support for Hapgood's decision to join the labor movement came from Roger Baldwin, the founder of the American Civil Liberties Union, who became a lifelong friend. Baldwin's background resembled Hapgood's. He was the product of a prosperous upper-middle-class family, had chafed under the authority of a domineering father, and disdained Harvard, where he had matriculated, as "restrained, sophisticated, and so, so genteel." Operating in a Thoreauian tradition that rejected the authority of the state, Baldwin served a prison term for draft resistance during World War I. Upon his release and immediately following his marriage, he took off on a bumming trip, declaring that "my whole training must be overturned." In order to overcome the "taint" of his comfortable background, he spent several months working at blue-collar jobs so that he could obtain personal knowledge of labor struggles.[24]

In Baldwin, whom he met in spring 1921, Powers Hapgood found a fellow "refugee" who had scorned his "plutocratic" background and the "emptiness" of middle-class parlor talk. More than Frank Tannenbaum, Roger Baldwin understood the world from which Powers Hapgood was attempting to escape. Especially during periods of doubt, Hapgood would seek assurance from Baldwin that his affinity for the working class was not misplaced. Baldwin's friend Scott Nearing, a prominent Socialist, teacher, and intellectual, was another source of encouragement. Here were men of Hapgood's own social class who believed that wealth and comfort destroyed initiative, encouraged passivity, and violated the principles of service and sacrifice that defined strong character. His encounters with Baldwin and Nearing affirmed Hapgood's critique of the middle class and his desire to pursue a strenuous life.[25]

Despite encouragement from Baldwin, Tannenbaum, and Nearing, Hapgood was not yet prepared to join the labor movement, a decision certain to generate opposition from his parents and also one that would be based upon limited experience. To learn more about working-class life without burning his bridges to the middle class, he joined the staff of the Bureau of Industrial Research in March 1921. The bureau, a liberal think tank with close ties to the labor movement, was headed by Robert Bruere, an economist and educator who welcomed Hapgood's interest in labor and encouraged his search for a calling. Although his work with the bureau exposed him to prominent Progressives, Hapgood was unimpressed by these contacts. He remained more interested in the labor movement, seeing it as the most appropriate arena in which to act upon his convictions. Therefore, Hapgood leaped at the opportunity when Arthur Gleason, one of the bureau's staff members, approached him regarding the possibility of conducting research in the Pennsylvania coal fields.[26]

Gleason had worked with Norman Hapgood at *Collier's* and took an interest in his idealistic young nephew. He and Bruere introduced Hapgood to John Brophy, president of UMWA District 2 in central and southwestern Pennsylvania and a major client of the bureau. Brophy would become Hapgood's mentor; they quickly forged a personal and political friendship that endured for the rest of Hapgood's life. Sixteen years Hapgood's senior, Brophy had emigrated from England to central Pennsylvania in 1892 and gone to work in the coal mines at the age of twelve. "The family, the union, and the community," along with a deep commitment to Catholicism, were the pillars of Brophy's worldview. Class-conscious miners from his native Lancashire had formed a community in central Pennsylvania upon their arrival in the United States, transplanting their ethnic and class solidarity to American soil. They regarded the union as their principal vehicle for maintaining a sense of community; it was not simply a device by which to improve the material conditions of work. In Brophy's words, the union remained a permanent fixture in the lives of the English miners, not something "strange, temporary, or erratic," as it often appeared among Americans.[27]

Describing himself as "an habitual rank and filer," Brophy rose from a series of local union positions to become president of the 40,000-member District 2 in 1916. He ran on a platform that stressed local autonomy from the dictates of the national union, a strong commitment to organizing, and independent political action. Brophy resisted the centralization of power within the UMWA and fought for the principles of local union and district autonomy. He viewed local unions and districts as "training schools" that prepared miners for the "larger social and industrial responsibilities that come with increased power." This position collided with the top-down approach favored by union president John L. Lewis but won Brophy considerable praise from outside the labor movement. He developed close ties with a network of New York-based intellectuals and activists who provided him with research capabilities and access to funding. Attracted to Brophy's formidable intellect and unimpeachable integrity, these liberals regarded him as one of labor's foremost advocates of industrial democracy and social reform in the post–World War I era.[28]

With the erosion of UMWA strength after World War I, Brophy began to articulate what he called the "larger program" for the union's resuscitation. The cornerstones of the larger program were expanded organizing, worker education, cooperative alternatives to company stores, and nationalization of the coal mines. Seeking to unite producers and consumers, Brophy argued that private ownership of the mines left both workers and the public at the mercy of rapacious, inefficient owners who lacked the incentive or imagination to stabilize their industry. Without the stability provided by public ownership, the UMWA would never be able to organize its jurisdiction or convince the industry to balance the production and consumption of coal. Brophy's relationship with the Bureau of Industrial Research reflected these interests. He was eager to establish links with liberals and intellectuals who could provide him with the technical assistance and broader contacts by which the larger program could be advanced.[29]

Brophy was impressed by the young Harvard graduate, recalling him as "a nice, sweet boy" with "a great deal of charm, and it was genuine." He also realized that Hapgood's connections to the liberal community might enhance his own standing within intellectual circles. For Powers Hapgood, John Brophy appeared as the prototypic worker-intellectual, an authentic son of the working class who combined rank-and-file experience with an avid search for knowledge. Brophy was self-educated, and Hapgood noted his "intelligence" and "refinement," middle-class virtues that he longed to find among the working class. Not only could Brophy hold his own with the intellectuals, but he never forgot his origins as an immigrant, a miner, and a union man. In Brophy's example, Hapgood found an inspirational synthesis that he sought to emulate. His discovery anticipated the Italian theorist Antonio Gramsci's hope that intellectuals might cultivate a "unity of manual and intellectual work," thereby gaining the credibility to influence working-class behavior.[30]

Energized by Brophy's vision and encouragement, Hapgood agreed to the District 2 president's request that he come to western Pennsylvania and learn more about the miners' problems. During spring and summer 1921, Hapgood worked on several projects under Brophy's direction. First he investigated the practice of car-pushing, whereby miners had to move heavy carts loaded with coal, often resulting in serious injury. Later he compiled an extensive report on the frequent failure of miners to receive adequate compensation for injuries suffered on the job. As Hapgood moved throughout District 2 attending union meetings and interviewing miners, his respect for the UMWA and its members continued to grow. At local union meetings, he observed the "intelligence" and democratic practice of the miners as they participated in vigorous debates over union policy and freely criticized leaders whose judgments they questioned. Here was industrial democracy in an embryonic form, spurred by informed workers and visionary leaders committed to civic participation and class solidarity.[31]

Hapgood's investigations resulted in a published article on car-pushing and a well-documented report on workers' compensation. Written in a muckraking style that would have pleased his Uncle Norman, both pieces focused on the injustices to social underdogs that had characterized his Uncle Hutch's most popular books. The compensation report embodied the naturalistic detail favored by muckrakers; Hapgood's extensive documentation of uncompensated injuries included reports of blood poisoning, ruptures, mangled hands, blinding, and one instance where an enraged foreman strangled a young Italian miner. He noted with dismay the machinations of attorneys and company officials who used their superior knowledge of legal procedure to manipulate the process and deny miners, especially those who were foreign-born, adequate recompense for their injuries. As a remedy, Hapgood proposed that District 2 establish its own compensation department and publish guides in foreign languages to assist immigrant miners in the filing of claims.[32]

Pleased with the results of Hapgood's investigations, Brophy offered his young protege a more challenging assignment. Somerset County had long been a staunch anti-union bastion within District 2, where large coal operators had successfully resisted the UMWA's attempts to organize. Brophy requested that Hapgood examine the conditions in nonunion mines within the district and assess the attitudes of miners toward union organization. Hapgood was eager to undertake a direct investigation. During July and August 1921 he traveled throughout the nonunion coal fields of western Pennsylvania via train and on foot, suitcase in one hand, lunch pail in the other, seeking work in the mines. Again, his findings were published, this time in a Bureau of Industrial Research pamphlet entitled "In Non-Union Mines: The Diary of a Coal Digger." The byline for the pamphlet described him as a member of the UMWA. Writing for the middle-class audience that the bureau's research tended to reach, Hapgood reveled in being identified as a miner and unionist who knew firsthand the issues that he was discussing.[33]

Beyond presenting the information he had gathered for Brophy, Hapgood informed his audience about the life of the miners. As he noted in his conclusion, "the nature of the work itself, which is so little known to ordinary folks who live their lives in the sunlight and freshness of the upper world, is hard and severe." The dangers of work underground were a recurring theme. In one entry, Hapgood asserted, "I will never forget the agony of mind and body" associated with shoveling coal in a contorted position created by a six-inch margin between the roof of the mine and the top of the loading car. On other occasions he experienced the rigors of car-pushing and was nearly grazed by a live wire while riding atop a loaded coal car through a mine. Yet he exulted in the combination of skill and judgment required in performing dangerous work and enjoyed the company of his "buddies," for it was customary to cooperate with another miner in preparing a "room" for the dislodgment and shoveling of coal. Underground, he suggested, there existed a strenuous life that the sheltered, effete middle-class could only imagine.[34]

Hapgood's political education deepened during his journey through the coal fields. With his exposure to such large nonunion operators as Berwind-White in Windber and the Cambria Steel Works in Johnstown, he learned workers were not exaggerating when they claimed that "the company owns the town and can do as it pleases." In Windber he was warned that he would face violent retribution from the coal companies if word of his mission became public. Hapgood encountered the long arm of corporate power on several occasions during his journey. In Vintondale he was dismissed from a job for asking questions about the pay and conditions of work in the mine. Later he had a run-in with the infamous coal and iron police, gun-toting guards employed by the coal companies who functioned as a private police force charged with protecting the operators' interests. For Hapgood, the coal and iron police were "one of the greatest evils of nonunion coal towns." They represented unaccountable, private power that stripped miners of their fundamental rights and made a mockery of democratic values.[35]

Among nonunion miners Hapgood found numerous grievances. They included wage rates far below the union scale, no payment for dead work (labor not associated with digging or loading coal), widespread cheating by operators in calculating the weight of coal on which compensation was based, and exorbitant prices charged at company stores. Although he met some former Wobblies and other union sympathizers in his travels, most of the miners appeared timid or apathetic when he broached the subject of unionism. Hapgood was frustrated by these attitudes, which ran counter to the superior intelligence he was accustomed to finding among miners. Lashing out, he characterized this group of miners as "inactive mentally" and "too lazy to exert themselves," a surprising departure from his usual environmental explanations for working-class apathy.[36]

Hapgood again seemed reluctant to analyze sentiments that deviated from the qualities he was searching for in the working class. Significantly, he gave scant emphasis to other evidence that suggested a more complex, socially rooted explanation for the miners' reticence. Some workers whom Hapgood met were constrained by consumer debt, including one miner who owed the company store for furniture he had purchased and another who was paying off a Ford automobile he had bought on an installment plan. Other miners were simply too engaged in the difficult task of finding work in a severely depressed coal industry to demonstrate interest in the union. Hapgood's conclusion was more to the point, incorporating his clear recognition of the climate of fear and social control that permeated nonunion mining towns. Although nonunion miners resented their mistreatment, they complained that "there is no organization to enable them to have an equal chance with the operators in the settling of differences" and "getting their rights." At the heart of the miners' struggle, Hapgood implied, were questions concerning the citizenship rights of Americans, rights that the operators were denying with impunity.[37]

What miners needed in order to overcome their sense of hopelessness was evidence of the union's willingness to fight on their behalf. "Some day," Hapgood predicted, "these Pennsylvania miners will begin to join organizations." His cohorts at the Bureau of Industrial Research and his patron John Brophy shared this view. The back cover of "In Non-Union Mines" displayed a map of the Somerset region under the heading: "Destined to be a Battle Map." Unbeknownst to Hapgood, Somerset County would soon became the setting where both his prediction and the assumptions of John Brophy's larger program were put to the test.[38]

After concluding his report on nonunion mines, Hapgood continued his work with the Bureau for Industrial Research and later vacationed at the family retreat in Rainy Lake, Minnesota. He took to the road again early in 1922 and hoboed his way through Illinois, Ohio, and West Virginia, looking for a mining job without success. Alarmed by their son's continuing attachment to vagabondage and his refusal to accept their offers of money, William and Eleanor Hapgood expressed concern for his safety and well-being. In an extraordinary thirty-page letter written on January 19, 1922, Hapgood attempted to allay their fears and explain his decision to pursue a career in the labor movement.[39]

The letter marked a culmination of Hapgood's search for a calling and illuminated the profound personal considerations guiding his political choices. The gravity of the letter was revealed in its opening line: "Here goes for the lengthy letter that I've known for some time I would have to write but which I've been putting off as long as possible." Unable to find work in a depressed coal industry, Hapgood confessed to his parents that he was down to his last $20.00 and would soon "be on the same plane as the other unemployed." "The thought of this only brings pleasure to me," he declared, for it would allow him to see if he could get by "without the help of my fortunate past." Knowing this revelation would cause his parents "pain," Hapgood hastened to explain the benefits of joblessness and hitching rides on trains. He pleaded for a two-week period of nonsupport, underscoring that there were clear limits to his incipient rebellion against parental authority.[40]

Hapgood attempted to explain to his parents how his unemployment reflected true fealty to the family's values. Invoking Walt Whitman, he insisted on a form of voluntary leveling and strict egalitarianism as the best means of fostering social empathy: "If all people were forced to play the game of life under the same rules, they would know, where they now do not know, what hardships the other fellow has to meet. As a result they would not only have a more tolerant and brotherly feeling for each other, but they would also understand just what they can do to better the living conditions of their fellows."[41]

Only by sharing the suffering of others, Hapgood insisted, could he put "his whole heart and soul and thus his best into the work of helping." By voluntarily accepting poverty, he would then be able to transcend the condescension of paternalism, achieve true understanding, and demonstrate his worth. Hapgood also emphasized the deeper personal meaning of being on his own, reflecting a broader cultural trend toward defining manhood as struggle and a readiness to suffer. He noted that at Andover, the "finer, stronger" boys were those who were working their way through school rather than relying on their family's largesse. Succeeding without parental assistance, he argued, "will make me a better man and consequently a better tool for the service of society." In addition to linking his quest for independence to his parents' values, Hapgood expressed his need to find a strenuous, manly alternative to middle-class comfort and security: "All my life I have wished I had an opportunity of meeting and striving to overcome something really difficult." Denied this opportunity in war, Powers Hapgood now sought to demonstrate his self-reliance and bravery, either in the mines or as part of the ranks of the unemployed.

He acknowledged that some self-made men had grown intolerant of weaker people but rooted his own quest for self-realization in the context of becoming a "better and more useful man."[42]

Although William and Eleanor Hapgood were disconcerted by their son's request, they encouraged him to "work out your life in your own way . . . and follow the course which will give you the most spiritual pleasure." Having instructed Powers on the importance of a life devoted to service, sacrifice, and cooperation, they realized that it would be counterproductive to attempt to dissuade him from acting on these values, even if they viewed his course as extreme. They might well have reasoned that in time, his need for adventure and proof of his mettle would diminish, and he would then be amenable to seeking "spiritual pleasure" from more conventional sources. Whatever the case, the issue for the moment became moot when several days later, Hapgood secured employment in a northeastern Pennsylvania anthracite mine.[43]

The January 19, 1922, letter revealed the complex set of influences shaping Powers Hapgood's commitment to labor. At the simplest level, he displayed an adolescent preoccupation to distinguish himself from his parents and assert his independence. Yet his personal declaration of independence remained painfully conditional, revealing the extent to which Powers Hapgood accepted his parents' definition of what constituted acceptable behavior. As a twenty-three-year-old adult, he still felt compelled to write a thirty-page letter justifying his plea for a two-week period of self-sufficiency. And at the end of the letter, he even offered to rescind his request if "being on my own" would "cause you too much worry."[44]

Hapgood's urgent request to "be on the same plane with the other unemployed" and "put his whole heart and soul" into easing the condition of the poor reflected an abiding sense of guilt over his fortunate past. He sought expiation by means of voluntary deprivation, which accorded with his personal need to demonstrate his ability to withstand suffering and his political commitment to the elimination of privilege. Yet he acknowledged that in contrast to his traveling companions, his "suffering" was self-imposed and obviated by his easy access to resources unavailable to the truly needy. At this stage of his development, there was a strong element of dilettantism in Hapgood's self-conscious attempt to approximate poverty and assume working-class status. His romanticization of unemployment and tramping neglected to consider the very real loss of self-respect and dignity working people experienced when they lacked the security of stable jobs or permanent homes.

The profound personal expectations that Hapgood attached to politics epitomized the secularization and politicization of impulses once largely satisfied via private or religious means. Hapgood's Uncle Hutchins had captured this sentiment tellingly in his 1907 book, *The Spirit of Labor:* "I am interested in trades-unionism, because it is the only thing which today seems to have any religion in it." By contrast, the politics of Hapgood's mentor John Brophy stemmed directly from the cultural and institutional moorings of work, church, ethnicity, union, and community. Not finding these connections in his secular upper-middle-class upbringing, Powers Hapgood looked to workers and the UMWA to satisfy his heartfelt need for membership in "shared communities of risk and high purpose." Whether or not the working class and the labor movement could fulfill the weighty personal demands Hapgood placed on them would remain a persistent question. His intense desire to gain acceptance within these communities compelled him to demonstrate continually the depth of his commitment and prove that he was not simply slumming or passing through the working class. This conflation of the personal and the political, a sentiment by no means confined to Powers Hapgood, tended to imbue middle-class radicalism with a self-absorption and level of expectation that were often ill suited to the complex demands of public life.[45]

At this time Hapgood also wrote several pieces in publications aimed at students and church people explaining the political rationale behind his decision to join the working class. He rejected business as hostile to liberal ideas and a difficult arena in which to gain influence. Having once considered becoming an "intellectual liberal" in the tradition of his uncles, he dismissed this option. Intellectual liberals reached only a limited audience and lacked a genuine understanding of working-class life. For example, the Bureau of Industrial Research, however well-intentioned, functioned merely as an adjunct to the labor movement and exerted little in the way of lasting influence.[46]

Hapgood leveled an even harsher criticism at intellectuals, one that underscored the personal dimensions of his political vision. He charged that in addition to being ineffectual, intellectuals lived off the labor of others, refusing to "fulfill their part of the ancient contract" with working people whose labor permitted them the leisure to theorize. This rigid view revealed an enduring anti-intellectual strain in Hapgood's thought, whereby direct experience and personal morality were elevated at the expense of critical social analysis. As a result, Powers Hapgood's appropriation of a producer identity was both self-conscious and contrived. He failed to consider that the producer ideology of the late nineteenth century was principally a defense against the encroach-ments of corporate capitalism and wage labor rather than an attack on intellectuals and the middle class. In fact, intellectuals and middle-class reformers were often welcomed by these movements for their theoretical contributions and political support. Devoid of these recog-nitions, Hapgood's definition of producerism signified a private, per-sonal vision that lacked broader public meaning.[47]

Unions, however, provided the synthesis that Hapgood had been seeking. They had the potential to reach a broad audience, to promote both "material and spiritual progress" through collective action, and to integrate productive labor with intellectual development. In contrast to the paternalism implicit in efforts that imposed change from above, unions promoted change from below, thereby extending democratic values and countering the trend toward centralized, bureaucratic au-thority. Ironically, Hapgood's vision of an expansive social role for unions was more often supported by the intellectuals he disparaged than by the labor movement he was preparing to join. While he was touting labor's potential to lead a progressive coalition, events were proceeding in precisely the opposite direction. Instead of reaching a broad audience, unions were forced to fend for themselves during the 1920s or induced to become junior partners in corporate attempts aimed at maintaining class harmony. Neither government, business, nor the public seemed inclined to grant labor an expanded social role, especially as the postwar economy boomed and the free market ushered in an era of unparalleled prosperity.[48]

Powers Hapgood was by no means alone in looking to the working class as an alternative to bourgeois convention. Many of his contempo-raries briefly hoboed or worked in factories in order to satisfy their curiosity about working-class life. Settlement houses, too, were filled with young people seeking to assuage their class guilt, share the suffering of the poor, and find a missing sense of community. A genera-tion earlier, this experience with charitable work propelled some young upper-middle-class women into the Women's Trade Union League (WTUL), where they sought more direct contact with workers and a closer connection to "real life." Yet while some of Hapgood's friends envied his adventures, most, like Hank Costigan, a college acquain-tance now in law school, wondered when he would relinquish his "glorious vagabondage for the slavery of the workplace." Generally, youthful explorers returned to professional and middle-class life en-riched but chastened by their encounters with working people and in Costigan's words, "were determined to turn bourgeois" even if they did not abandon their social ideals. As Clarence Darrow once quipped, "I'd rather be the friend of the workingman than be the workingman; it's easier."[49]

The intensity of Powers Hapgood's commitments and the duties imposed by his family's legacy combined to make his estrangement from the middle class more pronounced than that of his contemporaries. Most young liberals were content to read about the plight of working people in *The Nation* and the *New Republic* and empathize with their struggles while retaining the privileges and comforts of upper-middle-class status. Finding empathy and moral support an insufficient demonstration of his commitment, Powers Hapgood went further. The working class was the only place where he could find moral virtue and test his values in the laboratory of "actual life." As he explained to Roger Baldwin: "The brotherhood of man is far more nearly realized among manual working groups than among people of the middle class. . . . It is better for one to impart what little knowledge he has to these people than to study to get more knowledge for himself or to teach members of a class who are in a position to acquire all the knowledge they need for themselves."[50]

Whereas others like Roger Baldwin admitted that their "traditions" prevented them from becoming workers, Hapgood concluded that he could find fulfillment only by "submerging his interests with those of the masses" and joining the working class. He tied his personal search to working-class aspirations, resting content, in the words of Walt Whitman, his favorite poet, to "celebrate himself" only in concert with others. This sense of duty and collectivism distinguished him from most other middle-class radicals, who often agonized over subordinating their personal quest for meaning to the demands of social movements seeking political and economic reforms. Such vacillation between public commitment and private need was illustrated in Hapgood's extended dialogue with his friend Eloise Cummings, who was contemplating whether or not to work in a factory. Disagreeing with Hapgood's emphasis on collective action and structural change, Cummings, the disowned daughter of a wealthy Pittsburgh family, concluded that "the greatest revolution of all" needed to occur in "the hearts of men" before genuine social change was possible. Hapgood disagreed, insisting that a radical alteration of material conditions was the only way to transform individualistic cultural values and morally lax personal behavior. In order for service to triumph over greed, he argued, some form of socialism was needed to foster an atmosphere in which egalitarian values would replace selfishness and competition. In contrast to Eloise

Cummings and other conflicted young radicals, Powers Hapgood found productive labor, direct involvement with the working class, and political engagement to be the most appropriate ways to find inner harmony and change the cultural values that he found objectionable.[51]

The historic relationship between middle-class reformers and the working class has been described by Bernard Johnpoll as an "insoluble problem." According to Johnpoll, middle-class activists have invariably become disillusioned after prolonged contact with the working class, which has not always shared the utopianism or the moral fervor of its "benefactors." Although the cultural distance between the middle class and the working class may not be an insoluble problem, it has often sent reformers scurrying back to the comforts of more private, intellectual pursuits.[52]

Powers Hapgood remained largely unaware of this sobering history. He could cite his father's experience at Columbia Conserve as evidence that the relationship between middle-class reformers and workers did not have to end in disappointment and confusion. Moreover, his own experiences in mines, on boxcars, and around campfires had revealed the superior virtue of the working class. In John Brophy, he had found a mentor who confirmed his faith in the labor movement and provided him with an entree to acquiring influence within the UMWA. Tentatively, he had begun to assert his independence from parental authority and distance himself from the upper-middle-class world in which he had been reared. He was now determined to amass the five years of experience as a mine worker required to gain "the honor of being put up for office in the UMW of A" and complete his journey from college to the ranks of labor.[53]

Chapter Three

The Somerset Strike

He gave the best of his young manhood during
that stirring period.

—John Brophy, March 1949

Early in 1922 Powers Hapgood buckled down to work with his buddy in
the anthracite mines. But in April, the outbreak of a nationwide miners'
strike left him again among the unemployed. Hapgood reported that an
almost eerie calm spread over the coal fields as miners laid down their
tools. Nothing in his brief experience in the ranks of labor, however,
could have prepared him for the subsequent turmoil and the prominent
role he assumed in helping to lead one of the most significant strikes of
the 1920s. For the next seventeen months, the aspiring young coal
miner witnessed a remarkable display of union solidarity that captured
national attention and fundamentally shaped his relation to the working class, the labor movement, and the UMWA.[1]

The United Mine Workers faced adverse circumstances as they
prepared for contract negotiations in spring 1922. World War I had
spurred increased coal production and led to substantial wage in-
creases for miners, but conditions worsened after the war's end. The
demand for coal dipped sharply, resulting in falling prices, limited
markets, and overproduction. Responding to these developments, the
operators adopted a strategy that directly threatened the UMWA's

bargaining position. They began to transfer more of their operations to nonunion coal fields, especially those in West Virginia, where the union had met fierce resistance in its attempts to organize. This initiative was accompanied by a tough stance at the bargaining table. The operators proposed steep wage cuts and aimed to supplant the union's master agreement in the Central Competitive Field with a system of settlements on a district-by-district basis. The Central Competitive Field, which was established in 1897, covered mines in Illinois, Indiana, Ohio, and parts of Pennsylvania and constituted a landmark achievement in the UMWA's quest to gain uniform conditions throughout the industry. Without this master agreement as a standard, the districts could be played off against each other, and the union would no longer be able to bargain from a position of strength.[2]

The political context was equally daunting. Given coal's importance to the national economy, the stance of the government was crucial to the outcome of the negotiations. Unfortunately, the Harding administration was cool to the UMWA's cause, and Commerce Secretary Herbert Hoover concluded that wage cuts were essential to stabilizing a wounded industry. Nonetheless, the miners insisted that there be no backward steps. They approved bargaining demands that held the line on wages and proposed reducing hours in order to ensure adequate levels of employment.[3]

With negotiations deadlocked, the UMWA prepared to strike. Almost as an afterthought, the union decided to make a last-minute appeal for solidarity to nonunion miners. Although the union leadership had no clear strategy for implementing this approach, it knew that the operators would attempt to shift as much production as possible to nonunion areas once the strike was underway. If nonunion miners could be persuaded to honor union picket lines, the strike would be far more likely to hurt the operators at the point of production.[4]

John Brophy had long regarded organizing the nonunion mines in Somerset County and adjacent areas of his district as essential to the future of the UMWA. Although encouraged by Powers Hapgood's report that a serious organizing drive might attract support, Brophy had no illusions about the task ahead. The 140 companies in the area were affiliated with some of the sturdiest pillars of industrial capitalism, including Bethlehem Steel, United States Steel, and the powerful Berwind-White Company, one of the world's largest independent producers of bituminous coal. Many of the coal companies were interlocked with powerful railroad, banking, and insurance interests. In the words of Heber Blankenhorn, Hapgood's colleague at the Bureau of Industrial

Research and author of a subsequent book on the 1922 strike, the Operators Association advertised Somerset as a "non-union, American Plan paradise" and fully intended to maintain their tight control. Previous attempts to organize in Somerset had been aggressively resisted, leading John L. Lewis to conclude just eight months before the strike that the timing was inopportune for any new forays. Given this history and the industry's ravaged condition, Brophy and other union leaders had little reason to believe that their appeal to nonunion miners would be well received.[5]

Shortly after the national strike began in April 1922, Brophy asked Powers Hapgood if he would serve as a volunteer organizer in Somerset County. Hapgood hesitated initially. He was more inclined to work with the already organized "in solving functional problems" rather than devote his attention to attracting new recruits. Nonetheless, he appreciated the necessity for organizing the nonunion mines and calculated that direct involvement in the strike might further his long-range goal of seeking union office.[6]

Hapgood was suddenly thrust into the midst of an extraordinary confrontation. The 1922 strike became the largest in the UMWA's history: more than half a million miners, both union and nonunion, from the anthracite and bituminous segments of the industry, walked off their jobs. To the surprise of John Brophy and other veteran officials in District 2, some 90,000 miners in Somerset and neighboring nonunion strongholds heeded the union's call to strike. Somerset now became the battleground that Hapgood had predicted in his Bureau of Industrial Research pamphlet "Diary of a Coal Digger," exceeding the wildest expectations of the union leaders who had belatedly urged nonunionists to join their ranks.[7]

What accounted for the overwhelming response among nonunion miners to District 2's strike call? Certainly the grievances that Hapgood had identified in his report were deeply felt. Wage reductions, consistent cheating by operators in the weighing of coal, no pay for dead work, and exploitation at the company store—these complaints not only involved the quest for economic security but also spoke to fundamental issues of justice and equity. Many miners saw their action as continuing a familial tradition of union solidarity. As one miner observed, "We're only doing what our daddies did." There was in fact a long history of attempts to organize in Somerset. For several years before the strike, John Brophy had been deluged with requests from miners, merchants, and concerned citizens who saw unionization as the key to breaking the coal companies' stranglehold on political and economic affairs in their communities. Yet compelling job-related grievances and historical justification alone did not fully explain the outpouring of support that the union received in Somerset. Other influences were at work that lent the miners' cause an especially fervent sense of legitimacy and held particular relevance for Powers Hapgood.[8]

Many of the striking miners in Somerset were veterans of World War I. In Windber, a company town that was the stronghold of the viciously anti-union Berwind-White Company, 360 of the strikers had fought overseas. In the democratic rhetoric that Woodrow Wilson had used to legitimate American involvement, the miners found powerful justification for their cause. As one local union argued just before the strike, "The operators who preached patriotism to our Government and our contracts during the war do not hesitate now to make the effort to violate contracts to which our government was a party." Striking miners at Consolidation Coal elaborated on this theme: "We are fighting for the right to live as free American citizens and to live our lives in our own way, under the laws of the United States of America, not under the laws of a privately owned and tyrannical coal company." Assertions that the actions of the operators, the police, and the courts were un-American pervaded the miners' rhetoric and challenged the legitimacy of their opponents. This argument gave the strike transcendent meaning, raising issues of democracy, citizenship, and patriotism that Powers Hapgood could connect to his own heritage and the visionary aspirations he held for the labor movement.[9]

As the strike spread across Somerset County, the operators relied on injunctions and arrests of union leaders in order to stem the exodus of nonunion miners from the coal pits. The police presence during the strike, which included deputy sheriffs, coal and iron police, and special borough officers, was overwhelming. Several months into the strike, an investigation by the ACLU revealed that for every fifteen miners in Somerset County, there was one law enforcement official present. Hapgood was himself arrested over a dozen times in Somerset, occasionally jailed, doused with a fire hose, and threatened with a billy club by Jack Bentley, head of the Somerset Operators Association's notorious mine guards. Another antagonist, an enraged coal company official named D. B. Zimmerman, vowed to shoot the young organizer after reading his account of working in nonunion mines.[10]

Hapgood's prominent role in the strike infuriated the coal operators and the authorities. Somerset County Judge John Berkey, who presided over many of the court proceedings during the strike, summarized their attitude, observing that "the court feels the presence of Hapgood is obnoxious to the operators." A company lawyer lamented that "such a bright boy" was "seized with such a fad." Angered that the young Harvard graduate had defected to the working class, one coal operator was far less charitable: "He comes of a good family, has a good education, and doesn't have to earn a living by stirring up dissatisfaction." For his part, Hapgood was bemused by his treatment and the attention he received. Jailed on July 10, 1922, for attempting to persuade scabs to honor union picket lines, he informed his parents that he felt pampered as a jail trusty. He passed his time playing cards with the sheriff, receiving well-wishers, and sharing food he received from supporters with the other prisoners. In the early months of the strike when spirits were high and prospects for a favorable settlement appeared hopeful, Hapgood reveled in the drama of picket lines, strike meetings, confrontations with the authorities, and the relationships he was developing with militant coal miners.[11]

Throughout his encounters with the authorities in Somerset, Hapgood insisted on what one older organizer derisively referred to as his "constitooshnl rights," appealing to hostile courts to arrest operators and company police who violated the law with impunity. Many of the striking miners in Somerset were immigrants—Poles, Hungarians, Italians—to whom the language of rights was appealing but unfamiliar. The language of Americanism came much easier to Powers Hapgood, a midwestern, middle-class Protestant whose family had been in America for more than 250 years. Maude McCreary, a writer for the left-leaning *Federated Press* who was covering the strike, scoffed at the young organizer's recourse to the protections of citizenship: "Forgive me if I smile a little at your faith that your constitutional rights must in the end be recognized." Instead, McCreary hoped that Hapgood's rough treatment in Somerset would make him realize that class struggle was preferable to seeking justice under capitalist laws.[12]

Hapgood was by no means oblivious to the class overtones of justice in Somerset. He refused, however, to believe that constitutional rights existed solely at the pleasure of whomever held state power. Insistence on his constitutional rights allowed him to affirm the legitimacy of his own actions, and by seeking to extend such protections to the striking miners, he hoped to assure them of their dignity, self-worth, and acceptance as Americans. Therefore, he continued to protest what he called "un-American injunctions" and argued with armed guards that it was "not decent" to call himself or other "gentlemen" (striking miners) "s.o.b.s." Hapgood actually enjoyed some success in having several

Powers Hapgood in jail during 1922 Somerset strike.
His role in the strike infuriated coal operators and
authorities. A company lawyer lamented that "such
a bright boy" was "seized with such a fad."
(Courtesy of Lilly Library, Indiana University)

egregious violators of workers' rights detained for their transgressions.
His insistence on decorum amid class conflict resonated with the
strikers. As Heber Blankenhorn observed, it "gave a great many of the
simple people of many nationalities the new experience of having rights
and having them defended." Also, Hapgood won increasing respect from
colleagues who earlier had derided his preoccupation with rights but
now saw the powerful appeal of his references to citizenship and
Americanism.[13]

The miners' passionate assertion of their rights as Americans was
buttressed by shared notions of self-reliance and solidarity. Speaking at

countless meetings to hundreds of miners and sharing their travails, Hapgood was exposed to a culture of fraternity and solidarity that affirmed his faith in the labor movement. The language used by union organizers on the picket line reflected the importance that miners attached to notions of manliness, citizenship, and sacrifice. Hapgood joined his colleagues in urging miners to "be a man among men" and honor the strike. "Real Americans do not let others fight their battles," explained the union in its initial strike call. To be a man and an American, then, was synonymous with supporting the UMWA and its quest for industrial freedom. As Hapgood explained to his parents, these sentiments were so deeply ingrained that the daughter of an alcoholic miner had asked him "to keep her Daddy from being a scab." This ethic, which was demonstrated throughout the strike, reinforced Hapgood's belief that shared fraternal and moral values remained vibrant in Pennsylvania mining towns.[14]

Hapgood's attachment to the miners was further bolstered by the relationships he formed with several strike leaders, two of whom became lifelong friends. Albert Armstrong was an English-born miner who was elected president of a local union formed at Consolidation Coal, a large company closely tied to the Rockefeller interests. He became so attached to Hapgood that he named a child born during the strike after him. Hapgood also walked the picket lines with George Gregory, known as "Praying George" for his repeated use of religious rhetoric to inspire his fellow miners. Gregory had been a member of the fabled South Wales Miners' Federation and emerged as a prominent spokesperson for the strikers. In addition, Hapgood worked closely with John Kerr and Faber McCloskey, leaders of UMWA Local 1056 in Gallitzin, who led Labor Party efforts in Cambria County and were staunch advocates of John Brophy's larger program. These men, steeped in the traditions of English and Welsh miners, embodied the spirit of democratic, local unionism that Hapgood found so appealing. His friendships with Armstrong, Gregory, Kerr, and McCloskey signaled his acceptance into the fraternal culture of the union and his ability to gain the confidence of some of its most respected local leaders. As one local union official wrote John Brophy, referring to Hapgood and a fellow organizer, "they are men from the ground up and the kind that more ought to be."[15]

Beyond these relationships, Hapgood encountered aroused communities of miners and their families whose conflict with the operators assumed political and ideological overtones. As John Brophy explained in a letter to the U.S. Coal Commission, the Somerset strike was fundamentally concerned with preventing the destruction of "democratic community life." This theme was articulated throughout the strike by the acts of miners and their supporters. Hapgood wrote his parents about an Italian farmer who ignored coal company threats and allowed miners to meet on his property. Proudly, strikers informed him in November 1922 that they had invaded an operator's birthday party and proceeded to distribute pro-union literature. Merchants extended credit to the strikers, and ethnic organizations followed suit in making their halls available for union meetings. In Windber, priests who urged miners to return to work found the workers' tools left on their porches, receiving a clear message of their parishioners' refusal to accept the church's authority. Women and children were sometimes arrested for joining picket lines, in one instance defying a judge's warning to return to their "place in the home." Nor was the political establishment immune from the miners' activism. Hapgood noted that new union members were instrumental in breaking the Republican machine in Somerset County and electing their own candidates to office. In challenging authoritarian rule and accepted norms of behavior, the miners were asserting their rights as independent citizens and articulating alternatives to the ideological hegemony of the operators.[16]

Hapgood's jubilation over the strikers' heroism and courage was undercut by his introduction to the bruising world of UMWA politics as practiced by John L. Lewis. A shrewd political tactician as well as a consummate opportunist, Lewis was convinced that the UMWA lacked the ability to force concessions from the operators in 1922. While the operators intimated that they might be willing to renegotiate contracts in the Central Competitive Field, they refused to recognize the newly formed local unions in Somerset. Lewis had hoped for federal intervention, but an attack on scabs by striking miners in Herrin, Illinois, resulted in nineteen deaths and caused the Harding administration to tilt in the operators' favor. Faced with the government's hostility, the operators' unwavering resistance, and a depleted treasury, the UMWA president acted to preserve the union's base. In August, he brokered a deal that maintained the old wage scale but did not compel union operators to sign contracts covering their nonunion subsidiaries. This settlement was anathema to Brophy and Hapgood, who had assured anxious strikers from nonunion mines that the national union would sign no agreements that excluded their recognition.[17]

Lewis's resolution of the strike may have been the best settlement possible under the circumstances. In District 2, however, Hapgood,

Brophy, and other leaders saw the UMWA president's action as a "sell-out." Brophy later characterized the deal as one reached with "indecent haste," insisting that the coal companies were beginning to "feel the pinch" and eventually would have been forced to capitulate. Following the August settlement, he balked at negotiating with operators who refused to extend recognition to their nonunion affiliates in Somerset. One newly formed local eloquently captured the spirit of the strike in pleading with Lewis to reconsider. His action, Local 1347 charged, "means that this Weaver Co. will be more dirty and [we] will never be able to organize Revloc again." To no avail they urged the UMWA president to meet with them, declaring "it means real slavery for us if you do not."[18]

Lewis rebuffed these requests, leaving District 2 to fend for itself. Not surprisingly, Powers Hapgood was appalled by Lewis's deal with the operators, which he viewed as a betrayal of courageous strikers who had taken enormous risks in order to gain union representation. Here was a shocking example of the kind of hypocrisy that he had not anticipated finding in what he saw as an idealistic movement. Without fully appreciating the implications of his action, Hapgood joined the editor of District 2's newspaper in organizing opposition to Lewis's reelection in 1922. His efforts were undermined when a Lewis crony intercepted a telegram that the insurgents had sent to John Brophy requesting his advice. Lewis's agent then forged Brophy's signature on a reply that discouraged Hapgood and his collaborators from pursuing their activities. Upon learning that Brophy's response was a forgery, Hapgood's opposition to Lewis stiffened, and the die was cast for a prolonged showdown between the Harvard-educated miner and the powerful UMWA president.[19]

Powers Hapgood's insurgency stemmed from deep political and cultural differences with John L. Lewis, whose vision of the trade union movement revolved around the need to gather, exercise, and maintain power. This ruthless pragmatism clashed with Hapgood's ardent devotion to democracy and fraternity, ideals that were being defended at great cost by the striking Somerset miners. Craving a respectability often denied labor leaders, Lewis subscribed to American notions of upward mobility and acquisitive individualism, values that Hapgood had rejected. Further, Hapgood's firm ethical standards were offended by Lewis's unbridled opportunism and ruthless suppression of dissent. He took seriously the miner's oath that committed UMWA members to defend freedom of speech and recoiled at Lewis's cavalier disregard for any connection between means and ends. At root, it was the UMWA chief's dishonesty that repelled him, opening a breach between the two that lasted nearly fifteen years.[20]

Lewis was himself deeply suspicious of the Harvard-educated miner. He regarded Hapgood as a dilettante and troublemaker acting in league with his opponents. His distaste for Hapgood did not stem entirely from personal animus or fear that the young insurgent posed a threat to his position. Just as important, Lewis's debate with Hapgood and Brophy reflected a sharply different vision of how the union should respond to the hostile environment in which it was forced to function. Witnessing the government's suppression of the nationwide railroad shopmen's strike in 1922 and the employer-inspired open-shop offensive against the labor movement, Lewis calculated that his options were limited. In his judgment the union was in a constant battle for survival, and an excessive preoccupation with democracy was a luxury that the besieged institution could ill afford. Instead, he placed his hopes in working with large operators to maintain high wages and drive nonunion competitors out of business, preferably with the government's assistance. Given this vision, Lewis rejected the worker militancy and larger program advocated by Hapgood and Brophy as an unacceptable challenge to his strategy.[21]

Hapgood and Brophy, however, faced a more immediate problem. Unwilling to abandon their commitment to the Somerset strikers, they had to find ways of maintaining morale and exerting additional pressure on the company. In order to provide relief to miners who were being evicted from company housing, District 2 approved an assessment of its members to furnish additional funds. As winter 1923 approached and the union dug in for a long siege, sobering new responsibilities fell upon the young organizer's shoulders. Hapgood now was charged with finding tents for shelter, clothing for children, food for families, and funds to pay rent and other bills incurred by the striking miners. He drew on his family's wide range of contacts for support. Columbia Conserve sent canned goods, his Uncle Norman hosted a fundraising luncheon in New York, Roger Baldwin's American Fund for Public Service made a $25,000 loan, and such leading liberals as Elizabeth Brandeis and Dorothy Straight contributed to the strikers' cause at his behest. Clearly, the strike had become a cause celebre within liberal circles. As noted in a May 1922 letter to the *New Republic*, "men and women of the privileged class" were aiding the miners out of "sympathy for their American neighbors."[22]

Hapgood savored the opportunity to educate liberals about the realities of class conflict. The character of John McLoud, a worker-intellectual who appeared in Hapgood's unpublished novel "Coal and Men," echoed his sentiments. McLoud was not angry over being arrested in Somerset, rather, he looked forward to telling his liberal friends "what coal company repression was all about." Somerset enabled Hapgood to challenge the commitment of liberals to industrial democracy and civil liberties as he established his own credentials as a full-fledged participant in the miners' struggle. In spite of his concerns about the fecklessness of intellectual elites, Hapgood recognized the weight of liberal opinion, and he brought the problems of the miners to their attention. He also understood that opening the closed, authoritarian world of Somerset to outside scrutiny would lend further legitimacy to the miners' cause.[23]

Working with his old Bureau for Industrial Research colleagues Robert Bruere and Heber Blankenhorn, Hapgood now looked for a way to embarrass the coal companies in their own backyards. With the miners' morale sinking following Lewis's deal with the operators, Blankenhorn advocated "a dramatic and cracking stroke" that would rally public opinion and spur government intervention. In a precursor of what a half-century later would be called a "corporate campaign," he and Bruere devised a plan to pressure the coal companies by exposing their political and financial connections and spotlighting their blatant disregard of the public interest.[24]

The Bruere-Blankenhorn plan reflected the Progressive era's faith in exposure of corporate wrongdoing, aroused public opinion, and government as an arbiter of social conflict. As Blankenhorn explained, the plan aimed to enlist the "public as a partner" and demonstrate how the operators' intransigence was injuring the interests of consumers. The prime targets were Consolidation Coal and the fiercely anti-union Berwind-White Company. Bruere and Blankenhorn believed that John D. Rockefeller Jr., a large Consolidation Coal stockholder, was sensitive to publicity following his Colorado Fuel and Iron Company's massacre of miners and their families during a 1914 strike. Berwind-White supplied coal for the Interborough Rapid Transit Company (IRT), a major subway in New York City, and E. J. Berwind, the company's owner, sat on the IRT's board of directors. Due to diminished coal supplies, service on the IRT had been curtailed, and the city, which was a part-owner of the line, was paying much higher prices for coal. Here was a case where private power was subverting the public interest. As the striking miners explained in a statement before New York Mayor John Hylan and the city's Board of Estimate, both citizens and workers were victims of "the tyrannical policies of great transportation and coal companies linked together not to give public service but to smash workingmen."[25]

Hapgood assembled a delegation of striking miners, including his friends George Gregory and Albert Armstrong, and headed to New York to put the Bruere-Blankenhorn plan into effect. During a two-week visit, the Harvard graduate turned labor organizer took the miners' cause to leading New York politicians, liberal drawing rooms, and the corridors of corporate and finance capitalism. On September 26, 1922, he and several other miners addressed a public hearing of the New York City Board of Estimate, a meeting arranged by his Uncle Norman. At the hearing and on picket lines at the corporate headquarters of Berwind-White and Consolidation Coal, Hapgood and his delegation told horrifying stories of evicted miners living in chicken coops and stables, violent tactics employed by the operators and the coal and iron police, and even the rape of a striker's wife by a Berwind-White guard in Windber. The press dutifully noted these atrocities, but attempts by Mayor Hylan and other city officials to arrange a meeting with E. J. Berwind proved unsuccessful. Hapgood was more hopeful of influencing John D. Rockefeller Jr., who had a liberal reputation in business circles. Albert Armstrong met with several of Rockefeller's closest associates and gained public sympathy when his son was born during the delegation's visit. Rockefeller later issued a conciliatory statement conceding the legitimacy of the strikers' demands, but he lacked either the clout or the willingness to sway his fellow directors.[26]

At the urging of the miners, Hylan dispatched a committee that journeyed to Somerset to investigate the charges. The committee was brusquely treated; members reported that their hotel rooms were ransacked and their mail tampered with by Berwind-White officials. Hapgood organized hundreds of miners to attend a committee hearing in Windber, but Berwind-White refused to appear before this public gathering. The Hylan committee subsequently issued a report in December 1922, denouncing Berwind-White as a "soulless corporation," which refused to admit that collective bargaining "has become a fixed institution in this and many other lands." The committee did not recommend any action that would pressure Berwind-White, however. Rather than directly engage the company's entrenched power, it advocated full public ownership of the subways as the best way to protect consumers and the rights of coal miners. In John Brophy's words, Mayor Hylan "got his political capital out of the report, and that was all he was after."[27]

The failure of the Bruere-Blankenhorn plan to enlist the public as a partner raised serious questions about several key Progressive assumptions. Contrary to Bruere and Blankenhorn's expectations, the state had been unable to act as an effective arbiter. Hapgood did not react directly to this setback, but since he had initially "hoped and prayed" that the government would intervene, he was surely disappointed at the lukewarm response of liberal New York politicos. As John L. Lewis had come to understand, the wave of postwar strikes, the linking of unions with subversion, and the business community's vigorous pursuit of its open-shop drive had consigned the state to a role on the sidelines.

Bruere and Blankenhorn had also hoped to capitalize on the public's fear that distant, unaccountable corporate interests were failing to provide them with efficient, affordable service. Unfortunately, despite strong support from liberal activists, the miners' troubles seemed too distant to the majority of the middle class. As *The Nation* lamented, "the public is far more interested in getting coal than doing justice." Indeed, a college friend later complained to Hapgood that consumers had been hurt by the strike, and because they represented the "majority," they "deserve[d] more consideration than the miners." As members of a newly affluent middle class and not wholly secure in their status, they may well have regarded the workers' demands as extravagant. Also, middle-class consumers perhaps found the employers' justification of the open shop more attuned to their sense of Americanism than the miners' rhetoric of patriotism and citizenship. This tepid response revealed a widening gulf between consumers and producers that posed serious difficulties for sustaining cross-class alliances in a culture of abundance. Witnessing the failure of the Bruere-Blankenhorn plan to obtain public support and prompt government intervention, Powers Hapgood turned his attention to the internal affairs of the union and sought other means of advancing the miners' cause.[28]

Without the prospect of government intervention, the Somerset miners found themselves marginalized by the beginning of 1923. In January, the UMWA international suspended the strike in the adjacent coke region of Fayette County, leading Somerset strikers to fear that they would soon meet the same fate. Internal strife began to erode the solidarity that had sustained the miners. When District 2's executive board voted in February to grant back pay to staffers who had not been compensated during the strike, a groundswell of protest arose from miners who had gone without paychecks for months. Although Hapgood was not a target of such criticism (he had not been among those requesting back pay), he was surely disturbed when his friends John

Kerr and Faber McCloskey joined others in wondering if their leaders were "not men at their word of honor." Under the tension of a prolonged strike, shared understandings about loyalty and manhood were beginning to fray.[29]

As the strike wore on, many miners drifted away from Somerset in search of work, and the operators were able to find a sufficient number of strikebreakers to reopen many of the mines. On the first anniversary of the strike in April 1923, Hapgood joined others in a renewed effort to get scabs out of the mines. This initiative was unavailing, as was his attempt in May to protest an "unlawful and unAmerican injunction" by getting arrested yet another time. By summer 1923 the strike was crumbling, and John Brophy's political position within District 2 became precarious. John L. Lewis was angered not only by Brophy's refusal to call off the strike but also by District 2's fierce commitment to democratic and participatory procedures. As a UMWA international representative reported to Lewis in June 1923, District 2 leaders were guilty of "allowing the fullest measure of democracy in allowing the common layman to decide [such] important issues after instruction by the 'progressive' district organizers." District 2, then, represented an unacceptable political and ideological challenge to John L. Lewis, and he moved to neutralize this remaining outpost of opposition to his authority.[30]

Stepping up their efforts to discredit John Brophy, Lewis's loyalists found in Powers Hapgood a useful target. At a special district convention in April 1923, one delegate, possibly acting with Lewis's approval, denounced Hapgood as a "college graduate" who was "never a miner." "The Lord only knows where he comes from," the delegate proclaimed, depicting Hapgood's role in the union as illegitimate. Anticipating that his protege might be attacked, Brophy had advised Hapgood not to attend the meeting, even though a local union had elected him as a delegate. Brophy feared Hapgood's presence would only incite his rivals and leave him open to charges that the meeting was being packed with paid staff in order to override the will of the rank and file. But when these charges were made, Brophy vigorously defended Hapgood: "It is true that he has the misfortune of being a college graduate. . . . [Yet] guns have been shoved up against his body. He has been imprisoned. He has gone through the test of whether or not his conduct has been that of a man and a union man."[31]

Brophy explained that Hapgood had received only expenses during the strike and had been "willing to give his services without compensation." He also pointed out that Hapgood had raised thousands of dollars in relief for the strikers. Other delegates joined Brophy in defending Hapgood's honor and integrity. It was clear that Hapgood had become a respected figure within District 2. And, in describing Hapgood as "a man and a union man," John Brophy affirmed his induction into the fraternity of the union, thereby fulfilling the young Harvard graduate's most fervent dream.[32]

With the Somerset strike in shambles, the possibilities for government intervention bleak, and internecine struggle growing within District 2, Hapgood looked for new allies. His search led him to the American Communist Party (CP) and marked his formal entry into the world of left-wing politics. Committed to a policy of "boring from within," CP leader William Z. Foster sought alliances with "progressive elements" in key unions. Hapgood met with Foster several times during winter and spring 1923 and was impressed by his working-class background, tactical acumen, and commitment to opposing Lewis. John Brophy did not share Hapgood's attraction to the Communist Party. As the District 2 president explained, "my criticism of the communists is that their philosophy . . . is a repudiation of the democratic means of settling social and political problems."[33]

Hapgood innocently took Foster's offer of assistance at face value. Eager to rally all anti-Lewis forces under a common banner, he welcomed the CP leader's support but failed to consider the ramifications of his action within the union. In June 1923, he attended the Progressive International Conference of the UMWA, an attempt by Foster and the CP to unite Lewis's opponents. Hapgood was an active participant in the conference, promoting the cause of the Somerset strikers and approving plans to oppose Lewis at the UMWA convention in 1924. Recognizing the insurgents as a threat to his authority, Lewis wasted no time in condemning the conference participants as "dual unionists" and demanded that Brophy fire Hapgood from his staff position.[34]

Brophy resisted Lewis's demand, but he realized that the UMWA president's opponents would be crippled by the charges of dual unionism. Lewis's loyalists in District 2 stepped up their attacks on Hapgood, scorning him as a troublemaker and Communist sympathizer. These labels would stick to Hapgood throughout his decade-long battle with Lewis, yet he refused to back away from his association with the Communists. He perceived Foster and other party activists as supporters of union democracy and Brophy's larger program. In contrast to intellectual liberals whom he regarded as armchair activists, Hapgood respected the Communists as workers whose experience in the mines entitled them to speak on behalf of the rank and file. Like most young leftists of his generation, Hapgood was also sympathetic to the Bolshevik experiment. Although he later became far less charitable toward the CP, he valued the courage and toughness of individual party members. Ultimately, ideological purity mattered much less to Hapgood than evidence of character and commitment. For him, sectarian bloodletting violated the democratic, fraternal spirit that he associated with the labor movement's best impulses.[35]

Faced with the operators' resistance, Lewis's noncooperation, and rising internal strife, John Brophy suspended the Somerset strike in July 1923. The union's long struggle had resulted in few tangible gains, although in some nonunion mines, the operators raised wages and displayed greater responsiveness to the miners' grievances. In spite of these limited advances, nonunion miners had dispelled images of their docility, overcome the ethnic divisions that had plagued previous strikes, and sustained an impressive solidarity. Memory of this achievement would figure prominently when more propitious political circumstances appeared during the New Deal.[36]

The Somerset strike had a profound impact on the personal commitment and political development of Powers Hapgood. Red Doran, his old IWW mentor, asserted that the young activist's face-to-face encounters with the bitterness of the miners' lives would grant Hapgood the opportunity "to translate thwarted hopes into constructive effort and solidarity." Heber Blankenhorn's wife, Mary, who had been an investigator for the Hylan Committee, wrote Eleanor Hapgood that "he has grown older—much more grave—and if possible more earnest." In seventeen exhausting months on the picket line, the twenty-three-year-old Hapgood had faced personal danger and witnessed numerous other hardships. He had seen hundreds of miners evicted from their homes, observed the death of George Gregory's infant son in a tent colony, and read the UMWA burial rites for a miner murdered by a company guard. The suffering experienced by the striking miners remained etched in his memory. In Somerset, militancy and solidarity, however inspiring, had also proven costly. These sobering experiences led Hapgood to reconsider his views on how social harmony could be brought to the employment relationship.[37]

At the outset of the walk-out, Hapgood informed his parents that he abhorred strikes and hoped that the government would intervene in order to avert a protracted struggle. Noting his father's argument that fighting was an "evil" that should be replaced by cooperation, Hapgood assured him that he was not a "militant laborite." Having observed the intransigence of corporate power during the strike, however, he began to lose faith in peaceful means of settling industrial disputes. Even if lost, he argued, the value of the strike lay in the lesson it would teach the government about the need to reorganize the coal industry. Moreover, participation in strikes was invaluable in producing the educated leaders needed to establish industrial democracy. Questioning his father's Progressive view that conflict was inherently destructive, Hapgood now saw active struggle by workers as crucial for the achievement of social progress, even as he continued to admit that "industrial strife is a terrible thing."[38]

In spite of the horrors that he had witnessed on the industrial battlefield, Hapgood still sought to conduct class conflict by rules of engagement that were not socially destructive. In a letter he wrote after reading the burial rites for the murdered miner, he blamed the "system" rather than individual operators, whom he claimed simply had different interests from the miners and acted accordingly. In the unionized coal fields, he informed readers of the *New Republic* with some exaggeration, the strike had been waged "without bitterness or cruelty on either side." Conversely, in nonunion regions like Somerset, years of authoritarian rule by the operators had created deep feelings of anger and resentment that inevitably led to violent confrontation.[39]

In a letter published in the October 7, 1922, *New Republic,* Hapgood attempted to persuade a middle-class audience that acceptance of the UMWA would contribute to social stability. He insisted that American democracy could be revitalized only by the realization of industrial democracy. Although his recent experience suggested otherwise, he hoped that the mutual obligations embodied in a union contract would establish enduring bonds impervious to abrogation by momentary passions or outbursts of conflict. Nonetheless, Hapgood justified the miners' militancy given the operators' refusal to permit a fair fight: "I don't like to fight but when it is necessary I believe in doing it without bitterness. No one longs for peace more than I do. But when we're in a thing, we must play the game for the interests of all."[40]

This reflection attempted to reconcile two conflicting impulses—the Progressive, middle-class desire for social harmony and Hapgood's increasing commitment to working-class organization and militancy. The prospects for integrating these impulses were problematic. As the Somerset experience indicated, the fierce anti-unionism of the coal operators coupled with the laissez-faire attitude of government denied labor a substantive political or social role. Hapgood's argument (borrowed from Frank Tannenbaum) that labor was a stabilizing force gained little credence in a market-driven, open-shop setting, which denigrated unionism as an unacceptable restraint on both commercial freedom and individual liberty. With hopes for labor-management rapprochement fading in the aftermath of Somerset, Hapgood began to articulate more clearly his attachment to the UMWA and his larger aspirations for the labor movement.

Much to his parents' chagrin, Hapgood secured a job in a District 2 mine following the strike. Although they had supported his efforts on behalf of the miners, both were displeased over his desire to work underground. Eleanor Hapgood pronounced herself "very sad" over her son's decision. William Hapgood offered ideological objections to Powers's choice of occupations that were prompted by an unusual request he received soon after the strike had ended. Seeking to influence Powers Hapgood by currying favor with his father, John L. Lewis offered the elder Hapgood a position on the board of directors of a labor-run bank in Indianapolis. This action suggested just how seriously Lewis regarded the younger Hapgood's insurgency and his determination to derail sources of opposition to his authority.[41]

William Hapgood expressed grave reservations about accepting Lewis's offer, which he ultimately rejected. The bank, he suspected, was "run just like other businesses." As he wrote his son, "I see little more idealism on the part of labor than on the part of capital." In his judgment, labor was no paragon of either morality or character. As he asked Powers, "are labor leaders setting an example with reference to modest incomes and modest living?" These criticisms led the younger Hapgood to defend his attachment to the UMWA by aligning the labor movement with his father's values.[42]

Hapgood extolled industrial democracy as a means of inculcating the cooperative spirit by granting workers genuine responsibility and power in the running of business enterprise. He now placed his faith in the local union as the best vehicle for implementing this vision. Hapgood explained the role the local union in Greenwich, Pennsylvania, which he joined just after the strike, played in building character and establishing democratic values: "It is in this little local union that the coal miners of Greenwich get the most valuable part of their education, where they learn to transact their own business affairs, to think and make speeches about their problems, and, best of all, to look on life in terms of cooperation with their fellow man."[43]

The local union stood in sharp contrast to the centralized bureaucracies that characterized social organization in America. In Hapgood's conception, radical politics would be rooted in the little democracies formed by strong, local unions functioning as social, political, and educational institutions meeting a wide range of workers' needs. In addition to its political role, the union also performed the invaluable psychological function of developing self-confidence and expertise, thereby preparing workers to become industrial citizens. What was needed to advance the prospects of industrial democracy, Hapgood argued, was an expanded commitment to education on the part of the labor movement. He recognized that any scheme calling for public control of the mines required an informed group of workers prepared to accept new responsibilities and increased scrutiny from other social groups.

This vision paralleled what William Hapgood was attempting to accomplish at Columbia Conserve but with a crucial difference. Unlike the experiment initiated "from above" by his father, industrial democracy molded by unions came "from below." Change from below was free of the paternalism, however well intended, that inevitably accompanied change imposed from above. Hapgood's advocacy of robust local unionism served both the personal objective of distinguishing him from his father and the political aim of demonstrating how fraternal and democratic values could be extended among working people. Yet his uncritical praise of the local union in Greenwich ignored a larger context. Within the UMWA, John L. Lewis continued to centralize power and attack local autonomy, a trend that was also well underway in governmental and corporate circles. Hapgood did not address the challenge these developments posed to his vision of autonomous local unions, which he presented as islands of democracy safely insulated from their surrounding environment.[44]

In addition to strengthening Hapgood's commitment to the UMWA and refining his views on class conflict, the Somerset strike also secured him widespread public recognition. His exploits were reported in such leading liberal journals as *The Nation* and the *New Republic*, both of which devoted considerable coverage to the strike. As John Brophy later observed with a tinge of jealousy, Heber Blankenhorn and other liberals made Hapgood "the Jack Reed of the Somerset Revolution." The novelty of a Harvard graduate named Hapgood tangling with coal barons and consorting with striking miners endeared him to many liberals who sympathized with the miners and deplored the operators' authoritarianism. Hapgood's friends saluted his courage and decisiveness. Horace Davis, a Harvard chum, regretted his own "pleasant, easy" life in comparison to his classmate's derring-do. Eloise Cummings, still vacillating over committing herself to the working class, observed, "You seem to see and do while most of us hum and hah about and finally lose all pep to do." Applause for his efforts also came in numerous letters that his parents received during the strike. Alma Littell, the mother of a *New Republic* editor, concluded her letter to Eleanor Hapgood with unintended irony, proclaiming she must be a "very happy mother" to have such a courageous, committed son.[45]

Describing Hapgood as "tall and dark, with the austere, wilful thoughtful face of the New England puritan," the Communist writer Joseph Freeman illuminated the nature of his appeal. His credentials as an archetypal American were impeccable, allowing him to challenge native-born liberals to become active supporters of workers and inspire ethnic radicals like Freeman who were seeking to root their politics in American soil. Following his experiences in Somerset, Hapgood became a much sought after speaker before liberal church groups and youth organizations, giving him a platform from which to exhort others to consider a life of commitment to labor and the working class. Although many of his friends and acquaintances voiced respect for that commitment, few were willing to follow his lead. David McCord, a Harvard classmate who requested an article from Hapgood for an alumni bulletin, summarized these sentiments neatly: "You have chosen a lonely career and I admire your courage in doing it."[46]

Hapgood would have scarcely agreed with McCord's assessment. His contention that the working class was more virtuous than the middle class had been affirmed during the strike. As he wrote his parents after participating in a parade of striking miners and dining with their families: "How the well-to-do people who get together at their stiff, unnatural gatherings can call themselves a superior class of society I can't see." Later, he asserted, "I see nothing wasted in living and working with just plain ordinary people." Hapgood had gained acceptance in the fraternity of the UMWA and a position of esteem in the mining communities. Based on his direct experience he could speak with authority to a larger audience about the conditions of the working class and the promise of the labor movement. Finally, his character had been tested under the most extreme circumstances, and by all accounts he had met the challenge. He was now able to confidently proclaim: "The longer I live the more convinced I am that I want to help progress come from below rather than from above."[47]

This pronouncement reflected Hapgood's burgeoning loyalties to the working class and industrial democracy; it also signaled his distaste for Progressivism's attachment to administrative rule by managerial elites. Despite these deepening convictions, Powers Hapgood still felt compelled to seek additional evidence supporting his faith in progress from below. His search for new sources of inspiration would take him far beyond the mining towns of western Pennsylvania, exposing him to an international working class whose achievements fully met his highest expectations.

Chapter Four

"'Round the World Underground"

> I have faith, somehow that you will endure a child
> until you die—which means nothing perhaps,
> except that you have a faculty of finding the truth
> and not letting the world muddle things up for you.
> —Evelyn Preston to Powers Hapgood,
> February 9, 1925

Even though he had demonstrated his courage and commitment during the Somerset strike, Powers Hapgood confronted serious obstacles to rising within the ranks of the UMWA. With his reelection at the 1924 UMWA convention, John L. Lewis consolidated his control of the union and left his opponents in disarray. Lewis's forces in District 2 continued to snipe at John Brophy, undercutting his ability to rebuild the union. Increasing unemployment and the union's weakness following the strike enabled the operators to dictate the conditions of work. Faced with these constraints, Hapgood began to consider alternatives. Although he identified strongly with the miners, he was not prepared to remain mired in this bleak and constricted environment.[1]

During fall 1923, Hapgood discussed with his parents the possibility of an extended journey abroad. As he conceived it, the trip would permit him to study mining conditions in Europe and acquire knowledge to support his aspirations within the UMWA. His parents endorsed his plan but implored him to go as an observer and not exhaust his "strength and energy" by working underground. His father remarked that Powers had already lived more "abundantly" than most of his contemporaries and urged him to slow down. But if William and Eleanor Hapgood anticipated that their son would now be ready for a less strenuous life, they were sorely mistaken.[2]

Failing to dissuade Powers from his intention to be both observer and participant, William Hapgood pleaded with him to take his mother along so she could recuperate from an unspecified nervous condition. Hapgood rebuffed his father's attempt to make him feel guilty and dismissed his parents' concern for his well-being. Going abroad represented another opportunity to establish his independence from parental authority, although his independence remained conditional. As before, he obediently informed William and Eleanor of his daily activities and kept an extensive journal, which he entitled "'Round the World Underground." Nonetheless, he regarded the trip as a means of further demonstrating his self-reliance and earning greater credibility within the labor movement. Escaping the grim aftermath of Somerset, an option unavailable to his western Pennsylvania colleagues, was not mentioned as a motive. To acknowledge the distinction between himself and his Somerset comrades would raise troubling questions regarding the advantages afforded him by his "fortunate past," questions Hapgood was reluctant to consider.[3]

Hapgood obtained a list of overseas contacts from his Somerset friends, most of whom were of English or Welsh descent. Armed with letters of introduction from these miners (one described him as a "true and worthy companion," another as "honest, upright, and sincere"), he sailed for Europe in June 1924. His first stop was England, where he met some of the country's most renowned intellectuals and activists, including Harold Laski, G. D. H. Cole, R. H. Tawney, J. A. Hobson, and longtime miners' union leader Robert Smillie. These encounters excited Hapgood far less than his extended stay with a Welsh mining family, the relatives of a college acquaintance. In Ammanford, Wales, he saw a "mining community at its best" and told his Uncle Norman that "I am learning a great deal from these 'intellectual' miners." The miners that Hapgood met were represented by the South Wales Miners' Federation, popularly known as "the Fed." The Fed was one of Britain's most influential and powerful unions, having achieved, in the words of its historians, the "integration of pit, people and union into a unified social organism."[4]

For a young man seeking an ideal labor movement, the South Wales Miners' Federation was a breathtaking revelation. Welsh miners enjoyed social benefits—portal-to-portal pay, convalescent homes, well-kept mining towns—that were far superior to those attained by their

American counterparts. In sharp contrast to John L. Lewis's autocratic rule of the UMWA, the Fed honored local autonomy, a principle that Hapgood viewed as essential to the maintenance of democratic values. Attending a miners' union convention, Hapgood marveled that unlike the UMWA, Welsh unionists focused on issues rather than personalities and maintained cordial personal relations despite their political differences. Even the union's campaign for nationalization of the mines and the coal operators' determined opposition did not result in the level of bitterness between the parties that Hapgood had witnessed during the Somerset strike. This tolerant attitude was exemplified by Robert Smillie, who urged workers to direct their anger at capitalism instead of at individual employers, arguing that both workers and bosses were victims of the profit system. Here was class struggle conducted under Marquess of Queensberry rules, where each party acknowledged the legitimacy of the other and recognized a mutual obligation to preserve Britain's venerable tradition of stable, constitutional rule. Evolution toward industrial democracy seemed possible under these circumstances, offering Hapgood a model for the type of labor-capital relations that he hoped might be transferable to the coal fields of the United States.[5]

Among the Welsh miners in Ammanford, Hapgood found an inspiring role model in Jack Evans, a young miner active in workers' education. Evans had won a union-sponsored scholarship that freed him from work in the mines, provided he return upon completion of his studies and use his education to benefit his fellow workers. According to Hapgood's British confidants, only 2 of the 450 working-class students who had attended London's Labour College had chosen options other than returning to their workplaces and sharing their knowledge. This practice accorded with Hapgood's view that education belonged not to the individual but to the working class and should be directed toward social benefit rather than individual improvement.[6]

Jack Evans embodied a dedication and rootedness that appealed immensely to Hapgood. Evans was a younger version of John Brophy — a worker-intellectual who was anchored in a mining community and intimately connected to the politics of the miners' union, the Labor Party, and the cooperative movement. Attending classes conducted by Evans, Hapgood was impressed with the liveliness of the discussions, the miners' broad knowledge of political affairs, and the prevailing atmosphere of mutual respect in which divergent views were aired. Writing his parents in November 1924, Hapgood declared that on his return to the United States, he intended to live in a mining community where he could act as both a worker and an educator and participate in the labor, political, and cooperative movements. Witnessing Evans's ability to integrate work, politics, and community into a coherent identity, Hapgood was more convinced than ever that the possibility for leading a truly authentic life lay within his reach.[7]

Hapgood was especially moved by the "intelligence" he found among the Welsh miners. They are as "cultured as the owners," he informed middle-class readers in an article later published in the *New York Herald Tribune*. New social arrangements founded on workers' control and public ownership demanded a literate, informed working class untainted by consumer culture and individualistic striving. By developing their own class-conscious intellectuals, British unionists had apparently created such a group of industrial citizens. Workers, Hapgood implied, could now be entrusted with greater responsibility, for they possessed the character and expertise that entitled them to assume a more substantive social role.[8]

Hapgood's glowing impressions of the Welsh miners and the Fed were by no means romanticized or fanciful. In contrast to the UMWA's organizational fluctuation, the Fed's membership averaged approximately 60 percent of all South Wales miners during the first two decades of the twentieth century. This powerful organizational base permitted miners to create cultural and political vehicles for both individual development and collective advancement. Welsh miners established an elaborate set of institutions—chapels, libraries, sports teams—under popular and democratic control that enabled union leaders to function like village elders in their hold on the miners' loyalty. The Welsh miners were also able to express themselves politically through the Liberal and Labour parties, achieving far greater electoral representation than their American counterparts. And Hapgood accurately observed the profound effects of the union's commitment to workers' education, which helped to politicize many young miners and develop their leadership potential.[9]

Yet, in his eagerness to transplant British ideals to American soil, Hapgood neglected to consider crucial differences between the history and cultures of the two nations. Miners' union leader Robert Smillie acknowledged these distinctions following a visit to the United States in 1912: "The possessing classes of America would prove themselves a great deal more brutal and soulless than anything we have known over here." In Britain, where conciliation was regarded as a "manner of life," both the working and owning classes displayed a deep commitment to constitutionalism, respectability, and compromise. Far earlier than in

Powers Hapgood (right) with miners' union leader Robert Smillie (center) and unidentified man during Hapgood's trip to Wales in 1924. Hapgood found in the South Wales Miners' Federation a model for the type of labor-capital relations that he hoped might be transferable to the coal fields of the United States. (Courtesy of Lilly Library, Indiana University)

Powers Hapgood with unidentified Welsh miner after a shift in Ammanford in 1924. In Ammanford, Hapgood saw a "mining community at its best" and told his Uncle Norman that "I am learning a great deal from these 'intellectual' miners." (Courtesy of Lilly Library, Indiana University)

America, British authorities were willing to grant the labor movement legal and political legitimacy in order to preserve social stability. Hapgood understood that this mutual recognition of legitimacy had permitted class conflict to be conducted under agreed-upon rules of engagement. What he ignored was the fact that this modus vivendi had emerged from a political and cultural context that did not approximate historical developments across the Atlantic. Hapgood also failed to recognize that the Welsh miners possessed certain advantages unavailable to their American counterparts. A decentralized mining industry meant less operator control of civil society, thereby providing miners with the ability to create independent voluntary associations, and a mostly homogeneous work force spared the Welsh miners from the bitter ethnic conflicts that the UMWA had often struggled to overcome.[10]

Even Hapgood's new role model, Jack Evans, offered a view of Ammanford that conflicted with his friend's upbeat assessment. Evans complained that life there was "humdrum," and he felt stranded "in a kind of backwash far removed from the hub of the universe." Unlike Hapgood, he greeted industrialism far less cheerfully, musing that "the roughshod intrusion of highhanded capitalism into these beautiful vales savors of a desecration of things almost holy." By 1926, he made his escape complete by emigrating to the United States and joining the Columbia Conserve Company as its education director. Evans was a far more ambivalent role model than Hapgood was willing to acknowledge. His cosmopolitanism made him see Ammanford as parochial and conservative, while his distaste for industrialism led him to regret the conversion of farmers into proletarians. Hapgood was too taken with his view that Ammanford was "a mining town at its best" to consider Evans's more sober assessment.[11]

Continuing his journey, Hapgood spent fall 1924 and winter 1925 working in German and French mines. Working in a French mine, shoveling in a sitting position and breathing in large quantities of thick black dust, failed to dim his enthusiasm. As he wrote in June 1925: "the men and boys of the mine as they work and sweat with their lithe and active bodies, the solving of small engineering problems, problems of bad roof, derailed cars, water, and all the other hindrances to the work of getting coal, the talk and philosophy of the miners, and their playfulness and sense of humor at work underground are all wonderful and pleasing things."[12]

In mining Powers Hapgood saw the manliness of hard, productive labor; the overcoming of problems via both self-reliance and group cooperation; and an intimate camaraderie among miners. In his exuberant description of life underground, he was not only affirming his parents' values but also suggesting his own achievement in gaining acceptance among the most masculine of men. Yet his rhapsodic description of mining displayed a persistent romanticism that his coworkers did not always exhibit. As a miner's wife observed in a 1922 *New Republic* article: "Why should men work day after day in inky darkness, drenched with water, suffocated by dynamite smoke, cramped by low roofs when they could earn the same amount of money above ground at work where they could move and breathe freely and safely?" Primarily, she answered, because the wages in the mines were better than alternative employment above ground, not because there was intrinsic pleasure in the work. In his zeal, Hapgood continued to overlook this critical distinction between himself and his "buddies."[13]

The situation in France was less congenial, and Hapgood lamented the ideological splits that diminished labor unity and left French miners mired in working conditions reminiscent of those in Somerset. This experience reinforced his distaste for sectarianism and left a lasting impression regarding the pitfalls of dual unionism. Hapgood's experiences in Germany were more uplifting. He praised the generous social benefits afforded German miners, especially in the areas of pensions and compensation for injury. Hapgood could attest to the latter benefit personally. Having gashed a finger while he was unloading rock, he was paid a minimum wage until he was able to resume working.[14]

Even more impressive to Hapgood than Germany's advanced social welfare system were the manifestations of character and camaraderie he found among the miners. He noted that German beer halls were respectable establishments devoid of "painted ladies and lewd looking individuals." At a Christmas party, he observed men and women embracing each other in a spirit not "shallow" or "insincere" but "frank and spontaneous." In a Christmas 1924 journal entry he proclaimed: "They are wonderful, these German working people, and I love them." For Powers Hapgood, sexual purity was crucial. It embodied the all-important virtue of self-control and enhanced the possibility for honest male-female relationships untainted by drink or lust. Ignoring any evidence of working-class vice, he again remarked on the superiority of workers to a morally lax middle class.[15]

But it was the political attitudes of the miners that affected Hapgood most deeply. He was surprised to encounter no hostility from Germans over America's role in World War I. Rather, the German workers he met expressed sincere regret that they had renounced working-class solidarity and succumbed to nationalist appeals. Citing the pacifism of the German and French miners, Hapgood confessed that he had been "young and foolish" during the war and "stirred up" on behalf of the Allied cause. He now declared his loyalty to the workers of the world and embraced socialism as a unifying ideology. As he wrote to a mining friend in Pennsylvania, he had lacked "the understanding of a Socialist and the knowledge that wars are made by capitalists and princes and the workers only pawns in their games."[16]

Powers Hapgood and German miner Willi Bartels after a shift at the Tremonio Mine in 1925. The camaraderie Hapgood found among German miners fueled his own search for working-class fraternity. (Courtesy of Lilly Library, Indiana University)

Finding evidence of a transcendent, working-class fraternity was critical to Hapgood's evolving political thought, especially in the wake of a war where workers and even socialists had placed loyalty to nation over loyalty to class. This view grossly underestimated the depth of nationalist and ethnic feeling in Europe, which a decade later plunged the world into war. Because he had such a clear idea of what he was seeking, Hapgood failed to appreciate that workers might define their loyalties in narrower conceptions of ethnicity, race, or religion. As Standish Meacham, a historian of the British working class has observed, "loyalty and solidarity were more readily understood when preached with direct reference to bonds that were local, familiar, and concrete." Hapgood's experiences in both western Pennsylvania and Wales suggested the importance of such bonds in shaping working-class identity, but his overriding personal need for a sense of fraternity and belonging accentuated his eagerness to find commonality among workers regardless of their geographic or cultural milieu.[17]

Although Hapgood was moved by this vision of international working-class solidarity, his trip to the Soviet Union in summer 1925 provided him with the most compelling evidence to justify his faith in industrial democracy. Eager to see for himself the Bolshevik experiment, Hapgood received cautionary advice from an unlikely duo: Emma Goldman and William Green. Goldman, who was introduced to Hapgood by his Uncle Hutch, expressed her approval "that the younger Hapgoods were getting close to the masses not only in theory but by actual labor with them." Goldman's personal experience with the Bolsheviks had led her to denounce the Soviet regime and condemn its authoritarian practices. Exiled in London after her distressing sojourn in the Soviet Union, she despaired of convincing British unionists of the Bolsheviks' duplicity and sought to make Hapgood an ally in her new crusade.[18]

Ironically, the anarchist rebel invoked the language of character, writing Hapgood that, for the Bolsheviks, "truth, honesty, keeping a promise (and) respect for personality are all Bourgeois superstitions." There was a curious contradiction, she asserted, between the Bolsheviks' claims to toil for humanity and their failure to respect the sanctity of the individual. Meanwhile, AFL president William Green, who had furnished Hapgood with letters of introduction to French and German unionists, warned him about the perils of dreaming in a practical world and urged the young miner to avoid close contact with the Communists. Hapgood ignored Green's advice but did pose some questions suggested by Goldman to an English miner just returned from Russia, recording that he was satisfied with the traveler's response.[19]

Before visiting Russia, Hapgood had begun to clarify his attitude toward the Communist Party. While in Wales, he had met British Communists, attended their meetings, and found them "sensible," not "wild" or "erratic" like those he had encountered in the United States. When it came to Bolshevism's applicability to the United States, however, Hapgood demurred, insisting that "revolution by constitutional methods" was preferable to the Leninist model based on the use of force. This view reflected Hapgood's abiding commitment to constitutionalism and his desire to conduct class conflict within boundaries that preserved social stability. He also offered another reason for rejecting the Communist Party, one that illuminates the considerations shaping his approach to politics: "while I believed in Communism, I did not join the Party for the same reason I did not join the Church, namely that the Communist Party and its methods is as far away from Communism as the Church is from the teachings of Jesus."[20]

In seeking congruence between theory and practice, Hapgood was disappointed by both liberal Protestantism and the Communist Party.

Communists, as Emma Goldman had argued, disregarded fundamental standards of conduct, and their willingness to use force contradicted Hapgood's staunch belief in democratic means of political persuasion. Proponents of the social gospel, equally visionary in their professed desire to establish the Kingdom of God on earth, failed to honor Jesus' example of service and sacrifice as a matter of everyday practice. Essential to Hapgood's political vision was the quest for absolute consistency between word and deed, a quest that both he and his father grounded in the biblical command to "be ye doers of the Word, not hearers only." To achieve this consistency, Hapgood embraced such secular cultural concepts as the strenuous life and the superiority of direct experience rather than the spiritual imperatives of Christianity or the ideological certitude that often accompanied Marxism. As he prepared to visit Russia, he looked to the workers themselves as the purest source of evidence that the utopian promise of communism was being fulfilled.[21]

Evelyn Preston, a friend of Hapgood's (later to become Roger Baldwin's wife) who was herself a staunch upper-middle-class ally of labor, had urged him to go to Russia, where "people know what's important and face life simply and honestly." Preston's effusive characterization of Bolshevik virtue reflected the expectations that accompanied most American radicals in their pilgrimages to the Soviet Union. Powers Hapgood was no exception. He arrived in Moscow in July 1925 and first visited the ailing Big Bill Haywood, who had become a political exile there following government prosecution of the IWW during World War I. Whereas he had earlier thought of the Wobbly leader as "rough" and "coarse," Hapgood was now taken with Haywood's "kindness" and "gentleness." This uplifting encounter, which suggested the possibilities for personal transformation under the aegis of the workers' state, set the tone for the remainder of Hapgood's stay.[22]

Hapgood was immediately impressed by the accomplishments of the Bolsheviks, exulting that "Russia and its people are wonderful beyond description" and the Communists had "done wonders." In Moscow and elsewhere, he toured well-appointed recreational centers where workers and peasants could engage in leisure activities. Watching young Russian workers, both men and women, enjoying state-paid vacations comparable to those afforded the bourgeoisie, Hapgood was struck by their vitality and "fine comradeship." He was especially moved by the friendly intimacy displayed between male and female workers devoid of any sign of flirtation. Here, as in Germany, was further evidence of the sexual restraint and respectability that for Hapgood confirmed the moral virtue of the working class.[23]

Not content to be simply an observer, Hapgood decided to join the Kuzbas colony in Siberia in August 1925. Kuzbas was an experimental enterprise funded by American liberals and communists and staffed by some five hundred volunteers, many of them IWW members fleeing persecution in the United States. Intrigued by the colony's visionary aims and the opportunity to work in a Russian mine, Hapgood decided that he wanted to spend at least three months at Kuzbas. He explained that he did not want to "be considered a slacker or merely an agitator incapable of productive work the way so many of the American colonists turned out to be."[24]

Working in the Kuzbas mine, Hapgood praised its rigorous safety regulations, liberal compensation for injury, equal treatment for both sexes, and six-hour work day. Sidelined by a painful eruption of boils, he praised the Russian doctors who barred him from returning to work until he was healed. During his stay he combined work in the mine with participation in study groups ("Lenin circles") conducted by members of the colony. He also developed close relationships with many of the volunteers, most notably Anton Karachun, a Russian-born American with anarchist leanings. Karachun had joined the American army to help "make the world safe for democracy" but instead was sent to Russia as part of the Wilson administration's effort to aid counterrevolutionary forces. Unwilling to participate in this mission, Karachun deserted, was captured by American forces, and sentenced to die. His captors subsequently rescinded his death sentence and deported him to the Soviet Union. Karachun wound up in Kuzbas, where he complained about the subsistence conditions of the colony and the authoritarianism of the Communist Party.[25]

Although sympathetic to his friend's complaints, Hapgood defended the Bolsheviks' insistence on discipline and surveillance as necessary if unfortunate in the face of lingering political opposition. Speaking to party officials following Karachun's interrogation by the secret police, he urged them to recognize the legitimacy and usefulness of principled critics who would assist their "efforts towards perfection." He then quoted his favorite democrat, Walt Whitman: "From any fruition of success, no matter what, shall come forth something to make a greater struggle necessary." Like many American liberals, Hapgood was willing to relax his commitment to democracy to defend the Bolsheviks' apparent progress toward empowering workers and fostering social egalitarianism. Significantly, he was more offended by "some of the members of the Communist Party in high positions here who seem to be thoroughly bourgeois in their grasping for the comforts of life" than he was by any evidence of curtailed civil liberties.[26]

Hapgood and other American leftists faced a dilemma in approaching the new Bolshevik regime. As Roger Baldwin explained in an October 1925 letter to Hapgood, he abhorred the "persecution for ideas and autocratic dictatorship" that had surfaced in the Soviet Union. Nonetheless, Baldwin dismissed Karachun as having been spoiled by his years in America, suggesting that he was selfishly claiming privileges that contradicted the egalitarian ethos of the Bolshevik regime. Baldwin was so enchanted by the Bolsheviks' progress in eradicating economic exploitation that he submerged his usual commitments to civil liberties. Instead, he predicted that the workers themselves would eventually steer the revolution along a more democratic course. Hapgood agreed with Baldwin's assessment, citing the promise of the Bolsheviks and their elevation of the working class as an inspiring alternative to "moribund capitalism." As he wrote Joseph Freeman, "in other countries where I've worked—America, England, Germany, France—things are going from bad to worse. . . . Here, on the other hand, things are going ahead and there is hope."[27]

Above all, Hapgood was attracted to what the prominent Protestant liberal Sherwood Eddy described as "the experience of almost a whole people living under a unified philosophy of life." For Eddy and many other American liberals, the Russian experience filled the spiritual void that the expansion of laissez-faire capitalism had created in the United States. In Hapgood's case, he saw the integration of personal belief and public action in the creation of new men and women whose egos had been socialized and who were being prepared to assume leading roles as citizens in an industrial democracy. Although he was troubled by evidence of Bolshevik authoritarianism, he shared Eddy's need to see an entire society organized on the basis of cooperative principles and a mutual sense of sacrifice. Perhaps, too, Hapgood viewed the Bolshevik regime as living proof that the industrial democracy embodied in the UMWA local in Greenwich, Pennsylvania, and his father's experiment at Columbia Conserve could be extended to cover an entire society. Along with many other American liberals disheartened by developments in their own land, he found the prospect of Bolshevism's potential too exhilarating to question.[28]

Hapgood left Kuzbas in November 1925, having made quite an impression on many of his fellow colonists. A woman named Eva later wrote him that "I never had a friend like you and don't think I will

again." Ida Ado, a Finnish-born worker whom Hapgood had befriended during her bout with smallpox, marveled that "I cannot make out what the mystic power about you is that makes people so fond of you." In words that must have moved him especially, she lauded his "manly promise to always remain in the struggle of the classes."[29] Ado continued with an observation that Hapgood must have encountered many times in his quest for working-class acceptance: "Sometimes it seems impossible to me that you really are so enthusiastic about the welfare of the working masses as you claim to be. . . . I know you have a bourgeois family tree, and you think so much of your folks and friends and at times I feel certain that they will have a great influence on you and that you will turn against us instead of being with us."[30]

Hapgood's ability to overcome such skepticism testified to both his personal charm and his capacity to communicate the depth of his commitment to working people. His ongoing correspondence with German, British, and Russian workers whom he had met documented his acceptance within the ranks of labor, even if his working-class status was unusual by customary standards.

Hapgood concluded his world tour with a trip to the Orient, spending December 1925 and January 1926 in China and Japan. In a lengthy discussion with Japanese labor leaders, he summarized his evolving political views and offered his most extensive comments to date on the subject of race. Describing his politics to his hosts, Hapgood cast himself "neither as reactionary as most AFL officials nor as revolutionary as the Communists." Pressing his newfound faith, he touted international working-class solidarity "as a means of uniting the working people of the world against war, and in the event of war, the calling of general strikes among the workers." The Japanese officials scoffed at this suggestion, informing Hapgood that opposing their government during wartime was punishable by death. They were also unconvinced by his assertions that opposition to Japanese immigrants in America was not widespread among workers and reflected class antagonism rather than overt racism.[31]

Hapgood condemned the National Origins Act of 1924, a racially inspired law that sharply curtailed immigration to the United States from Eastern Europe and Asia. Although he denounced racist practices by unions, he insisted that most American workers were not biased but simply resented Japanese immigrants for undercutting their wages. There was an element of truth in this argument; few workers would accept low-wage competition with equanimity. Still, the fierceness of the attacks on Asian immigrants and the unvarnished racism that

often accompanied political movements to limit their numbers revealed troubling attitudes that Hapgood was reluctant to engage. Typical of most socialist thought during this period, his analysis refused to grant race a special status or consider that it might distort notions of class unity. Undeniably, Hapgood abhorred racism and cited the nondiscrimination clause in the UMWA's obligation as evidence that intolerance would not be condoned. Yet his attachment to mythic visions of international solidarity, worldwide general strikes, and an almost saintly rank and file evaded the tough questions posed by Japanese labor leaders who were operating in a forbidding political environment. Hapgood was unwilling to allow his shining vision of working-class virtue to be tarnished, even when confronted with clear evidence of racism within labor circles.[32]

By the end of his eighteen months abroad, Hapgood's political orientation had grown increasingly clear. He now denounced the evils of capitalism and consistently described himself as a socialist. In his journals he recorded his voracious reading of diverse texts, including Marx, Lenin, Trotsky, and Kropotkin, along with books on psychology, history, and political theory. The author who influenced him most profoundly, however, was Edward Bellamy, the nineteenth-century social critic, whose utopian novel *Looking Backward* and other writings condemning the emerging corporate state had won him a wide following.[33]

Describing Bellamy's analysis of the "Economic Suicide of the Profit System" as the "best thing on economics I've ever read," Hapgood was able to wed socialism to his family's ethical heritage. Paralleling Marx, Bellamy argued that capitalists left workers with insufficient purchasing power by expropriating excessive profits from the wages of producers. But instead of investing in glutted industries, capitalists sank their profits into the purchase of luxuries that Bellamy derided as "refined sensualism." As Hapgood explained in a letter home, "These industries cater to their [capitalists'] own extravagances or to the bad habits of the workers." Because capitalists failed to invest profits wisely, their control of the economy led to a misallocation of resources, the impoverishment of the working class, and worst of all, the transformation of workers from virtuous producers into squandering consumers. Although Bellamy's analysis may have exaggerated the extent of capitalist profligacy and working-class deprivation, it did reflect the growing disparities of wealth and power that simmered beneath the surface prosperity of the "roaring twenties."[34]

For Hapgood, productive labor and modest living were crucial emblems of personal worth and social commitment. As he wrote his mother before meeting her in Hawaii at the conclusion of his journey, "extravagant living has grown so distasteful to me that I can't enjoy it any more for even a few days." Edward Bellamy's powerful moral indictment of capitalism helped convince him that character and thrift could be upheld only under a socialist system that rewarded productivity and curbed private power. Hapgood proclaimed that socialism was necessary in order to preserve the values his family held dear. "Yes," he wrote, "I'm a Socialist, but contrary to many uninformed people's beliefs, I don't advocate giving people something for nothing or dividing equally among worthy and unworthy." By rewarding productive labor, discouraging wasteful consumption, and allowing workers to supplant bureaucrats in governing industry, socialism represented the best means of upholding personal character, public morality, and democratic values.[35]

Powers Hapgood neglected to consider how much the political and cultural landscape in America had changed since Edward Bellamy's day. Many nineteenth-century Americans had responded to industrialism by asserting alternative notions of moral economy, but by the 1920s, uneasy citizens tended to focus on cultural rather than economic issues. The reform impulse often followed a fundamentalist direction, climaxing in campaigns on behalf of Prohibition, creationism, and the maintenance of white supremacy. Far from embodying the cosmopolitan sentiments that Hapgood encountered abroad, the mood at home since his departure had grown insular and defensive. Nonetheless, in his travels both domestic and foreign, Hapgood had found numerous sources that sustained his belief in the possibilities for moral economy and industrial democracy—District 2 of the UMWA, the Welsh miners and the Fed, the Bolshevik Revolution, his father's experiment at Columbia Conserve. On his return to the United States, he hoped to extend these beachheads but seemed oblivious to the diversion of populist impulses in a more conservative direction.[36]

Hapgood could not claim total ignorance of this shift in the public mood. Throughout his months abroad, he received extensive correspondence from his UMWA friends documenting rampant Ku Klux Klan activity in District 2. John Kerr informed him of violent incidents fomented by the Klan, and U. S. G. Gallagher claimed in an October 1924 letter that "most all American Protestant miners have went into the KKK." Especially troubling was a letter Hapgood had received from George Gregory, his Somerset comrade, a veteran of the South Wales Miners' Federation, and now a worker at Columbia Conserve. Besides announcing that he had returned to the church, Gregory declared that the KKK "started out all right." He went on to underscore his susceptibility to racial appeals, explaining that "blacks will take advantage of you if you leave them. You can see that in this city." There is no record of Hapgood's responding to these disturbing disclosures, all of which suggested that the fraternity and solidarity achieved during the Somerset strike were unraveling. If a man of George Gregory's pedigree could have his outlook distorted by racism, Hapgood's visionary dream of universal working-class solidarity appeared to rest on fragile foundations.[37]

Such thoughts were far from Powers Hapgood's mind as he prepared to return home in early 1926. His trip had met all his expectations. He had worked in mines throughout the world, underscoring his commitment to productive labor and reinforcing his credibility as an analyst of working-class life. Although still within the parameters of parental authority, he had been on his own for a year and a half, extending the boundaries of his independence. He had acquired new friends in the labor movement throughout the world who affirmed his belief in the working class's virtue and potential. Among Welsh miners he had seen industrial democracy in its embryonic form; in Russia, he had witnessed the thrilling possibilities for social transformation under the aegis of a workers' state. Anxious to emulate Jack Evans, he joyfully anticipated a homecoming party in his honor being organized by friends in District 2. To his deep dismay, he encountered a world far different from the one he had left, one that posed formidable challenges to his visionary plans.

Chapter Five

Save the Union

Nothing is ever done for the benefit of humanity,
however, unless strong characters are willing to
take risks.

—Powers Hapgood to Pat McDermott,
September 21, 1926

Conditions in the coal industry had worsened dramatically while Hapgood was abroad. The old cycle of overproduction, falling prices, reduced profits, and severe unemployment reemerged as demand fell for bituminous coal. In spite of John L. Lewis's best efforts to present the UMWA as cooperative and his strategy to drive inefficient, low-wage competition out of business, coal operators resisted the union's demands for wage protection. The union's weakness led to an upsurge of such grievances as car-pushing, neglect of safety rules, and cheating on tonnage rates. Making matters worse, the open-shop movement that had been sweeping the nation forcefully invaded District 2. The operators unleashed an ideological offensive to undermine the UMWA's strong community support, conducting what John Brophy described as a "well-organized propaganda drive" to press the union to accept wage concessions. Many of Powers Hapgood's friends contemplated "quitting the mines for good," as they saw both union and community subverted by the operators' relentless attempt to destroy their unity and standard of living.[1]

Brophy's forces in District 2 fought back aggressively. The district launched a major initiative in workers' education, using the vehicle of the "labor chautauqua." Modeled after the lyceums of the nineteenth century, the chautauquas featured entertainment, lectures, and classes aimed at both the wives and children of miners. The goal of the chautauquas was to revive the miners' flagging spirits and build support for the larger program that Brophy insisted was necessary for the UMWA's survival.[2]

The education of workers also spurred concerted political action within District 2. Joining much of the labor movement, miners backed the Progressive ticket of Robert LaFollette and Burton Wheeler in 1924. In Nanty Glo, the site of John Brophy's home local, labor was able to elect many of its candidates to municipal office. Keeping faith with their supporters, these newly elected officials deputized miners in order to block attempts by the coal and iron police to assist scabs in breaking strikes. The union also resisted operator-aided attempts by the Ku Klux Klan to destroy community solidarity by ousting KKK members from union office and forming a citizens' committee of labor, fraternal, and religious organizations that countered the Klan's divisive message.[3]

The educational programs and political mobilization in District 2 were exactly the types of initiatives favored by Powers Hapgood. The labor chautauquas in particular constituted a grassroots alternative to employer propaganda in the form of mass-produced entertainment that was directed at a working-class audience. Unfortunately, these efforts had a limited effect. The defeat of the LaFollette-Wheeler ticket soured many miners on the possibility of finding a political solution to the instability of the industry. Even such a union stalwart as John Kerr told his friend Hapgood that he was "disgusted on politics" following the defeat of the Progressive ticket. Another problem, as one miner noted several years later, was "the poison that was injected during the flourishing days of the KKK," which made organizing much more difficult. Paul Fuller, education director of District 2, reported to Hapgood that many miners were indifferent to education after the 1924 election. Although they believed in schooling for their children, miners above all else wanted work for themselves. These disquieting developments suggested that the close relation between union and community that had so inspired Hapgood during the Somerset strike was beginning to erode.[4]

Hapgood's ambitions were not solely confined to union politics. During his time in Somerset, he had met Margaret McDowell, the daughter of a mining family in Windber, and he now hoped to establish a long-term relationship with her. Just as he sought ideal labor in his political quest, Hapgood had thought much about finding the ideal woman with whom to share his life. Until now, his search had been unsuccessful. "Most of the empty young things I met in college didn't interest me particularly," he later recalled, and he found himself drawn more to "older women who had done something." While in New York working for the Bureau for Industrial Research, he had been attracted to Gertrude Mathews Shelby, a Progressive writer many years his senior and a married woman. But as expressed by his alter ego, John McCloud, in the draft of his autobiographical novel, Hapgood "had enough of a sense of the fitness of things" not to pursue a relationship with Gertrude Shelby.[5]

Trim, clean-cut, sincere, and unaffected, Hapgood aroused considerable interest among many of the women he encountered, including a New York journalist he met during the Somerset strike and a teacher whom he briefly escorted in Europe. Hapgood's constant movement and exacting standards prevented him from developing any lasting relationships. Now, upon his return to Pennsylvania, he decided that it was time to find a mate and sought to win Margaret McDowell's affections.[6]

Hapgood was uncharacteristically tight-lipped in discussing his feelings for McDowell, leaving the nature of his attraction to her something of a mystery. Perhaps subconsciously, he hoped that their relationship would further validate his commitment to the working class and complete his escape from the middle-class world. Yet his frame of reference continued to be the educated middle class. In one of the few allusions to McDowell contained in correspondence with his parents, he directed them to send her subscriptions to *New Republic* and *The Nation,* leading organs of enlightened middle-class thought. McDowell did not respond positively to Hapgood's attempt to broaden her social awareness. As he cryptically commented following his long-awaited homecoming in Gallitzin, his prospective mate had "not developed the interest and enthusiasm about the labor movement that I hoped she would." Instead, McDowell focused on giving an "exhibition of the Charleston" at the dance that followed Hapgood's recounting of his experiences abroad.[7]

Margaret McDowell's lukewarm response to Powers Hapgood's attempt at political education illustrated important tensions in his relationship with working people. For Hapgood, the mining community embodied a union culture of cooperative stores, labor chautauquas, and independent political action that contrasted favorably with the escapism of popular culture. Yet he sought to augment the virtues of the working-class community with infusions of liberal culture and saw neither contradiction nor condescension in his attempt to lift a coal miner's daughter to a higher level of "intelligence" and "refinement." But Margaret McDowell did not find the ethos of the small mining town or the UMWA as romantic or inspiring as did Hapgood. For a young woman who was perhaps stifled by the insularity of a mining town, popular culture may have been an important source of comfort and release. Whatever the case, McDowell's unwillingness to seek self-improvement along the lines proposed by Hapgood shattered his image of her as the ideal woman. This left him deeply disappointed and denied him both the intimacy he sought and confirmation of the working-class credentials that were so central to his self-image and political ambitions.[8]

An incident following Hapgood's homecoming party in Gallitzin highlighted the pressures facing mining communities and the distance between Hapgood and the workers. Immediately after the Gallitzin gathering, Hapgood went with Paul Fuller to address striking miners in Sagamore, a mining town north of Somerset. The town had been "one of the most pleasant mining camps in the District" until the operators abrogated the UMWA contract, imported African-Americans as strikebreakers, and proceeded to break the union. The impact of these actions was profound, violating the implicit understandings that had governed relations between the miners and the coal operators. As John Brophy noted, "when confidence in the pledged word fails, the social structure is endangered."[9]

Nonetheless, Hapgood reported that "it is sad to see the suffering but wonderful to see the spirit of the people." Visiting miners in their homes, he encountered "many intelligent and refined people among the strikers." In numerous cases, workers proudly displayed pianos, played classical music, and, in this "very religious community," sang hymns. The Presbyterian church in which Hapgood spoke had become a community church, and he praised the multi-ethnic crowd that gathered to hear him describe his experiences abroad. The speech of Paul Fuller, a former minister, especially stirred Hapgood; it was "a regular socialist speech, calling upon the 'God of labor' to bring in justice and brotherhood." Here was Hapgood's beloved community—humble, faithful, and unscathed by the impurities of ethnic rivalry, mass-produced commercial entertainment, or consumer culture.[10]

Hapgood joined the striking miners and their families in imploring scabs to honor their call for solidarity. Barred from picketing by an injunction, the strikers dramatized their plea by singing a song written by a school teacher who was the daughter of a miner. The lyrics moved Hapgood profoundly:

> oh stranger why did you come here
> and take our homes and bread away. . . .
> we need you in our ranks today
> now come and be a man we say. . . .
> so why oppose a cause that's right
> for God will lead us in our fight.[11]

Hapgood noted that most of the African-American strikebreakers were "man enough to leave Sagamore," perhaps moved by the strikers' characterization of them as intruders. "Farmers and professional scabs," however, refused to heed their pleas. As the strikebreakers entered the mine, the strikers began to recite the Lord's Prayer. Hapgood was anguished by this scene: "It was too pathetic. I'm not usually soft because I've seen so much but I could scarcely keep back the tears, in fact, I shed a few." When the strikers and their families prayed to "forgive those who trespass against us," Hapgood felt tempted to "pick up a rock" in despair over the miners' weakness and their reliance on prayer as a last resort. "How the strikers stand for as much as they do is a mystery," he proclaimed, lamenting the pressures that threatened to destroy union solidarity and the bonds of community life.[12]

Yet the strikers' capacity to endure and suffer was not altogether mysterious. As was the case in the nineteenth century, miners, their families, and their fellow citizens fiercely resisted intrusion by outside forces. Recognizing the power of the forces arrayed against them, they drew on familiar sources to sustain their dignity and project a sense of moral superiority over their opponents. Powers Hapgood, however, was unable to comprehend a religious culture where God was not a politicized "God of labor" but embodied a personal relationship whose meaning was not reducible to a social or political construct. His inability to appreciate the meaning of faith in the strikers' lives spotlighted the chasm between his cosmopolitan, secular outlook and the spiritual orientation of these Pennsylvania coal miners. In defense of family, community, and union, they utilized resources whose legitimacy was widely accepted rather than drawing on unfamiliar imagery (socialism, international working-class solidarity) that was inaccessible to them.[13]

Having observed the miners' deteriorating circumstances firsthand,

Hapgood's euphoria from his European trip evaporated. His romantic designs had failed to materialize, his beloved mining towns were in disarray, and the militancy of the miners was proving ineffective. These setbacks were not entirely unanticipated, for even before his return to Somerset, Hapgood had expressed doubt about the willingness of rank-and-file miners to fulfill his visionary expectations. He confessed these uncertainties to Roger Baldwin, who attempted to allay his fears: "Don't you ever despair over the ignorance of these simple people you love. They have more real wisdom than the learned. When the conditions are ripe for them to express power, they will rise just as the industrial workers in Russia rose."[14] Affirming Hapgood's decision to work in the mines, Baldwin continued: "It is right for you because you really prefer it to any other life. Your satisfactions are so much greater than any halfway job of ease would give you."[15]

Baldwin was far more candid than Hapgood in acknowledging the personal and even selfish motives that attracted his friend to the miners. When confronted by a less than heroic working class, he and Hapgood felt compelled to insist upon the superior wisdom of "simple people" in order to validate their personal rebellion. This romanticization of workers revealed a marked unwillingness to appreciate the diverse influences that both shaped and circumscribed the attitudes of workers towards collective action and union involvement. Hapgood, however, was not inclined to seek sources of advice that might affirm or illuminate his momentary pessimism. Comforted by Baldwin's encouragement, he put aside his doubts about the rank and file and began to contemplate other possibilities for reviving the UMWA.

Most of Hapgood's time during spring and summer 1926 was consumed by an active schedule on the lecture circuit; he addressed a variety of middle-class audiences, spreading his message of social commitment, international working-class solidarity, and the achievements of the Soviet Union under Bolshevik rule. His listeners included urban civic clubs, college groups, and church-affiliated social service organizations across the United States. Eleanor Copenhaver, a national YWCA official, praised him as someone "who is young yet can speak with authority." Hapgood's lecture topics—"Evidences of the Peace Spirit among European Workers," "A Harvard Graduate's Experiences as a Coal Miner in Russia," and "My Adventures in Search of Social Justice"—invoked his personal experience as a means of establishing his credibility. In spite of his concerns about Bolshevik authoritarianism and warnings that favorable assessments of the regime would expose him to red-baiting, he continued to praise the Soviet

Union's labor policies and its bold attempt to move from feudalism to communism. Middle-class audiences responded enthusiastically to his talks; Hapgood was booked solid for nearly five months following his return from abroad.[16]

Hapgood also sought an outlet for the journal he kept while overseas. Several prominent publishers, including Bobbs-Merrill and G. P. Putnam, expressed interest but ultimately declined to award him a contract. As a vice president of Bobbs-Merrill explained, his style was too "flat, bare, and commònplace to tell your interesting and human experiences." Similar criticism could be made of his attempted novel, a thinly veiled autobiography of a worker-intellectual that came off as stiff and one-dimensional. Vivid reporting, comparative analysis, and tailoring his work to commercial dictates were less important to Hapgood than conveying the experience of workers to middle-class audiences and exhorting them to engage in a life of social commitment. Yet his eagerness to publish his journal suggested that he had not rejected the literary heritage of his family or written off the desirability of communicating with a middle-class audience.[17]

Given his ongoing quarrel with the alleged hypocrisy of intellectual liberals, why did Powers Hapgood continue to reach out to the middle class? Although Hapgood was not seeking anything so grandiose as a formal cross-class alliance, he well understood a besieged working class's need for middle-class allies. Like his father, he sought to convince a skeptical middle class that workers had the ability to govern industry and represented the best hope for the fulfillment of democratic ideals.

Hapgood's outreach to the middle class was also shaped by personal considerations. Demoralized by his recent setbacks in the coal fields, he surely appreciated the admiration of a friendly audience. Whereas workers were too preoccupied to embrace his message, middle-class audiences applauded his exploits and welcomed his glowing characterizations of the international working class. As the pages of liberal journals suggested, the coal miner had achieved iconographic status, both as a symbol of an oppressed working class and as an agent capable of reforming an unjust economic system. Hapgood, whose credentials as both an eyewitness and an activist were well known to his listeners, confirmed these perceptions. Yet the fact that his most receptive audience was composed of middle-class liberals and church people did not strike him as ironic or prompt any reevaluation of his relationship with workers. Rather, his ongoing contacts with liberals underscored his continuing need to justify his personal choices and demonstrate his virtue before a jury of his former peers.

Revitalized by his stint on the lecture circuit, Hapgood returned to Gallitzin in summer 1926, secured a job in the mines, and boarded with the family of Tom McCloskey, another District 2 friend who was a UMWA activist and chair of the Labor Party in Cambria County. He now had to face the reality that District 2 was no longer a pristine enclave of democracy and militancy. Given the no-holds-barred offensive being waged by the coal operators and what he regarded as a tepid response by John L. Lewis, Hapgood and other dissidents within the UMWA concluded that a larger program could only be advanced by replacing the union's leadership. Certainly Hapgood understood the larger implications of challenging John L. Lewis. With the failure of the LaFollette-Wheeler campaign in 1924 and the minimal results gained from the AFL's initiatives to promote labor-management cooperation, attempting to install new leadership at the helm of America's preeminent union would be viewed as a fight not only for the soul of the UMWA but for the entire labor movement.[18]

Hapgood spent much of summer 1926 attempting to persuade John Brophy to run against Lewis. "If Brophy only has the courage to make a fight," he declared, "he can defeat Lewis." Hapgood offered no evidence to support this sanguine prediction, preferring to depict Brophy's decision as a simple matter of individual will. This analysis reflected Hapgood's intense frustration and his tendency to assess complex political problems in personal terms. He ignored the profound difficulties involved in attempting to oust an incumbent with Lewis's formidable political skills.[19]

The more level-headed John Brophy was understandably cautious. Whether or not the splintered opposition to Lewis could be united remained problematic, and Brophy was wary of the Communist Party, which had assumed leadership of the anti-Lewis forces. He feared that the CP was an unreliable ally with ulterior motives and antidemocratic tendencies that contradicted his own fundamental commitments. Brophy also knew only too well how harshly Lewis would respond to a challenge and feared inflicting further pain on his already beleaguered membership. But he was finally convinced by Hapgood and other Lewis opponents that it was imperative to offer an "intellectual and social answer" to inertia and demoralization. By fall 1926, Brophy put aside his reservations and agreed to mount an insurgent campaign for the UMWA presidency.[20]

Operating under the slogan "Save the Union," Brophy's platform

Hapgood returned to the United States in February 1926 and spent nearly five months on a lecture circuit, spreading his message of social commitment and international working-class solidarity to middle-class audiences. Here Hapgood is pictured in December 1926 after returning to the mines of western Pennsylvania. (Courtesy of Lilly Library, Indiana University)

revolved around his larger program—no wage reductions, nationalization of the mines, aggressive organizing, workers' education, and support for a labor party. He emphasized the importance of a national program, asserting that only public ownership was capable of stabilizing a chaotic industry and providing "mine workers the opportunity to govern and administer their lives and labor." Both Brophy and Hapgood acknowledged that simply ousting Lewis would not solve the miners' problems. Still, they depicted the larger program as an ideal that would keep alive the spirit of Somerset and place the quest for industrial democracy at the forefront of the union's agenda. For Hapgood, Save the Union carried an additional meaning. It was not only an effort to advance a political program but also a personal crusade to preserve the ideals that had attracted him to the UMWA and which he believed John L. Lewis was violating.[21]

Hapgood became Brophy's campaign manager and assumed a visible role in advancing his candidacy. His first task was to unite the disparate elements in the anti-Lewis fight and deter the wily UMWA chief from dividing the opposition, a skill that Lewis had honed over years of bare-knuckled political infighting. Hapgood moved quickly to win support from the Communist Party, which had made insurgency within the UMWA its most important initiative within the labor movement. Attending a July 1926 CP conference in Pittsburgh, Hapgood was warmly received by the delegates. Whereas Brophy accepted Communist support as a necessary evil, Hapgood reported his unqualified willingness to cooperate with "sincere, hard-working, and intelligent" party activists in the labor movement.[22]

While the commitment of the Communists stemmed from ideological certitude, Powers Hapgood's political will was animated by the demands of his personal code. If he harbored any doubts about the wisdom of challenging John L. Lewis, he submerged them in open appeals to principle and individual sacrifice. As he explained later in attempting to persuade a fellow miner to run for Brophy's old post as District 2 president, "real trade union leaders must always be willing to sacrifice . . . personal convenience for a set of principles. . . . Nothing is ever done for the benefit of humanity . . . unless strong characters are willing to take risks."[23] Strong character and the willingness to sacrifice remained the yardsticks by which Hapgood measured political commitment. In his continuing search for comrades who were willing to sacrifice all, he regarded CP activists as among the select few whose dedication matched his own. This conviction induced Hapgood to work much more closely with the party than most non-Communist radicals, a stance he maintained throughout his political career.

Hapgood's own relationship with the Communist Party is a matter of some controversy. Documents recently made available from the Profintern (Red International of Labor Unions) archives claim that he was a secret member who joined the party in 1926. The report offered no further details on the nature of his membership, however, and must be viewed in light of other evidence suggesting that Hapgood placed clear limits on his associations with the Communists. Years later, he recalled that CP factions led by Jay Lovestone and William Z. Foster had attempted to recruit him and even offered him a seat on the party's Central Committee, provided that he keep his membership secret.

Hapgood admitted being tempted by the CP offer, explaining that "the only thing that kept me from joining the CP instead of the SP . . . is because I was instructed to deny my membership if I joined so as to hold my membership in the miners union."[24]

On numerous occasions thereafter, both publicly and privately, Hapgood denied that he was or ever had been a member of the Communist Party. In a July 1926 letter to his parents, he explained that he would not join the CP but would work with Communists when their "policies are sound." In an open letter to miners in District 2 written during Brophy's campaign, he denied party membership while simultaneously denouncing the "deliberate and malicious lies" that critics used to discredit the CP. Given Hapgood's policy of telling his parents everything and the place that personal integrity occupied in his moral code, it seems reasonable to question the Profintern account of his secret party membership. What perhaps made critics suspicious of Hapgood's sympathies was his ongoing defense of the Soviet Union and his continuing willingness to work with Communists, a position that was rejected by most others on the non-Communist left.[25]

As John Brophy had anticipated, John L. Lewis fought his challengers with unbridled ruthlessness. Intercepting a letter that Albert Coyle, a left-wing unionist involved in the Save the Union campaign had sent to Hapgood, he read portions of it to the AFL convention in October 1926. In what a front page *New York Times* story described as an "excoriating attack," Lewis highlighted Coyle's references to Communist support for Brophy's campaign by pointing to William Z. Foster, who was sitting in the gallery, and denouncing him as the "arch-priest of Communism." By implication, Hapgood was smeared with the same brush, and his relations with the Communist Party became a campaign issue that damaged Brophy's cause.[26]

The full wrath of Lewis's machine was now turned against Hapgood and Brophy. In the *UMWA Journal,* Hapgood was described as the "sort of coal miner who digs little coal and spreads a good deal of Red poison." Hapgood responded vigorously to these charges, denying that he was a Communist but defending the Soviet Union's labor policies. In an October 15, 1926, letter to AFL president William Green, with whom he had previously enjoyed friendly relations, Hapgood began to burn his bridges to the official labor movement. He charged that AFL leaders were inclined to "believe capitalists more readily than their own members" and sought to impress employers so that they could have comfortable careers after leaving the labor movement. Again, Hapgood cast the issue as one of morality and character, taking pains to depict himself as more virtuous than his opponents. He concluded his letter to Green defiantly: "John L. Lewis and others may think they can get rid of me, but no matter what happens I expect to lead my entire life in the front lines of the movement for a better world."[27]

Green lamented Hapgood's evolution towards radicalism: "I had long hoped that you would see the futility of following vague and visionary policies. You ought to know that nothing substantial can be accomplished except through the application of practical and constructive policies." Hapgood's endorsement of the Bolsheviks and his attack on the moral character of his opponents exceeded the limits of tolerable dissent. He was now declared persona non grata by the heads of both the UMWA and the AFL. In the short span of five years, the aspiring labor leader had gone from institutionalist to insurgent. Having made powerful enemies who were determined to deny him any substantive role in the labor movement, Hapgood's hopes of seeing if a college man could rise to union leadership dissolved.[28]

More painful for Hapgood than the attacks of Green's and Lewis's toadies was the dissolution of support for Brophy in his home district. Most of District 2's officers, including James Mark, who had accompanied Hapgood on the delegation to New York during the Somerset strike, defected to Lewis's camp. His old Somerset friend John Kerr also deserted the Brophy ticket in favor of Lewis. Kerr, Mark, and other former allies had been convinced by the UMWA president that the Brophy ticket was consorting with dangerous and disreputable outsiders. Their defection suggested a darker side to the communal environment of Hapgood's beloved mining towns, an insularity and parochialism that John L. Lewis was able to turn to his advantage.[29]

One of Lewis's favorite tactics was to find technicalities that invalidated the union membership of his opponents. He was then able to declare them ineligible to run for office. In Hapgood's case, Lewis's cronies were able to uncover a bookkeeping error in the transfer of his membership from one local union to another when he first entered District 2. His membership was revoked by an investigating committee, restored by a vote of the local union, and finally rescinded by the District leadership, which was now in Lewis's pocket. Adding insult to injury was the fact that John Kerr had betrayed their friendship by cooperating with Lewis's forces in helping them to deny Hapgood's membership.[30]

Through a combination of red-baiting and challenging the credentials of his opponents, Lewis was able to split Brophy's once unified base of support. The UMWA president went on to defeat his challenger in December 1926 by a vote of 173,000 to 60,000. The election was marred by opposition charges of widespread fraud, fueled by a six-month delay in releasing the final vote count. Near unanimous tallies for Lewis in some districts and evidence of phantom votes in others lent credence to the insurgents' allegations that the election was fraudulent. In one district where Brophy was able to check actual vote totals against Lewis's tally, he found that his opponent had stolen 477 votes from him in order to secure an overwhelming majority.[31]

Yet Brophy found little support within the union for his attempt to overturn the results, and most liberals outside the union were unwilling to take on Lewis publicly. The fact that Brophy was able to garner so many votes testified to the genuine appeal of his program and the distaste that many rank-and-file miners held for Lewis's tactics. Still, Lewis's ability to undermine the legitimacy of his challengers suggested that his opposition to local autonomy and his advocacy of centralized leadership were shared by substantial elements within the rank and file. Beyond revealing differing visions of which principles should guide the UMWA, the defeat of Save the Union had other implications. The most eloquent and thoughtful critics of not only the UMWA's but also the AFL's leadership had been repudiated, driving those who were suggesting alternatives to the margins of the labor movement.[32]

As he prepared to attend the UMWA convention in January 1927, Hapgood saw his dreams for a revitalized UMWA crumbling. He remained determined, however, to expose Lewis's wrongdoing and protest the election results. "Otherwise," he explained, "the honest people might as well leave the labor movement. Of what use will it be to vote?" Without the possibility for change via the ballot box, the UMWA risked becoming a one-party state, and Hapgood feared that the ensuing demoralization would destroy any chance for reasserting the union's democratic traditions.[33]

But Hapgood had only begun to feel the full implications of John L. Lewis's wrath. Defeating his opponents electorally was not enough for the vindictive Lewis; he had to ensure that Brophy, Hapgood, and their allies would never again be in a position to challenge his authority. There was nothing subtle in Lewis's approach to the Save the Union advocates at the 1927 convention held in Indianapolis. Several days before the opening gavel, Hapgood was lured to a hotel room, threatened with a loaded automatic, and beaten by three of Lewis's goons. When police arrived to break up the fight, the assailants charged Hapgood with being a Communist, and the authorities arrested him.

Following a raucous trial, the charges were dismissed by a local judge. These events were only a preview of the treatment Hapgood would receive at the actual convention proceedings.[34]

Hapgood was undeterred by his beating. Membership in the UMWA was not only his umbilical link to the working class but also a symbolic loss of his industrial citizenship. He persisted in attempting to speak before the convention, but Lewis gaveled him out of order as a noncredentialed delegate. Underscoring his determination to render Hapgood illegitimate, the UMWA president twice told the delegates that "the man who just disturbed this convention is not a member of the United Mine Workers of America" and thundered that "any man who thinks he can abuse the privilege of the convention and defy the chairman . . . is merely a fool." Hapgood then scuffled with Lewis's sergeant-at-arms and suffered another beating right on the convention floor. Although Hapgood was not the only Lewis opponent to be subjected to violence, his enemies seemed to take special pleasure in brutalizing the Harvard graduate whom they regarded as an outsider and a subversive.[35]

These events received substantial publicity and cemented Hapgood's image as a courageous middle-class crusader seeking to reform a corrupt union. But the convention left John L. Lewis in total control of the UMWA. Worse yet, Brophy, Hapgood, and their fellow insurgents had been cast as traitors by Lewis. In a besieged organization that valued loyalty as the highest virtue, this accusation was especially telling. Loyalty was a linchpin of Powers Hapgood's personal moral code, and he now stood condemned as treasonous by the entire institutional apparatus of the UMWA.[36]

The 1926 election indelibly shaped Hapgood's career. As John Brophy's campaign manager, he had held the legitimacy of union membership and retained the esteem of many miners within District 2 who remembered his role during the Somerset strike. The Save the Union banner had permitted him to crusade for a coherent political program that embodied his deepest aspirations for industrial democracy. Now, branded as a pariah by Lewis and having relinquished his base in District 2, Hapgood faced the chilling prospect of political exile. Hapgood also paid a profound psychological price following Save the Union's defeat. He would experience prolonged feelings of loneliness and despair as he struggled to regain his working-class credentials and recapture the fraternal spirit that he had discovered in Somerset and Ammanford.

An exhausted John Brophy left the field of battle to recuperate, but Hapgood sought ways to continue the fight. After the convention, he returned to Pennsylvania, hoping to rally the remnants of Save the Union. He also drew closer to the Communists, writing a lengthy analysis of the convention in *New Masses,* a leading party organ. Having failed to change the UMWA at the national level and suffered rejection by District 2 leaders who had once been his allies, Hapgood expressed his faith in the rank and file. Looking ahead to the expiration of the national coal agreement, he predicted that "internal dissensions will be subordinated in the event of a strike and a united front can be expected from the miners." These brave words reflected the memory of Somerset and his hope that the miners' visceral sense of solidarity would emerge once battle lines were drawn. But even Hapgood must have sensed the wishful thinking contained in his forecast, for he was well aware of the hard realities facing miners in Pennsylvania's depressed coal fields.[37]

In April 1927, Hapgood and his fellow insurgents were summoned to aid striking miners at Berwind-White in Windber. Revealing a new caution regarding militancy, Hapgood discouraged the Windber miners, fearing that they were not strong enough to sustain a successful walkout. Ultimately, he bowed to the "enthusiasm of the strikers" and led 500 miners onto the picket lines. Predictably, the new District 2 leadership undercut his efforts by denying his requests for assistance and working to cool the strikers' ardor. More alarming for Hapgood was the response of the rank and file itself. Many miners, recalling their bitter defeat five years earlier, crossed the picket lines, despite being "good union men at heart." For these men, the memory of Somerset differed markedly from Hapgood's. Rather than regarding the strike as a stirring display of courage and solidarity, they remembered it as a crushing loss that they did not wish to repeat.[38]

In Windber, Powers Hapgood was forced to acknowledge that the once-powerful language of manhood had lost its power. He pleaded with miners not to be "cowardly" or "fainthearted" by "calmly allowing your leaders to be crucified." Imploring scabs not to cross the picket line, he asserted that "*real men* [italics added] would never work under armed guards except in the penitentiary." These once stirring appeals went unheeded. The attenuated meaning of his moral code also extended to his relationship with the coal operators. Attempting to gain an agreement with a mine superintendent at Berwind-White, Hapgood thought him to be "honorable" and "refined" because he had a "nice, white house" and "daughters studying in Paris." But this cultural affinity between Hapgood and the superintendent did not extend to political matters. Much to his chagrin, the mine official reneged on a previously agreed-to deal, leaving both Hapgood and the workers without a contract.[39]

It was wrenching for Powers Hapgood to witness the collapse of the rich union culture of District 2. A scant three years after Somerset, he had been betrayed by old friends, smeared by his enemies, and disregarded by "good union men at heart." The coal operators' willful abrogation of contracts, which overrode the pledged word that miners had come to regard with reverence, eroded the sense of mutual obligation and honorable conduct that had, however imperfectly, structured workplace and community relations in the coal fields. The fact that "good union men at heart" rebuffed Hapgood's appeals illustrated that even the miners' deeply held fraternal culture could not withstand such serious pressures. Many young miners, Hapgood reported, were leaving the Pennsylvania coal fields to seek work in the mills and factories of Detroit, Dayton, and other cities. He now found himself almost totally isolated, as the communal culture of the mining towns disintegrated into a Darwinian world where survival took precedence over solidarity.[40]

Nor was the collapse of mining unionism a phenomenon restricted to the United States. Through Jack Evans and other friends in Wales, Hapgood learned of the General Strike and subsequent lockout of miners in England that occurred in 1926. Facing circumstances similar to those across the Atlantic, the Fed mounted a fiercely militant strike. In Jack Evans's words: "There were us—young men—realizing in our youth the dream of our life," as miners took over their communities, and local strike committees briefly assumed political control. Yet the British government refused to yield to what it regarded as a political strike and, after a bitter seven-month conflict, was able to subdue the union. The Fed's communal institutions were shattered by the strike's defeat. As one of Hapgood's Welsh acquaintances wrote, "all customs which were of real value to the workers are gone or going fast." Fleeing the wreckage of Hapgood's revered Welsh mining villages, a sobered Jack Evans joined Columbia Conserve as its education director, seeking a more evolutionary approach in developing alternatives to capitalism. Everywhere it seemed, the political and cultural foundations for working-class fraternity and industrial democracy lay in ruins, leaving radical activists adrift and detached from the constituencies they sought to mobilize.[41]

The defeat of Save the Union, the fracturing of the miners' communal culture, and his growing sense of marginalization led Hapgood to ruminate about his search for a political synthesis. Seeing the need to declare formally his loyalties, he had joined the Socialist Party (SP) when he returned to the United States. By the time Hapgood joined the SP, it was struggling to emerge from an extended period of decline. Under the leadership of Norman Thomas, the party was shifting away from its working-class base and beginning to attract disaffected intellectuals and middle-class professionals to its ranks. There was a certain irony in Hapgood's joining the SP at the time this transition was underway given his persistent critique of the intellectual liberals who were rapidly becoming the party's mainstays.[42]

Hapgood explained that he was most politically comfortable with the Socialist Party. In contrast to the dogmatism, dishonesty, and lukewarm commitment to democracy that he had witnessed in his dealings with the Communists, the Socialists were "honest and fair." Yet he chided Norman Thomas and the Socialists for their lack of political courage in allegedly abandoning John Brophy when John L. Lewis and the AFL launched their red-baiting attacks on his candidacy. Despite their faults, Hapgood declared, the Communists far surpassed the Socialists in their personal willingness to forego respectability and "give up everything" in loyalty to the cause. Hapgood's emphasis on personal sacrifice was an extension of his father's view that socialism was advancing fitfully because there were few people prepared "to live the life which such a belief calls for." The problem with the SP was not a matter of a limited working-class base or an outdated political message. Rather, Socialists lacked the intense personal commitment that for Hapgood defined meaningful politics.[43]

This diagnosis reflected Hapgood's ongoing quest for an ideal politics that would combine the "courage, devotion, and enthusiasm of the communists" with the "tolerance and tactical honesty of the liberal-progressives." In seeking a synthesis between the Socialists' moral commitment to democracy and the Communists' devotion to sacrifice and militancy, Hapgood was searching for a "muscular socialism" whose decency would not be mistaken for weakness. Even though he admired the Socialist Party's decency, he feared that Norman Thomas and his cohorts lacked the manly virtues that, for Hapgood, imbued politics with the moral attributes of the strenuous life. His criticism of the Socialist Party anticipated charges made during the 1930s, when intellectuals like John Dos Passos derided its politics as "near beer" in comparison to the confident assertiveness of the CP.[44]

Hapgood faced a difficult task because his critique of the SP faulted both its dominant wings. On one hand, he was asking middle-class Socialists, who were becoming a majority in the party, to identify with the working class and imbue their politics with a harder edge. On the other, he was imploring trade unionists within the party to support insurgencies against established union leadership, an action that few of them could condone. Many Socialists, especially those in the needle trades who had seen Communist machinations nearly destroy their unions, were loath to appreciate what Hapgood saw as the "courage, devotion, and enthusiasm" of the CP. Meanwhile, his friends in the Communist Party questioned his affiliation with an organization that in their view lacked the political will and discipline needed to supplant ruthless capitalist adversaries and reactionary union leadership alike.

Caught in a political no-man's-land and consigned to the margins of the labor movement, Powers Hapgood found himself adrift by summer 1927. Joining John Brophy in Pittsburgh, he attempted to secure funding for a newspaper that would publicize the cause of dissident miners. Unfortunately, such liberals as Eleanor Roosevelt, while sympathetic, were unwilling to provide financial support. The reluctance of liberals to aid an insurgency that Hapgood regarded as a test of democratic values and a barometer of political commitment further distanced him from their ranks. He perhaps hoped, in the words of Adolph Germer, a Socialist and fellow UMWA dissident, that a "hurricane" would somehow hit the rank and file and galvanize them into action. Hapgood was not disposed to await such a cataclysm. Having failed to save the union, he now looked to save two individuals whose persecution raised fundamental questions about America's commitment to justice and morality.[45]

Chapter Six

Exile at Home

You have convicted me without either hearing or
trial in a manner that even the corporation
controlled courts of this country would be afraid to
do and have sentenced me to life imprisonment in
a non-union mine as a political exile, and this
has occurred in America and by decree of the
International Executive Board of the United
Mine Workers, whose watchword has always
been justice, equality, and brotherhood.
— Powers Hapgood to
UMWA International Executive Board,
March 30, 1929

After the defeat of Save the Union and his marginalization within the
UMWA, Powers Hapgood embarked on a course of action that he later
described as "freelance agitation." For the next three years, Hapgood
confronted injustice wherever he found it, sometimes in concert with
others, more often acting simply as an individual.[1] His first foray in
freelance agitation was spurred by one of the defining political events of
the 1920s: the Sacco-Vanzetti affair. For many American liberals and
radicals, the execution of the Italian anarchists Nicola Sacco and
Bartolomeo Vanzetti climaxed a decade of bigotry, xenophobia, and
attacks on workers' rights that mocked America's commitment to democratic values. For the educated upper middle class, the case posed a
special dilemma. Some of New England's most respected citizens had
determined Sacco's and Vanzetti's fate, including the presidents of the
Massachusetts Institute of Technology and Harvard, who served on an
investigating committee that rejected the anarchists' bid for a new
trial. Even though Powers Hapgood constantly railed against middle-
class hypocrisy, he expressed shock that the governor of Massachusetts
and the president of Harvard would refuse to honor standards of justice

and decency. As was the case in the coal fields, those in positions of authority continued to disregard such standards in making decisions about working-class lives. Describing his soul as "ravaged," Hapgood rushed to Boston in August 1927 at the request of the Sacco-Vanzetti defense committee, which was waging a desperate protest in an attempt to avert the execution.[2]

Hapgood now began to doubt the efficacy of nonviolence and constitutionalism, confessing that "little by little, my faith in peaceful evolution vanishes." Denouncing the authorities who had condemned Sacco and Vanzetti, he declared that it would be "warm-hearted and sentimental" not to respond violently to "sleek, well-fed hypocrites" who "wear good clothes and pass as respectable." All the disappointments he had experienced during the past four years coalesced in what Hapgood described as a "hopeless feeling of helplessness" and a clear crisis of faith. The shrillness of his rhetoric underscored his despair. In both public appearances and private correspondence, he branded Massachusetts governor Alvan Fuller and Harvard president A. Laurence Lowell "murderers" and pronounced that Sacco and Vanzetti were the "innocent victims of as foul and brutal a murder plot on the part of supporters of a decaying social order as the world has ever seen."[3]

In Boston, Hapgood was arrested on four separate occasions. After his final arrest, on the eve of the execution, Hapgood was taken from his jail cell and transported by state police to a Boston psychiatric hospital where he was held incommunicado for more than twenty-four hours. Although the authorities' action was clearly illegal and designed to discourage protest, Hapgood's frenzied behavior suggests that he may well have been on the verge of a breakdown. Alarmed by both his son's rough treatment and his apocalyptic rhetoric, William Hapgood pleaded with Powers to regain his "lost faith in the processes of peace." The ensuing dialogue between father and son revealed differing assessments of their shared values and reflected Powers's growing sense that class conflict might well be irreconcilable. Just as he worried that the tolerance and decency exhibited by the Socialist Party might be mistaken for softness, Hapgood brooded that adherence to his family's moral code could be construed as sentimentality. The Communist Party, he observed, did not cling to quaint notions about honor and decency in the face of "capitalist brutality." His father cautioned him against the superheated rhetoric of class struggle, observing that "permanent satisfaction" came not from provocative language but rather from "the kind of life you lead and not from deeds irrespective of conduct." Adhering to an ethic of personal discipline in the face of social upheaval, he urged his son to return to "your most effective weapon—self-control."[4]

Deeply distraught, Hapgood viewed his father's faith in self-control as misplaced if not irrelevant. The authorities who condemned Sacco and Vanzetti had acted without restraint; continuing to play by their rules had not saved two innocents from the electric chair. Seared by the memory of Sacco and Vanzetti, Hapgood developed an abiding distrust of the state, a distrust he retained even when the political climate in America became more liberal. Nonetheless, he could not escape the influence of his familial and cultural legacy. Despite his flirtation with the language of class war, Hapgood was too much the middle-class gentleman to objectify his enemies or embrace violence as a morally justifiable tactic.

In fact, Hapgood adopted a more restrained tone in recounting his incarceration for readers of *The Nation* in a September 7, 1927, article. Again, he sought to explain to upper-middle-class liberals how constitutional rights and democratic principles were being violated by the very authorities pledged to uphold them. In Boston, Hapgood argued, the authorities did not confine their transgressions to the working class. By pointing out that middle-class supporters of workers were now fair game, he hoped to make liberals understand that their civil liberties were potentially endangered in such a poisoned political environment.[5]

Coming on the heels of his battle with John L. Lewis, Hapgood's tussles with Massachusetts authorities cemented his image as a crusader for both workers' rights and civil liberties. He did not stop, however, at pointing out the consequences of liberal hypocrisy; the executions of Sacco and Vanzetti also led him to reformulate his political identity. While the Communists pointed to the anarchists' fate as a predictable example of class justice and stunned liberals retreated into a mood of resignation, Hapgood crafted a new political persona: the moral man in an immoral society. Quoting Bartolomeo Vanzetti, Hapgood endorsed "speaking at street corners to scorning men," a position that reinforced his solidarity with the outcast, affirmed his disdain for middle-class complacency, and invested his freelance agitation with overtones of nobility. This self-image offered Hapgood personal consolation, but the political effectiveness of his new identity remained to be seen.

While he was in Boston Hapgood met Mary Donovan, the secretary of the Sacco-Vanzetti defense committee, a woman whose passion and commitment rivaled his own. Donovan's working-class heritage was as rich as Hapgood's familial connections to Puritan ancestors and middle-class reformers. Some of her forebears were Irish revolutionaries who had fought against British rule, and her father was a class-conscious Massachusetts shoe worker who had been a member of the Knights of Labor. Donovan, however, had higher aspirations: she attended the University of Michigan before World War I, working her way through college and becoming an active member of the Young People's Socialist League. But Donovan was also a staunch Catholic, and her affiliation with a group of Socialists presented problems for the church. She was summoned before the bishop of Detroit who ordered her to shed her Socialist membership or face excommunication. Donovan refused, and the bishop made good on his threat, thereby severing a vital strand of her cultural identity.[6]

Mary Donovan grew eternally bitter toward the official church and assuaged her anger by plunging into liberal politics. While working as a state factory inspector in Massachusetts, she became interested in the Sacco-Vanzetti case, served as secretary for their national defense committee, and developed close relationships with the anarchists and their families. Donovan's loyalty to the working class, commitment to social struggle, and aspirations as a worker-intellectual (she hoped to write novels about working-class life) all endeared her to the young Harvard radical, who wrote his parents that he was "more and more in love with her." In contrast to Margaret McDowell, here was a daughter of the working class whose commitments were untainted by popular culture or individualistic aspirations. Barely a month after they had met, he asked Donovan to marry him, a decision that was not well received by his parents. Whether they disapproved of Donovan's working-class background, the fact that she was ten years older than their son, or the haste in which marriage was being contemplated, William and Eleanor Hapgood now faced a profound change in their relationship with their only child.[7]

Hapgood remained undeterred by his parents' coolness toward Donovan. Marrying her represented an important assertion of his personal independence: in one of the most crucial decisions of his life, he had rejected the counsel of his parents. His choice also reinforced the depth of his commitment to his adopted class and further distanced him from the middle-class world. Yet his subsequent admission that he married Donovan for reasons of "comradeship" over physical attraction underscored the extent to which the need for self-validation guided even his most intimate personal choices. This is not to deny that Hapgood genuinely loved Donovan or to claim that he married her simply to demonstrate his solidarity with workers. Still, Hapgood's insatiable need to find an ideal woman led him to ignore warning signs (their ten-year age difference, sexual problems, parental disapproval) that might have suggested caution to a less psychologically driven suitor.[8]

For her part, Donovan was drawn to Hapgood, whom she found "sincere, ardent, and so young." She did express concerns over the fervor and pace of their courtship, wondering if the heat of the moment was obscuring sound judgment. Perhaps worrying over their age and class differences, Donovan asked Hapgood not "to love her so much," fearing that she was "undeserving" and might disappoint his high expectations. She also worried about his parents' reaction and promised to send Eleanor Hapgood a photograph in order to convince her "that I am not an ogre." Donovan's protests were muted, however. She obviously valued the attentiveness of her suitor, especially in the aftermath of Sacco's and Vanzetti's deaths, which remained for her an unalterably traumatic memory.[9]

Having seen so many of his personal attachments severed since his return to America, Hapgood took great comfort in establishing an enduring relationship with a woman. Following the favorable dispensation of legal proceedings against him in Boston, he and Donovan were wed in a civil ceremony in New York on December 28, 1927, Hapgood's twenty-eighth birthday. He convinced a reluctant Donovan, who had strong family ties in Massachusetts, to spend their honeymoon in the Pennsylvania coal fields. There she could pursue her writing while he continued the struggle against John L. Lewis. As he explained, the mines had become his world, and he felt out of place when away from them for too long. He also feared that striking miners in Pennsylvania would accuse him of abandoning them when the going got rough, one of the few times that Hapgood acknowledged his unusual working-class status. This return to the mines, coupled with the fact that there was no indication of parental approval or congratulations for his wedding, signified new tensions in the relationship between William and Eleanor Hapgood and their son, who now wrote them infrequently and seemed less susceptible to their influence.[10]

By the beginning of 1928, conditions in the UMWA and the Pennsylvania mines had reached their nadir. The 1927 strike, which had adopted as its slogan "No Backward Step" on wages, ended disastrously, not because of John L. Lewis's lack of nerve but because of the operators' staunch refusal to yield to the union's demands. Hapgood joined the remnants of the Save the Union movement, which was now dominated by the Communist Party, in supplying relief to miners

Powers Hapgood with Mary Donovan and members of her family. Seated from left, Mary Donovan Hapgood, Mary's father Dennis, and Mary's sister Elizabeth Donovan. Powers is in the back row, flanked by Mary's brother Dan and his wife Anna. Ronald and Betty, Dan's and Anna's children, are next to Coleen and Sheila, Irish terriers whose puppies were a source of income. In Donovan, the secretary of the Sacco-Vanzetti defense committee, Hapgood found a companion whose passion and commitment rivaled his own. The two married in 1927. (Courtesy of Lilly Library, Indiana University)

dispossessed by the strike. This strategy, which the dissidents hoped would affirm their credibility as opponents of John L. Lewis, brought them into direct conflict not only with the UMWA hierarchy but also with the AFL and the Socialist Party, which were both reluctant to sanction the provision of relief outside official channels. Since he was persona non grata in District 2, Hapgood moved to the anthracite region of northeastern Pennsylvania. He hoped to establish a new base of operations there but soon discovered that Lewis' forces were conspiring with local operators to deny him employment. He now began to experience the full meaning of political exile, as the UMWA degenerated into a state of war where survival was the highest virtue and dissidence was tantamount to treason.[11]

The anthracite region of Wilkes-Barre and Scranton had been a hotbed of militancy directed against both the coal operators and the UMWA leadership. In some areas of anthracite, an exploitative system of contracting—where miners acted as bosses in collusion with sympathetic operators—had taken hold. This system especially infuriated immigrant Italian miners, who associated it with the padrone of the old country who wielded tyrannical, unaccountable power. Dissent against this system's patent unfairness and its perversion of union solidarity was often accompanied by violence. Just before Hapgood's arrival in Wilkes-Barre, insurgents had succeeded in ousting corrupt union officials who were notorious contractors. Shortly thereafter, thugs employed by the defeated contractors engaged in running gun battles with the victorious dissidents, resulting in several deaths and the filing of trumped-up charges against those who had fought back in self-defense.[12]

Denied the right to speak at a public gathering on behalf of the dissidents, Hapgood warmed to his new role as a freelance agitator. He and Mary Donovan paraded through the town of Pittston wearing armbands proclaiming "we mourn [the loss of] free speech." This action led to their arrest and incarceration where, Hapgood informed his father, he shared quarters with "murderers, embezzlers, pimps, panderers, bigamists, thieves, and non-supporters." Hapgood's cheerful, even romantic description of his cellmates masked a deepening despair as he was again stymied in his attempt to reenter the coal fields and reclaim his cherished identity as a coal miner. His individual act of dissent was ineffectual against ruthless UMWA leaders and local authorities, both of whom branded him an "agitator" and "alleged communist."[13]

Hapgood's principal ally became the Communist Party, which almost singlehandedly continued to rally opposition against John L. Lewis. By summer 1928, however, Hapgood was forced to reexamine his relationship with the Communists. The Communist Party's approach toward trade unions had shifted abruptly. Abandoning its earlier policy of "boring from within," the Comintern (Communist International) ordered its American affiliates to establish dual unions and challenge the authority of existing labor organizations. This directive coincided with the judgment of many American Communists, who had concluded that changing the UMWA from within was impossible. Disturbed by this new strategy, Hapgood demanded an explanation from William Z. Foster, who just a year earlier had opposed dual unionism. In Hapgood's recollection, Foster offered no strategic or political rationale for the turnabout but replied: "Powers, the Communist Party decided that policy. As a good Communist, I just have to go along." This limp response from someone he respected shocked Hapgood, who now saw the extent to which even top CP leaders were forced to toe the Comintern line.[14]

Whereas John Brophy had always been uneasy about working with the Communist Party and rejected dualism as unworkable, Powers Hapgood engaged in an extended dialogue with the Communists, who pleaded with him to join their ranks. Given Hapgood's reputation for integrity among dissidents and his profile within liberal circles, the Communists had a potential recruit whose support would do much to legitimize their new political course. Despite their best efforts to persuade him, Hapgood remained unconvinced by the Communists' rationale for forming a new miners' union. Acknowledging the limits of insurgency, he declared that the failure "to capture leadership in the UMWA was not alone due to Lewis's strong arm methods and suppression of democracy." As he explained in a response to Mother (Ella Reeve) Bloor, a Communist leader, "Had our following been large enough, . . . he could not have gotten away with the things he did." He disagreed with the CP's claim that the "worsening of economic conditions" would inspire worker militancy and denounced their apocalyptic strategy as a pipe dream: "To try to evade the task of educating the masses by starting a propaganda sect of those who agree with oneself is fatal." He insisted that it was crucial to "be inside the organization that controls the American thinking masses" (that is, the AFL or the UMWA) rather than "splitting off into little sects" who lacked the ability to influence workers.[15]

This frank admission of the insurgents' weakness, the folly of sectarianism, and Lewis's standing among the miners signified a pronounced shift in Hapgood's political thinking. Even more telling was his memory of the Somerset strike, which he poignantly recalled in his letter to Mother Bloor: "But I had enough of wasted effort and futility in the 18 months Somerset strike and saw too much suffering of men, women, and little children to no avail to go through with it myself again or to ask others to unless I think that the chances are at least fair that it will not mean futility."[16]

In contrast to the CP, Hapgood was reluctant to subject miners to greater hardship in the interest of hewing to a party line or fulfilling a political vision. More important, he rejected the Communists' approach as antithetical to his belief in personal independence and participatory democracy. "I have not reached the point (and this is one of the reasons I'm not a CP member)," he wrote party activist Tony Minerich, "where I can let someone else do my thinking for me or accept the discipline of those who are not closely enough in touch with things to understand reality." Invoking the language of character, he explained to Mother Bloor that although he accepted the necessity for political discipline, it had to be accompanied by "some decency, some honesty, some fairness and democracy." For all his qualms about the timidity of the Socialist Party, Hapgood noted that Socialist policy was "democratically made" and not unilaterally imposed from above. Through their insensitivity to democratic values, the Communists were aping the behavior of their adversaries and ignoring "America's peculiar conditions" where the rule of law and the authority of the people enjoyed widespread social legitimacy, however much these principles were sullied or ignored. Moreover, by refusing to accept "some standard of word that will pass as legal tender," the Communists reduced politics to simple questions of power and discipline. In Hapgood's eyes, this approach robbed public life of the ethical foundations on which the values of fraternity and democracy could be extended and preserved.[17]

Nonetheless, Hapgood retained a grudging respect for the Communists and could not resist observing the inaugural meeting of the party's new organization, the National Miners Union, in September 1928. Uncomfortably occupying a position on the political sidelines, he lamented his status: "From one who used to be in the forefront of things, I'm now considered dead." Despite his doubts about the Communist Party, Hapgood saw it as the only hope for political change: "I'm afraid one can't be of much use to the movement without being a Communist, for one won't be given a chance to decide policy and fight unless one belongs to the machine. And after all, a machine is almost essential in this age to combat the capitalist machine. These boys are going to win where individuals fail."[18]

Hapgood's reference to the "capitalist machine" alluded to a larger context, the dramatic shift toward institutions whose size, centralization, and bureaucratic structure threatened to overwhelm individual apprehension. Driven by an ideology that viewed class struggle as the defining theme of social existence, the Communists were willing to embrace the cult of efficiency and create their own machine capable of competing with the dominant structures of political and economic power. In spite of his acceptance of a class analysis, his respect for Communist discipline, and his recognition of capitalism's unyielding resistance to popular challenge, Powers Hapgood could not embrace such mechanistic symbolism. Instead, he clung to an older tradition defined by a producer identity; small, cooperative institutions; and strict adherence to a personal code of moral conduct. Yet he acknowledged the quaintness of these notions in his reflections on the power of the capitalist machine. By his own admission, Hapgood was left dangling as an individual in an age that seemed to respect only organization and regimented collectivity.[19]

Denied the ability to act in concert with others, Hapgood was forced to seek a personal solution to his political marginality. Early in 1929, he was able to return to work in a coal mine. At the invitation of Josephine Roche, a wealthy liberal who had recently acquired ownership of the Rocky Mountain Fuel Company in Colorado, he found employment as a miner and an adviser to the management of this new experiment in labor-management cooperation. Roche had been shocked by Rocky Mountain's complicity in the infamous 1914 massacre of women and children in Ludlow, Colorado, during a coal strike. When she assumed control of Rocky Mountain, the second largest coal company in Colorado next to the Rockefeller-owned Colorado Fuel and Iron, she offered the UMWA a contract that the *Kansas City Times* described as a "charter of economic justice and decency." This was one of the few instances during the 1920s where the cooperative approach between labor and management advocated by the AFL was successfully implemented. Hapgood got on well with Roche and her advisers, one of whom had led the strike that culminated in the violence at Ludlow. And he hoped that he would be beyond the reach of John L. Lewis, in an outpost distant from the UMWA's primary concentrations of membership.[20]

A photograph in the February 13, 1929, *Denver Post* featured a smiling Hapgood clad in mining clothes, accepting his lunch pail from Mary Donovan before leaving for work. Donovan later recalled this period in Colorado as one of the happiest of their lives, noting a "great contrast between this life and the struggles and disappointments of past years." In Josephine Roche, Hapgood found the enlightened "liberal boss" he had vainly sought in Pennsylvania. Like his father's experiment at Columbia Conserve, Rocky Mountain was a cooperative alternative to class conflict and union fratricide, a setting where the pledged word was honored by both labor and capital. The fiery rhetoric of class war that Hapgood had recently spouted was replaced by the the language of civility, and he regained a much-needed sense of personal efficacy. Hapgood's joy was short-lived, however. Less than three months after he arrived in Colorado, the UMWA executive board revoked his union membership, charging that Hapgood was a dual unionist and therefore barred from employment in Roche's mine.[21]

John L. Lewis justified this expulsion in terms that were especially painful to Hapgood. He claimed that Hapgood was "not a bona fide miner," questioned his "loyalty and adherence to the principles of the United Mine Workers of America," and doubted the "propriety and advisability of conferring membership upon a man of means." In a lengthy letter to Lewis and the UMWA executive board, Hapgood responded angrily to these charges. Stung by Lewis's insinuation that he was a dilettante, he asserted that "I have worked under practically every condition known in the industry . . . and in no place that I've worked have I been unable to cope with conditions." Besides affirming his manliness, Hapgood insisted that his claim to be a member of the working class was legitimate in spite of his education and background: "I consider myself a part of the working class," he proclaimed, "and my fortunes will either rise or fall with those of the other workers."[22]

Although Powers Hapgood and John L. Lewis both used the language of loyalty and character, each invested it with different meanings. In his Darwinian view of the world, Lewis defined loyalty in narrow, personal terms. Powers Hapgood offered a far more expansive interpretation, insisting, in his Uncle Hutch's words, that labor needed to embody an "independent moral code" that would bind workers to a set of ethical standards. The fundamental principles of the union—justice, equality, brotherhood, freedom of thought—which Lewis devalued and violated provided miners with an alternative form of morality that in Hapgood's view was central to the UMWA's social legitimacy and popular appeal. The irreconcilable issue between Hapgood and Lewis, then, was whether power or morality should be the principle that guided labor in a modern business culture.[23]

In language that reflected his anguish, Hapgood accused Lewis of having convicted him of "high treason" and "sentencing him to life imprisonment in a non-union mine as a political exile." Awaiting action on his appeal of the expulsion order, he took a job as a surveyor in one of Josephine Roche's mines, a post that while not managerial was exempt from union membership. But this proved untenable: the price of his remaining and not endangering Roche's relationship with the UMWA was to refrain from criticizing Lewis. Hapgood was unwilling to remain silent, and in February 1930 he prepared to leave Colorado.[24]

Despondent over his expulsion from the UMWA and wearied by repeated political defeats, Hapgood began to consider what would have previously been an unthinkable move—going to work for his father's company. Before he took action, he was presented with a new opportunity to strike back at John L. Lewis. The Illinois district of the UMWA, long a center of fierce opposition to Lewis, had obtained a court ruling barring the UMWA president from placing the district under provisional rule. Emboldened by their legal success, the Illinois miners gathered together a loose coalition of anti-Lewis forces. Instead of forming a dual union, the insurgents cast themselves as the "legitimate" UMWA and held a founding convention in March 1930.[25]

Along with John Brophy and other Lewis foes, Hapgood attended the convention. Encouraged by his fellow Socialists and non-Communist leftists led by Brookwood Labor College's A. J. Muste, Hapgood reluctantly ran against Adolph Germer, a staunchly anti-Communist Socialist and longtime Lewis rival, for the vice presidency of the new union. He lost decisively after being termed too young by some delegates and too "red" by others. It was not his defeat, however, that sobered Hapgood on the new union's prospects. The convention's seating of Frank Farrington, a corrupt and opportunistic Illinois UMWA leader, led John Brophy to bolt the Reorganized UMWA, as the new union was called, and prompted Hapgood to doubt its integrity. Yet he rejected Mary Donovan's qualms, ignored John Brophy's advice to leave gracefully, and decided to work for the new union. His decision reflected a familiar sense of duty but was now accompanied by an irrepressible feeling of despair: "I can't stand the thought of being an organizer but it seems to be expected of me and I don't know what else to do."[26]

Hapgood was reassured by Roger Baldwin, whose advice he often sought during moments of personal crisis. Baldwin discouraged Hapgood from going to work for his father and urged him to assist the new union. "Your place in American life is in unions and coal," Baldwin averred. "Your change to a business identified with your family would never be understood. What you stand for would lose force." He also assuaged Hapgood's guilt over taking a staff position and abandoning physical work in the mines, asserting that "you owe it to the union and yourself to get out of rank and file labor . . . [and] into work that will use your major talents." Torn between his sense of duty to old comrades, his fear of losing the moral validation of productive labor, and his desire to be with his family, which now included a daughter, Barta (named after Bartolomeo Vanzetti), Hapgood accepted Baldwin's advice and joined the staff of the Reorganized Union. Despite his misgivings he could not resist the opportunity to resume combat with the Lewis machine and reestablish his connection to the miners. Also, leaving the ranks of labor for his father's company would have been an admission of defeat whose implications he preferred to avoid.[27]

In spring and summer 1930, Hapgood journeyed throughout the coal fields of Pennsylvania, Illinois, and Kentucky attempting to win support for the Reorganized UMWA. John L. Lewis responded to the effort with his customary ruthlessness; his thugs disrupted meetings organized by the new union and used violence to intimidate the insurgents. Hapgood's contacts with the miners revealed a working class that was riven by the misery and poverty of the Great Depression and which he gloomily characterized as "divided, discouraged, and afraid." Especially distressing was his visit to the site of his glory days in Pennsylvania. Hapgood hoped to organize support for a strike in Somerset, but other leaders in the new union rejected that strategy as suicidal under the circumstances. In Pittston, he found that the insurgents in the anthracite had been routed and were simply struggling to survive. As an alternative, he looked to find an "intelligent" operator like Josephine Roche who might be willing to recognize the new union but found no takers—there were no enlightened owners who felt the need to make common cause with unions. Hapgood's assessment of the miners' attitudes grew increasingly bleak, a far cry from the romantic imagery that he had formerly attached to coal diggers.[28]

Dismayed by the dissolution of both union and community, Hapgood was nearly ready to give up the fight. "It's just the same old argument," he concluded wearily, "trying to get timid, beaten men—needy and greedy"—to do something. Hapgood's encounters revealed a welter of conflicting attitudes among the miners: an abiding loyalty to the UMWA, the renunciation of collective action as futile, and above all, a profound demoralization caused by the collapse of the union, the lost cohesiveness of the mining community, and the devastating effects of the Great Depression. The proud fraternity of the UMWA lay in shambles. There was simply no foundation on which to rally workers on behalf of the new union or revive the political ideals that had proven so potent during the Somerset strike just eight years earlier.[29]

By June 1930 Hapgood again considered resigning from the Reorganized UMWA. Speaking to a meeting of John L. Lewis's home local in Panama, Illinois, Hapgood was told by one elderly miner that he reminded him of the famed UMWA leader John Mitchell. The miner went on to predict a great future for him. The poignancy of the moment was not lost on Hapgood, whose dream of becoming a leader in the UMWA now seemed out of reach. "It's sad to disappoint anyone who really has faith," he mused. He noted that the Panama miners had remained true to the mutualistic ethic of the UMWA. They shared work in slack times, owned their own homes, and had a "real union," in short, that rare combination of self-reliance and solidarity that Hapgood found so appealing. But there was no place in this community for an insurgent like Powers Hapgood. Now thirty years old, with a family to support and no chance of finding work in a mine, his options had narrowed. On July 16, 1930, Hapgood resigned from the Reorganized UMWA to join his father's company.[30]

Hapgood's political friends regarded his decision skeptically. Tom Tippett, a former miner, Brookwood Labor College instructor, and Illinois insurgent, complained, "I can't help but feel that the C.C.C. is a pretty negative factor in combating old man capitalism." But Tippett also acknowledged the precarious condition of the new union and conceded that "everything seems to be futile." Hapgood justified his choice in cautious terms, reflecting the erosion of his romanticism after nearly a decade in the labor movement: "To go to Columbia wouldn't mean abandoning the cause of labor. It would merely mean transferring one's energy to a field where constructive, if less romantic and spectacular work, was sure." As Hapgood realized, the conditions for romantic and spectacular work hardly existed in a country and an industry gripped by the Depression, not to mention a union from which he had been expelled.[31]

Just a few months after rejecting employment at his father's company, Powers Hapgood could no longer avoid acknowledging the futility of his freelance agitation. More tellingly, he had nearly lost faith in the "kindliness and courage of the masses," the mythic image of working-class virtue that had guided his political quest. His profound belief in change from below had been shaken; ironically, his greatest fulfillment during the last five years had occurred in a setting where change had been initiated from above. Still, Hapgood must have harbored powerful feelings of ambivalence in returning to Indiana. Having fought for so long to establish his personal independence, he was now forced to reenter the orbit of his father's authority. Also, his unquenchable need for "romantic and spectacular work," while momentarily subordinated, was not easily abandoned. For his part, William Hapgood welcomed the opportunity to convince his prodigal son that Columbia Conserve represented industrial democracy in its purest form. In reuniting with his father, Powers Hapgood's odyssey entered a new phase, one that provided a different form of exposure to the working class, unmasked submerged tensions in his relationship with his parents, and profoundly influenced his subsequent political choices.

Chapter Seven

Debacle at Columbia Conserve

The company now represents only a family
corporation being conducted with rather more
autocracy and less social responsibility than many
a "soulless" corporation making no claims to
industrial pioneering.
—*Christian Century* editorial, December 13, 1933

The 1920s had been a banner decade for the Columbia Conserve Company and its ambitious experiment in industrial democracy. Between 1917 and 1929 the company secured its niche in the canning industry, conducting business in 240 cities and 35 states. Most important, Columbia Conserve generated profits in all but two years during this period. This steady growth and profitability enabled William Hapgood to be more generous in sharing the fruits of Columbia's success. He instituted a profit-sharing program, offered his employees fully paid medical coverage, and virtually guaranteed employment to all salaried workers. These policies placed Hapgood in the vanguard of enlightened employers and were especially noteworthy given the seasonal nature of the canning industry.[1]

Spurred by his egalitarian commitments, William Hapgood moved to eliminate hierarchical distinctions among employees and to institutionalize workers' control. Employees were trained in a variety of tasks in order to diminish the distinction between "brain work" and "factory work" and to reinforce Hapgood's conviction that "we are all of one kind." Instead of being appointed by top management, department leaders were elected by their fellow workers. By the late 1920s, salaried employees were eligible to serve on "the Council," Columbia's supreme governing body, which made all decisions regarding salaries and working conditions. Hapgood launched his boldest initiative in 1926, introducing a plan whereby Columbia employees would achieve majority shareholder status. This goal was reached in July 1930, when Columbia's approximately one hundred salaried employees gained ownership of 51 percent of the company's common stock. Columbia Conserve now publicized itself as a "business without a boss" where "every employee was a boss and every worker an owner." As Jack Evans, Powers Hapgood's Welsh mining comrade and now Columbia Conserve's education director observed, William Hapgood appeared to have succeeded in his quest to link "technical and business skill with the spirit of the social good."[2]

As the onslaught of the Great Depression raised serious questions about the viability of contemporary capitalism, Columbia Conserve was widely praised for its humane managerial practices and democratic commitments. Yet in the space of a few short years, William Hapgood's experiment was shattered, destroyed by cutthroat competition and internal squabbling. The unraveling of Columbia Conserve left both Hapgood and his son deeply shaken. Powers Hapgood was forced to question the father he revered and reconsider the viability of small-scale alternatives to industrial capitalism.

Hapgood could not have chosen a less auspicious time to begin work at his father's company. Columbia Conserve had built its reputation and profitability by furnishing canned soup products to wholesalers, who then sold them under private labels. This practice served "as a means of protecting the independent grocer and jobber against the ravages of the chain store" by offering them quality products at fair prices. But with the onset of the Depression, the demand for canned soup plummeted, and Columbia began to lose market share to Campbell's, whose superior size and economies of scale posed a serious threat. Banks began to demand more stringent terms for the company's outstanding loans, evoking howls of protest from Columbia's worker-owners over finance capital's lack of regard "for the welfare of the community in which they operate." These sobering conditions left Powers Hapgood undaunted. After his disappointing tenure as a freelance agitator, he relished joining some of his most trusted colleagues at his father's business and promoting Columbia Conserve as a model of industrial democracy.[3]

Hapgood's old Somerset comrades Albert Armstrong and George

Gregory had both become long-term Columbia employees. Armstrong had especially distinguished himself, chairing the company's employee council and later advancing to a position on Columbia's sales force. Other refugees from the class struggle had also joined Columbia Conserve at Hapgood's urging. As the company's education director, Jack Evans proclaimed his commitment to the "very difficult task of making co-operative individuals." Facing options as bleak as his protege's, John Brophy became a salesman at Columbia, along with Hapgood's brother-in-law, Daniel Donovan, an ardent Socialist and trade unionist. Surrounded by old comrades and family members in a cooperative setting, Hapgood was now the moral man in a moral society, a welcome change from his recent wanderings as a political outcast.[4]

The worsening of the Depression confirmed Hapgood's belief that capitalism's days were numbered and reinforced his desire to advertise Columbia Conserve as a cooperative alternative to a bankrupt competitive system. With a deep sense of urgency, he sought to convey that message in his capacity as a Columbia salesman and publicist. Traveling across the country, he spoke to groups ranging from Rotarians and chambers of commerce to churches, unions, women's clubs, and student organizations. After making fifty-four speeches in just two weeks during February and March 1931, he described the work as "tiresome and lonesome." Yet via speeches and radio talks, he and his father reached nearly 15,000 people on their midwinter publicity tour, a far larger audience than he had ever attained in his years as a labor activist. To "sleek Rotarians" in the Midwest, Hapgood preached a form of repentance, declaring that "the only way out was for capitalism to cease to be capitalism." Addressing a women's club in Emporia, Kansas, he rooted Columbia's mission in the social gospel: "We decided if there was anything to the fatherhood of God and the brotherhood of man it meant just one thing to us—from each in accordance with his power to each in accordance with his need." By conducting its business according to democratic, egalitarian, and Christian principles, Columbia Conserve suggested the possibilities of a new society and what might be accomplished if industrial democracy were practiced on a broader scale.[5]

Hapgood remained ambivalent, however, about his new role away from politics and the heat of class conflict. Recounting his lecture to a group of students in Nebraska, he joked to Mary Donovan that "I'm doing more good for socialism than for soup, I think, although perhaps some students will get their parents soup-conscious." He tried to retain some connection to the labor movement, following a January 1931 morning talk to the Portland, Oregon, chamber of commerce with an evening speech before the local labor council. After visiting imprisoned labor militant Tom Mooney in California and meeting with supporters of jailed Wobblies in Washington state, he was himself briefly detained in Council Bluffs, Iowa, in October 1931 for defending the free speech rights of George Papcun, a Communist acquaintance from Save the Union. The latter action garnered front-page headlines in Indianapolis and resulted in sharp criticism of Hapgood by some Columbia employees, who feared that their company was being linked with communism.[6]

Arlie Myers, a senior Columbia employee, bluntly told Hapgood that he was no longer a "free-lance coal miner" and had to think carefully before engaging in actions that could damage the company's interests. Hapgood apologized for the bad press Columbia had received but defended the need to uphold the fundamental principle of free speech. Freedom of expression remained the yardstick by which Hapgood measured democracy, for it illustrated the extent to which social institutions were willing to subject themselves to scrutiny and permit popular participation. But his dismissal of Arlie Myers's criticism unveiled a chasm between Hapgood and some of his fellow employees. The fundamental principle that mattered most to them was a cooperative, consensual spirit, which they suspected their headstrong new coworker of violating.[7]

The quarrel over the Papcun episode was overshadowed by Hapgood's fears that Columbia Conserve's basic principles were being compromised. As the economy plunged, workers agreed to a series of pay cuts and other belt-tightening measures. Initially, there was widespread approval for these steps, which were aimed at ensuring guaranteed employment. Hapgood touted the virtues of personal sacrifice in order to continue providing the benefits that defined Columbia as an industrial democracy. He endorsed workers absorbing further wage cuts, which he likened to "strike pay." As Daniel Donovan observed, strike pay conveyed the notion of personal sacrifice for the common good and signified Columbia's willingness, in contrast to typical capitalist firms, to maintain its social commitments despite economic hardship. Hapgood also opposed attempts to limit medical coverage for dependents and lay off workers as economic conditions worsened. Such concessions, he charged, violated "our principles" and encouraged "idealism chiselers" whose proposed cutbacks undermined Columbia's visionary aims. Writing his father in April 1932, Hapgood insisted that the company had to "maintain the safeguards and guarantees necessary to keep ourselves a socialist organization" or "the idealism I thought was inherent in Columbia will have been killed for me."[8]

For a frustrated Powers Hapgood, Columbia Conserve was the embodiment of values that were disregarded in the capitalist world, and he was dismayed to discover that not all Columbia employees shared that vision. Many, he charged, were unwilling "to give everything to the Columbia cause." In a harsh 1931 letter to the Council, he accused some Columbia employees of failing to uphold the company's ultimate purpose as a cooperatively owned and democratically managed enterprise. His use of capital letters suggested the depth of his anger: "IF THESE PEOPLE REALLY HAD A COOPERATIVE ATTITUDE THEY WOULD GET MORE PLEASURE FROM SUCH ACTIVITIES [discussions, lectures] THAN THEY WOULD FROM DANCING PARTIES OR BOWLING, which seem to be the only after-working hours activities that some of this group are interested in." "Now is no time for play if civilization is not to be destroyed by war or revolution," Hapgood continued. He recommended that workers who did not support Columbia's ultimate purpose either shape up or be replaced.[9]

Hapgood's petulant, accusatory tone revealed an unresolved tension in his attitude toward workers. He consistently needed to discover evidence of working-class virtue in order to validate his personal sacrifices. When Columbia employees failed to meet his exacting standards for cooperative behavior, he denounced them as ingrates. Curiously, William Hapgood, though more forgiving than his son, expressed similar criticism of his employees. As middle-class men seeking to exorcise the "burden" of their comfortable past, both Hapgoods could not escape a sense of noblesse oblige in their relationship with workers. They demanded that the recipients of their generosity demonstrate their gratitude and prove their worthiness. When the workers fell short of his expectations, Powers reacted like a scorned prophet: "The group can't expect me to give my entire life to them unless they cooperate by keeping all of the principles of Columbia alive." This self-righteous attitude prevented him from analyzing the reasons for the workers' apathy and from developing a more nuanced response.[10]

Most Columbia employees were not driven by a personal need to give everything to the Columbia cause. They tended, in Daniel Bell's words, "to live 'in parts,' parceling out their lives amidst work, home, neighborhood, fraternal club, etc." Especially in an urban setting, they enjoyed numerous options for fulfilling leisure activities outside the workplace. And in spite of being offered educational opportunities and being encouraged to participate in management, most Columbia employees were reluctant to assume such responsibilities. Reflecting older patterns of deference to authority and expertise, they were generally content to leave decision making to their elected officers and department leaders. Still, workers were committed to Columbia Conserve, not only for its generous social benefits, but more important, for psychological reasons. As the wife of one worker explained, "I never thought that a public place of this sort could be run so much like a family."[11]

A significant portion of Columbia Conserve's salaried employees had recently migrated from farm to factory. Discovering the comradeship they had known in agrarian communities recreated at Columbia Conserve helped ease their transition to a fragmented industrial world. The "spirit of harmony" and the "feeling of good fellowship" was cited by such veterans of class conflict as Albert Armstrong and George Gregory, who contrasted their experience at Columbia with the bitter strife they had seen in the coal fields. This spirit of harmony was abetted by Columbia's racial and ethnic homogeneity. Most of the workers were native-born Protestants; therefore, Columbia was spared the racial and ethnic strife that so often marred the American workplace. When company liberals proposed in 1930 that Columbia consider employing African-Americans, salaried workers rejected the proposal by a five-to-one margin, insisting that the feeling of good fellowship could only be achieved among "social equals."[12]

Feelings of family and fellowship were more meaningful to most Columbia workers than such concepts as equality, socialism, or even trade unionism, which seemed to violate Columbia's harmonious spirit. When Hapgood attempted to persuade the Council to affiliate with a union, his father spoke for many employees in rejecting the proposal. Identification with a union, William Hapgood feared, would signify a shift in Columbia's culture "from discussion through peaceful means to one of struggle and warfare." Besides, he proclaimed, "we have a labor movement that is altogether more far-reaching than any labor movement that is labelled trade unionism."[13]

For Powers Hapgood notions of fellowship and harmony seemed too tepid at a time when capitalism appeared to be on the ropes. Like many on the political left, he was convinced that economic deprivation would soon prompt workers to stir. He wanted Columbia Conserve to challenge capitalist hegemony by directly identifying with union struggles and socialist politics. It now became clear that Hapgood's identity as a trade unionist and socialist was incompatible with his father's vision of Columbia as a classless institution, a vision most employees supported. His Uncle Norman was not far from the mark when he later charged that "Powers is frankly and honestly interested in our company only as a step toward organized Socialism," an expectation that was rebuffed during his tenure with the company.[14]

The image of family assumed special irony for Hapgood as conflict with his father intensified. In a letter to his brother Norman, William Hapgood explained what he regarded as his son's principal shortcoming: "He has for so long had a completely open hand with respect to the appeals of unfortunate manual workers that it is hard for him to refuse many requests even when they are made by wholesale grocers whose economic position is stronger than ours." This criticism suggests the younger Hapgood's difficulties in mastering the demands of business, which conflicted with his personal loyalties to his clients. While acknowledging mistakes which he attributed to overwork and stress, Powers objected to his father's scrutiny, protesting that "it makes me feel that you lack confidence in me." He questioned William's attempt to fire an employee under his (Powers's) supervision, asserting, "I think we have got to review our thinking and actions a little if we want to give publicity to the Columbia Conserve Company as a democratic organization." These exchanges, couched in qualified, civil terms, scarcely concealed the long-simmering tension now surfacing between father and son. In part, it appears as if Powers was rebelling against his loss of personal independence by criticizing his father's purported lack of commitment to democratic principles. Meanwhile, William Hapgood was feeling the strain of managing Columbia Conserve under extremely trying circumstances, which were exacerbated by disputes with his son.[15]

By summer 1932, Hapgood leaped at the opportunity for a sabbatical. Securing a leave of absence, he returned to the political arena as the Socialist Party candidate for governor of Indiana. Inspired by evidence of unrest in the state's coal mining regions, Hapgood hoped to locate a more politically conscious segment of the working class than he had encountered at Columbia Conserve. He employed the language of solidarity in urging workers not to "scab at the ballot box" by supporting the candidates of the mainstream parties. Despite an energetic campaign, the Socialists fared poorly at both the state and national levels. Most workers, however sympathetic, feared that voting Socialist would divide the opposition to Herbert Hoover and permit the reviled Republican president to win reelection.[16]

As Hapgood and his fellow Socialists conceded in an election postmortem, "the breakdown of the capitalist system does not help automatically to make socialists." This rueful admission begged the question: if a collapsing capitalist economy could not dislodge workers from their traditional political loyalties, what was the future for American socialism? How, in fact, were socialists to be "made"? Although Hapgood left behind no public musings, he must have been disappointed at still further evidence of the working class's unwillingness to support radical social reconstruction.[17]

With few other options, Hapgood prepared to resume work at Columbia Conserve. His return was interrupted when he was wounded while taking target practice at his father's farm in December 1932. In the course of exchanging firearms with a companion, Hapgood was shot in the abdomen, and only quick medical attention prevented a life-threatening loss of blood. With only slight exaggeration, Boyd Gurley, an editorial writer for the *Indianapolis Times,* noted that "all over the land, men and women are asking about the condition of Powers Hapgood." Gurley's editorial, entitled "What Is Success?" pointed out that Hapgood had "deliberately chosen privation and sacrifice above ease and comfort" and suggested that his life was worthy of emulation by Depression-era youth "who may be puzzled over their own destinies." The attention given Hapgood's injury underscored his visibility as a social reformer whose dedication and commitment were admired and respected.[18]

Considerable evidence suggests that Hapgood was not engaging in target practice for sporting purposes but rather was preparing for armed resistance in the event that fascism emerged in the United States. Throughout the 1930s he spoke of the need to "keep in trim" and train with "defense weapons." Like many leftists, he cited the fate of the German Social Democrats as an example of the perils of failing to resist fascist incursions with countervailing force. Yet, for all their dire warnings that "it could happen here," few others accompanied their militant rhetoric with actual practice in acquiring sharpshooter's skills.[19]

Hapgood's attraction to firearms was not simply a political judgment. In part, his war games represented an attempt to overcome his continuing disappointment in the working class. Workers had been unwilling to demonstrate the militancy and solidarity that he had come to expect. Preparing for battle perhaps offered Hapgood a sense of efficacy that had eluded him in his political work. Detached from the working class, denied the opportunity for collective action, and yearning for fraternal bonding, he substituted the fantasy of armed resistance as his personal moral equivalent of war. Hapgood's contrived image as a heroic warrior assuaged the profound discouragement he felt. It also signaled a profound self-absorption that contradicted his fervent desire to be at one with the masses.

While Hapgood was recuperating from his gunshot wound, the tensions at Columbia Conserve erupted into what his father later described as civil war. As the company's economic position continued to deteriorate, William Hapgood proposed an expanded publicity campaign to promote Columbia's products under its own label. A group of salesmen led by John Brophy and Daniel Donovan criticized this plan, denouncing such expenditures as wasteful and unwarranted in light of the company's growing indebtedness. The clash between the Brophy-Donovan forces and William Hapgood became vitriolic, with Brophy charging that for the company president, "the love of publicity has become a form of intoxication."[20]

The dispute over publicity was accompanied by accusations that a special committee appointed to oversee Columbia's finances usurped the powers of the Council, resulting in "the setting aside of the fundamental principle of democracy." In a rebuke that must have especially stung William Hapgood, John Brophy asserted at a November 27, 1932, Council meeting that "democracy should not abdicate to a person who puts on the cloak of expert." William Hapgood responded vigorously to these charges, reflecting both the strain of the company's precarious financial status and his pent-up frustration over the failure of workers "to develop the psychology of ownership." Hapgood was quoted in the minutes of the November 27 meeting as complaining that "for sixteen years . . . he has had to cram information into an unreceptive group of workers." William Hapgood had hoped to shift power from technicians to workers and had seen this transfer as the defining element of industrial democracy. Now, he argued that "citizens of a democracy should abide by the judgment of experts if they have no definite opinion of their own." The tensions underlying Hapgood's experiment, especially those involving fundamental questions of power and authority, had become contested issues that threatened Columbia's familial sense of harmony. The debate between Hapgood and his critics culminated on January 30, 1933, when Columbia's board of directors voted to fire John Brophy, Daniel Donovan, and another antagonist, bypassing the Council, which had previously made all final decisions regarding discipline.[21]

Powers Hapgood watched this dispute between his father and his friends with growing alarm. According to William Hapgood, he had "broken down twice" in recent weeks, anguished over the fratricidal war raging at Columbia. Powers initially defended his father. He fired off a telegram denouncing the "Brophy-Tearney faction" as "cowardly" for attacking William Hapgood when he [Powers] was absent. Even after the firings, he remained reluctant to separate himself from his father, although he was clearly disturbed by the summary dismissal of his friends.[22]

Still not fully recovered from his injury, Powers attended the February 3, 1933, Council meeting, telling the gathering that William Hapgood "was interested in democracy in spite of the fact that people here felt he was not." Attempting to resolve the dispute "without bloodshed," he proposed a deal that would reinstate his friends and establish a committee to investigate "how a business could combine democracy and efficiency." Yet Hapgood undercut his effort to assume a mediator's role. He declared his allegiance with "those who desire more democracy" and charged the board of directors with subverting "real democratic control" at Columbia. His father recoiled from these statements. William had boycotted Council meetings to protest what he regarded as a poisoned atmosphere and had asked Powers to present a proposal for an outside group to mediate the conflict. William Hapgood later accused his son of sabotaging that proposal by preceding it with his own judgments and "placing all the blame on one side." Apparently, the qualified support of his son was insufficient for William, who demanded absolute loyalty in the face of attacks on his character coming from Powers's closest friends.[23]

Because Columbia Conserve had a reputation as a pioneering experiment in industrial democracy, these bitter rifts within the company had repercussions beyond the factory floor. Hoping to mobilize support from allies in both the liberal and religious communities, William Hapgood's proposal for mediation designated a "Committee of Four" to investigate the Columbia crisis. The committee included such prominent liberals as Sherwood Eddy and Paul Douglas, a well-known economist with strong left-wing convictions. At the committee's recommendation, Brophy and the other fired employees were reinstated, the famed labor relations specialist William Leiserson was appointed to arbitrate subsequent disputes, and a cease-fire was declared in the personal attacks that had dominated Council meetings. But as William Hapgood later complained, these arrangements violated his attempt "to make ourselves a family" and imported legalistic mechanisms that were antithetical to the cooperative spirit. In May 1933 he forced the issue, threatening to resign unless his antagonists were dismissed. The Council, by a 58–1 vote, complied with his request, abrogating the agreement with the Committee of Four. This lopsided vote clearly indicated that the vast majority of Columbia workers, however sympathetic to Hapgood's critics, desired a return to the customary rhythms of a familial atmosphere.[24]

In a subsequent report, the Committee of Four condemned William Hapgood's actions as autocratic. The committee concluded its report with an assessment that undoubtedly coincided with Powers Hapgood's conclusions about Columbia Conserve: "the injustices of capitalistic industry will not be corrected nor a new social order built by a few employers handing down certain privileges to the workers in individual concerns, but rather that justice and a cooperative order must be won by organization of the workers on an industry-wide and national scale."[25]

The findings of the Committee of Four prompted an outpouring of regret and dismay among liberals and religious leaders who had been attracted to the Columbia experiment. Reacting to its report, the *Christian Century,* a leading journal of liberal Protestantism, declared in a December 12, 1933, editorial that "few more melancholy documents have appeared in recent years" The *New Republic* rejected an article on the controversy that its editor, Malcolm Cowley, had requested from Hutchins Hapgood, declaring that the piece "has a distinctly anti-labor union slant." These statements reflected a growing conviction among liberals that individual corporate experiments like Columbia Conserve were insufficient to repair the damage caused by a rapidly crumbling capitalist economy. Witnessing William Hapgood's willingness to discard democratic procedure when it suited his purposes, the Committee of Four and other liberals distanced themselves from a cooperative arrangement that was out of touch with the militant mood of class conflict surfacing on shop floors and city streets throughout the country. Given the backdrop of worldwide depression, the rise of fascism, and the ever increasing consolidation of capital, a small-scale experiment in industrial democracy appeared inadequate to liberals and intellectuals now drawn to the explanatory power of a Marxist analysis. Corporate power would now have to be broken by the countervailing power of mobilized workers harnessed by large institutions, not by a small cooperative experiment that sought to blur class differences.[26]

Columbia Conserve, which Powers Hapgood had extolled for so long, now appeared to resemble a traditional employer rather than an experiment in industrial democracy. On March 17, 1933, he resigned his position, explaining that he could no longer split his loyalties among the labor movement, the Socialist Party, and his father's company. "I feel that I can no longer be either happy or useful here," he wrote in a letter to the Council. "There was a time that I could give up many of my activities in the labor movement because of my interest in the Columbia plan, but unfortunately, that is no longer the case." His decision was praised by an editorial in *The World Tomorrow,* a liberal Protestant journal, which declared that he had displayed a "deeper wisdom" by leaving Columbia and going to work for the Socialist Party.[27]

The class-conscious pronouncements of radicalized liberals and their endorsement of his resignation were of scant comfort to Powers Hapgood. The debacle at Columbia Conserve called into question his most deeply held political assumptions and personal loyalties. The experience diminished his faith in the ability of small institutions to challenge corporate power and reinforced his earlier conviction that only a disciplined machine possessed the capability to rally workers effectively in defense of their vital interests. Beyond the political ramifications of the dispute at Columbia, Powers Hapgood was faced with an extraordinarily painful personal choice—whether to demonstrate loyalty to his father or to his mentor. John Brophy's criticism of William Hapgood's domineering personality and paternalistic tendencies mirrored the ongoing private conflict between Powers and his father over precisely the same issues. Brophy, a judicious man who had admired William Hapgood, now judged him harshly: "William P. could never stand criticism or equality; he must have adulation and subserviency. . . . The workers were never permitted to forget the 'generosity' of the Hapgoods and the eternal debts they owed them. The expression of any difference of opinion was considered ingratitude." Although Brophy's jabs at William Hapgood's generosity perhaps hit too close to home for Powers to consider, he could no longer avoid a wrenching acknowledgment of his father's shortcomings.[28]

It was deeply embarrassing for Hapgood to see his father's integrity impugned by his friends, his mentor, and leading liberals. Despite their disagreements, Powers had continued to honor William as a moral compass and political confidant. His father's example had consoled him throughout his string of political defeats, assuring him that their shared quest to make fraternity and democracy "a manner of living" was not in vain. Now the man he most admired had revealed a profound gap between his professed beliefs and his public morality, committing a cardinal sin according to the family code. Relations with his parents, already strained as a result of his marriage to Mary Donovan, became more distant and formal, eroding the sense of familial intimacy and virtue that had so long sustained him. The task of "living the [family's] principles" fell to Powers, a task made more lonely and more desperate by the shock of his father's "betrayal." As a result of the debacle at Columbia, Powers rededicated himself to the quest for fraternity and democracy, pursuing these goals even more fervently.

Powers Hapgood had come to the Columbia Conserve Company seeking refuge from what appeared to be the hopeless task of mobilizing a demoralized working class. With the dream of promoting Columbia Conserve as an alternative to corporate capitalism shattered, he was again thrust into the traditional arena of industrial relations. Amid a rising tide of class conflict, he began a new quest, seeking to reestablish his connections with resurgent workers who were making claims on both their employers and the New Deal state.

Chapter Eight

"Lone Wolf Crying in the Wilderness"

The people in charge because of their power and fighting ability are more likely to make a success than the average "class-conscious thinker," who unfortunately usually is a lone wolf crying futilly in the wilderness.

— Powers Hapgood to John Battuello, December 31, 1935

Between 1933 and 1935, Powers Hapgood struggled to understand and respond to the events that were transforming domestic and international politics. Like many on the political left, he watched in horror as fascism rose in Europe and once powerful socialist movements fell before the onslaught of Nazism. Closer to home, American capitalism seemed close to collapse, workers manifested genuine signs of militancy, and Franklin Roosevelt was just beginning to articulate the "new deal" that he envisioned for the American people. One did not have to be a die-hard Marxist or a hopeless romantic to believe that capitalism was imperiled and a socialist alternative might well be at hand.

After he left Columbia Conserve, Powers Hapgood attempted to take advantage of new opportunities for union organizing and independent political action. He became active within the Socialist Party, playing a leadership role at the national level and participating in policy debates that had important implications for the party's future. Simultaneously, he sought direct involvement with newly aroused workers. In such venues as western Pennsylvania, Kentucky, Massachusetts, and Arkansas, he searched for workers willing to act with courage and solidarity. But despite his best efforts, Hapgood remained a "lone wolf crying in the wilderness," isolated and marginalized even as the American labor movement was experiencing a resurgence. His demoralization eventually led him to a stunning decision, a rapprochement with his archenemy John L. Lewis, which granted him a substantive role in organizing the fledgling industrial union movement.

In early 1933 Hapgood was immersed in the politics of the Socialist Party. He had been elected to the party's National Executive Committee in 1932 and was closely aligned with the "Militant" faction that swept the SP's "Old Guard" out of power. Younger, more middle class, and newer to the party, the Militants denounced the cautious politics of their elders, favored a more agitational Socialist presence within the trade unions, and advocated exploring a united front with the Communist Party. Like Hapgood, the Militants were eager to prove their revolutionary credentials and feared that fascism would emerge in the United States unless strong working-class resistance were mobilized. Hapgood seized upon the rise of the Militants to press some of his pet issues, urging his fellow Socialists to support a new insurgency within the UMWA.[1]

In 1932, the Progressive Miners of America (PMA) had emerged in Illinois, a pocket of ongoing resistance to Lewis's hegemony. The introduction of mechanization by the Peabody Coal Company, which many Illinois miners saw as a violation of dignity, and Lewis's imposition of an unacceptable contract triggered the formation of the PMA. Several of Hapgood's most respected political friends—including veteran UMWA activists Agnes Burns Wieck, her husband Edward, and Tom Tippett—were important figures in the PMA. In its earliest incarnation, the PMA manifested clear democratic, egalitarian commitments. These included limited tenure for organizers, the ability of local unions to call for special conventions, work-sharing as an alternative to layoffs, and an aversion to domination by paid staff and attorneys. The PMA also featured a powerful women's auxiliary that was able to mobilize 10,000 female participants for a January 1933 rally at the Illinois state capitol. Hapgood urged the Socialist Party to support the PMA "if the Socialist Party is [to be] a working class organization instead of one composed of intellectuals." Intensifying his effort to make the SP more muscular, he demanded: "Do we wish to build our party out of sincere people who will be real Socialists or out of reactionary and corrupt hangers-on of the Lewis Machine?" Commenting on this letter, which was written while Hapgood was recuperating from his gunshot wound, sympathetic party leader Darlington Hoopes wryly commented: "He seems to have recovered with a bang."[2]

Ever wary of fomenting union factionalism, the Old Guard rejected Hapgood's proposal. Faced with yet another failure, Hapgood redirected his attention to the coal fields of western Pennsylvania. Section 7(a) of the National Industrial Recovery Act (NIRA), passed in June 1933, endorsed the right to organize, and inspired by this, formerly quiescent miners were beginning to stir. Affirming the profound importance he attached to mining and the UMWA, Powers Hapgood, along with John Brophy, returned to western Pennsylvania in July. There he met many old friends and found a "mass movement" of miners flocking to the union. Hapgood decided to seek employment in a mine and reestablish his membership in the UMWA, hoping John L. Lewis would be reluctant to incur bad publicity by suppressing his old rivals now that the NIRA codes were in place. At the same time, Hapgood joined others on the left in expressing grave suspicion regarding the NIRA, denouncing it as a code designed to uphold "maximum hours and minimum wages" while doing little to enforce the right to organize. He predicted that the coal operators in Somerset would resist the union, new members would be hesitant to strike, and "the best ones will be crucified again."[3]

His assessment was wrong on several counts, for both the state and the union were acting in ways that posed important challenges to Hapgood's political assumptions. His grave distrust of the state led him to underestimate the galvanizing effect that governmental encouragement for union organizing had on coal miners. As one miner in Windber, the stronghold of Berwind-White, wrote John L. Lewis, "we are going to put up a good fight as we consider it our turn to get what belongs to us as American citizens, and we give all credit to our representatives on the labor board and our President Franklin D. Roosevelt." Another Windber miner put it more succinctly: "We knew it was finally safe" to organize. Here was the rhetoric of citizenship rights that had resonated so powerfully during the Somerset strike legitimated by government sanction which had previously been absent.[4]

By the time Hapgood arrived in Somerset, Vintondale and Revloc, the impenetrable nonunion towns he had visited twelve years earlier during his reconnaissance mission for John Brophy, were now organized, as was most of the district. Between September and December 1933, organization in District 2 swelled from 10 locals to an all-time high of 298. Pennsylvania alone contributed some 128,000 new members to the UMWA's ranks, with District 2 providing many of these new recruits. Miners in Windber, where a decade earlier Berwind-White had exerted totalitarian control, began to settle old grievances and establish vibrant local unions. What Powers Hapgood had not foreseen was John L. Lewis's adeptness in seizing the opportunity presented by Section 7(a); the coal operators' uncertain response, which muted their customary resistance; and the subsequent willingness of "good union men at heart" to return to the UMWA. Lewis's success also undercut his critics' argument that he was a do-nothing leader disinterested in organizing. Unencumbered by the ideological qualms and personal doubts of a Powers Hapgood, the UMWA president, a master of power relations, was able to move expeditiously where his old rival feared to tread.[5]

Local agents reported to Lewis on his former rivals' attempt to resurrect themselves. In spite of the union's revival and the weakness of his "bitter enemies," Lewis was unwilling to allow John Brophy and Powers Hapgood to "come home again." Having tamed the unruly District 2 and rebuilt its ranks, Lewis had no place for dissenters who might question his strategy or threaten his authority. Denied the opportunity to rejoin the miners, Hapgood went to work as an organizer for the Amalgamated Clothing Workers in August 1933. Although he did not explain the rationale for this choice, he needed employment and was able to capitalize on the Socialist Party connection of Frank Rosenblum, the Amalgamated vice president who hired him. The post with the Amalgamated was Hapgood's first political job outside the UMWA or the Socialist Party, and it placed him in a union where he lacked an institutional base and direct knowledge of the workers he was attempting to organize. He was dispatched by Rosenblum to work in Mayfield, Kentucky, a small town in the southwestern part of the state. There the Clothing Workers hoped to take advantage of the militancy sweeping the country and organize a large shirt factory owned by the Curlee Clothing Company. The task would not be easy. Curlee's owners led a national organization of open-shop manufacturers and showed little willingness to abide by the new legal requirements that granted workers the right to organize.[6]

In Mayfield, Hapgood faced a group of workers whose political sentiments and cultural proclivities were alien to his experience. Miners were, he felt, "good union men at heart" who would stir when conditions were ripe, but in southern Appalachia he found native-born Protestants whom he characterized as "docile," "backward," and "scared." A previous organizer had been threatened with a knife, and Hapgood received a death threat soon after he arrived. Here, he concluded, were workers who lacked any knowledge of the labor movement or the "duties they have" regarding class solidarity. Lamenting the low level of union consciousness, he complained to Frank Rosenblum that "this is the first town in my life that I have ever been in, where in a week's time I could not find anybody with both the intelligence and the courage to help in an enterprise of this kind." Typically, he analyzed the problem in individual terms, chiding the workers for lacking the awareness that he expected to find within the working class.[7]

Some of Hapgood's observations of Mayfield were more sociological, even if he was reluctant to consider their implications. He noted strong religious sentiment in town, with the local church "crowded to overflowing," which made Sunday visits to workers' homes nearly impossible. Although he "hate[d] to compromise," he decided to request that an organizer of "American stock" be sent in to assist him. Unlike other organizers who appealed specifically to the ethnic and cultural identity of workers, Powers Hapgood resisted making such "compromises." Committed to cosmopolitan values and determined to find evidence of working-class virtue, Hapgood became disenchanted with the parochialism and fear of Mayfield clothing workers. He grumbled about the dullness of his work and confessed that he "almost wish[ed] someone would start some rough stuff."[8]

It was not long before Hapgood chose a different approach. To persuade sympathetic workers who doubted the ability of either the government or the union to defend their right to organize, he tapped the imagery of patriotism and invoked the support of the state. In September 1933, he distributed a leaflet in which he "wrap[ped] himself in the Blue Eagle," the ubiquitous symbol of the NIRA. Appropriating the language of Americanism, he urged "patriotic" clothing workers not to be "slackers" but rather to act as "good Americans" and join the union, thereby helping to improve wages, increase consumer spending, and revitalize the American standard of living. Later, in "An Appeal to Intelligent Americans," he noted that some Mayfield merchants "have had the courage of our American pioneers" and refused requests to sign anti-union advertisements. Hapgood then cited presidential endorsement of union membership, solemnly proclaiming that "it is President Roosevelt's and your government's wish that you do so." This declaration earned him a rebuke from no less a figure than Amalgamated president Sidney Hillman. Responding to an National Recovery Administration (NRA) board member's complaint, Hillman admonished Hapgood "not to quote the President unless you have authority for it." But although Hillman and other labor leaders felt compelled to issue official denials of Roosevelt's support, they did little to discourage organizers' proclamations of presidential backing.[9]

At one level Hapgood was replicating the approach of other unionists who recognized the powerful appeal of the NIRA's guarantee of the right to organize. More significantly, he had begun to engage the possibilities offered by the New Deal, reconsidering how radicals should respond to the developing apparatus of liberal reform. As he had done in Somerset, Hapgood employed images of patriotism and citizenship that symbolized universal moral ideals and were recognizable to workers. He also acknowledged the importance of governmental sanction on other grounds, admitting that "it is only the NRA that has enabled me to stay this long in town without being ganged up on in some way." Hapgood now began to contemplate a more extensive use of NRA procedures, seeking to win reinstatement for fired workers as a means of convincing others that their right to organize would be respected.[10]

Hapgood encouraged Mayfield workers to file complaints with NRA boards and urged his fellow Socialists to seek punishment of code violators as a means of advancing union organizing. Therefore, he was disappointed when the Amalgamated terminated the campaign, citing its return to the AFL and the ceding of jurisdiction over shirt workers to another union. The cultural obstacles to unionization in this region of Kentucky may ultimately have proven too much for Hapgood to overcome. His willingness to appropriate patriotic imagery and cite the support of the state, however, signaled the tentative beginnings of an important shift in his political approach. But Hapgood's engagement with the New Deal was put on hold while he turned his attention to internal politics within the Socialist Party, which reached a boiling point at the SP's 1934 convention.[11]

Among workers, Hapgood had begun to display ideological flexibility, but within SP circles his rhetoric grew more strident, as if to assure both himself and his fellow Socialists that his revolutionary credentials remained intact. Hapgood allied himself with the Revolutionary Policy Committee (RPC), a small but vocal group within the Socialist Party that was agitating for a more militant party platform. Fearful of being outflanked by the Communist Party, the RPC in April 1934 issued "An Appeal to the Socialist Party," a fiery manifesto declaring that there was "no longer a middle road" in American politics. If the Socialists were to be relevant, the RPC argued, they would have to consider disavowing electoral politics and embrace direct action in order to ensure success in the antifascist struggle.[12]

Although Hapgood did not sign the RPC appeal, he accepted its analysis without reservation. When the SP approved a diluted version of the RPC's proposals in a "Declaration of Principles" at its July 1934 convention, he argued in favor of a more militant stand. Rebutting critics who charged that the declaration flirted with illegality and violence, he asserted to loud applause that "the working class in this country is waiting at the present time for a political party which will not quibble about these phrases." He went on to proclaim in a fanciful burst: "The workers that I come in contact with say that their objection to the SP is not that it is too radical, but that it is not radical enough." If the Socialists were to declare unequivocally their opposition to "capitalist war," Hapgood insisted that workers would flock to their ranks.[13]

Such rhetoric would be understandable coming from party members who had had minimal contact with the working class and based their arguments on a millennial sense that Armageddon was near. These young Socialists looked upon the rising tide of militancy in the first half of 1934—successful strikes among auto workers in Toledo, truckers in Minneapolis, longshoremen in San Francisco—as clear evidence that workers were beginning to play their prescribed historic role as the agent of capitalism's demise. In contrast to most members of the RPC, Powers Hapgood had spent over a decade among working people and could not claim ignorance of their attitudes. Certainly his experiences with workers, whether in Pennsylvania, Kentucky, or at Columbia Conserve, offered little evidence that they would embrace socialism if only the Socialist Party unabashedly expressed its revolutionary commitment.

Hapgood's stance at the SP convention reflected a long-festering frustration over his political marginality and separation from the working class. He wanted to believe that apocalyptic circumstances could override the working-class hesitancy he had so often encountered. At a time of social crisis, he also feared that the Socialists were missing a historic opportunity to lead workers who were finally acting on their class consciousness. Ironically, their revolutionary rhetoric took Hapgood and his fellow radicals further away from the recognizable American symbols of patriotism and citizenship that perhaps represented their strongest suit in the fight against fascism. Instead, he and his comrades concocted a revolutionary scenario that would instantaneously link them with the newly galvanized masses. The martial, cataclysmic spirit that permeated the SP convention, however, stemmed more from the personal and ideological needs of young radicals than from an accurate reading of working-class sentiments. Along with Powers Hapgood, they preferred to invent a heroic working class rather than engage workers' often complex attitudes toward mobilization and direct action.[14]

Hapgood was soon forced to reconsider his assumptions regarding working-class militancy. As a Socialist organizer in Massachusetts, he participated in the largest industrial conflict in American history—a September 1934 nationwide strike of textile workers that at its peak involved nearly 400,000 millhands. Angered by deteriorating working conditions and the ineffectuality of a New Deal oversight board headed by Hapgood's old Bureau of Industrial Research colleague Robert Bruere, the United Textile Workers (UTW) authorized a general strike. Both Hapgood and Mary Donovan assisted the UTW in the Worcester area, leading flying squadrons that roamed from mill to mill urging workers to join the picket lines. These efforts were supported by many textile workers and their community allies, especially in the South, where economically ravaged local merchants had begun to endorse the workers' quest for higher wages. Nonetheless, following frequent violence perpetrated by employers and police, a wave of injunctions, and lukewarm support from the Roosevelt administration, the UTW leadership felt compelled to end the strike after three weeks. Although many elements on the left denounced the union's move as a sellout, Powers Hapgood, who spent ten days in jail for violating an injunction during the strike, defended the UTW's move.[15]

Hapgood noted that the strikers had faced injunctions, clubs, and guns, enjoyed minimal support from the state, and received little assistance from either the labor movement or the left. Faced with such obstacles, he asserted that continuation of the strike would have been disastrous. His assessment concluded prophetically, observing that UTW leader Francis Gorman had attempted to use the concept of industrial unionism as a weapon. Ultimately, Hapgood predicted, this tactic would succeed in rallying workers effectively. Hapgood's sober, clearheaded postmortem underscored the bravado accompanying his pronouncements at the SP convention just two months earlier. For all his revolutionary rhetoric, he could not dispel the painful memories of working-class suffering that he had seen at Somerset. When confronted by superior force, Hapgood proved unwilling to sacrifice workers simply to accommodate his own apocalyptic yearnings.[16]

The strike did encourage Hapgood in his quest to recruit workers into the Socialist Party. Believing that he and Mary Donovan had established their credibility by aiding the UTW, he decided it would now be possible to promote the SP's agenda more openly. Initially, Hapgood's expectation seemed justified. Following the 1934 election, he proudly reported that in the towns of Warren and West Warren, areas where Socialist candidates had previously received no support, the party garnered eighty votes. Yet Hapgood failed to acknowledge the contradiction between his hailing the party's limited electoral achievement (it was unable to elect any of its candidates) and his rhetoric scorning the ballot box just four months earlier. This paradoxical attitude demonstrated Hapgood's intensifying need to see his faith in socialism and the working class tangibly rewarded. After absorbing repeated defeats, he demanded clear evidence that workers were prepared to manifest the qualities that had inspired him to join their ranks. Eighty Socialist votes, however, were a slender reed upon which to brace a faith that showed increasing signs of deterioration.[17]

An incident in April 1935 illuminated the anguish of Hapgood's status as a wanderer in the political wilderness. After he spent weeks of painstaking work arranging an SP meeting in West Warren and importing a Polish-speaking organizer to address the strongest ethnic contingent in the area, only four people attended the gathering. When faced with such displays of apathy, Hapgood would usually accuse workers of lacking courage or character. In this instance he attributed the small turnout to cultural factors, most notably opposition from the local Catholic church and competition from the "moving picture show." In his April 26, 1935, organizational report, he confessed his profound disappointment: "for the first time in my life I begin to realize why so many radicals get tired—not that there is any danger of my doing it—but I'm frank to say that West Warren was a much crueler blow than anything I've ever had from reactionary courts, gunmen, labor fakirs, and all the other things I've run up against."[18]

To Hapgood's chagrin, Worcester's workers, bound by a complex web of parochial identifications and loyalties, did not respond to the universal cadences of democratic socialism. The working class in the Worcester area was ethnically and occupationally diverse, factors that inhibited it from sustaining an enduring sense of solidarity. Facing staunch employer resistance, Worcester had never developed a strong labor or left-wing movement. For workers in West Warren, the moving picture show was a far more accessible, even communal form of leisure than the meeting of a small, left-wing political party. Working-class political loyalties in the Worcester area were also shaped by the church and the appeal of the popular radio priest Charles Coughlin, an ardent anti-Communist whom many Catholics perceived as a champion of labor rights.[19]

In this atmosphere Mary Donovan's checkered past with the church and Powers Hapgood's identification with the SP loomed as insurmountable obstacles to establishing their credibility. Confounded by working-class religiosity, ethnic particularism, and the lure of popular culture, Hapgood felt powerless to communicate with yet another set of workers. Contrary to his disclaimer, he was beginning to feel like a tired radical, who despite his best efforts remained estranged from his cherished constituency. Hapgood's fear of descending into political irrelevance led him on an even more feverish search to align himself with a militant segment of the working class.

In February 1935, Hapgood embarked on a lecture tour of southern states sponsored by the League for Industrial Democracy. During his month-long journey, he explored the possibility of assisting the fledgling Southern Tenant Farmers Union (STFU), an interracial organization of sharecroppers backed by the Socialist Party. Involvement with the STFU satisfied all Hapgood's criteria for political action—an uphill fight against terrible odds, an aroused membership prepared to fight, the democratic virtue of a small, participatory organization, the opportunity to face danger personally—and permitted him to avoid the troubling questions raised by his experiences in Mayfield and West Warren. As he explained to STFU leader Howard Kester, "I would rather anyday encounter opposition from owners than apathy from workers. . . . I am anxious to get to Arkansas, where you don't have to argue with the workers." Continuing his eternal search for ideal labor, Hapgood looked to the stark conflict in Arkansas between sharecroppers and planters in order to restore his faith in the working class and recover his coveted place on the political barricades. By June 1935, he left Massachusetts and began working with the STFU.[20]

Hapgood's experience with the sharecroppers was short-lived. To meet the threat of violence, he proposed that the STFU purchase a bullet-proof vehicle and prepare itself for armed self-defense, citing his experience in Somerset as justification for such steps. Blunt-spoken union leader H. L. Mitchell rejected this suggestion: "If we get in that thing and go to Arkansas, the planters will dynamite it and blow us all to hell and back." Disappointed in Mitchell's response, Hapgood left the STFU. After all his recent frustrations, he could not be content with anything less than a definitive showdown with clearly drawn battle lines. To his colleagues, however, he was a liability, too self-possessed to be of use in a volatile political situation.[21]

Hapgood drifted back to Indiana in July 1935, so desperate for a job that he briefly worked as an hourly employee at Columbia Conserve. He once again flung himself into the role of freelance agitator during an August 1935 general strike in Terre Haute. After workers at Columbia Enamel and Stamping were locked out during their fight for union recognition, the company imported private armed guards to keep them at bay. This action prompted a spontaneous outburst of violence from strikers who were supported by the rest of Terre Haute's labor movement. The strikers' sense of outrage was fueled by a recent Supreme Court decision that declared the NIRA unconstitutional. The workers concluded that the chamber of commerce and local authorities had been emboldened by this ruling, which threatened to weaken the right to organize. Here was the stirring event that Powers Hapgood had been seeking, although the workers' sentiment stemmed less from a revolutionary awareness than a fear that state sanction for unionization was being subverted.[22]

Defying the martial law order issued by Indiana's governor, Hapgood was arrested several times and punched in the nose by a police officer, who branded him an "un-American bastard." Reflecting both his attachment to the meaning of citizenship and his enduring Victorianism, Hapgood replied: "I'm a better American than you are and I'm not a bastard." To his delight, some women strikers signed SP membership cards, and the local central labor union, which had previously attacked him as too radical, now supported his activities. But Hapgood lacked any organic connection to these workers and knew that his acceptance would be short-lived. He was forced to acknowledge the ineffectuality of his efforts as a freelance agitator and began to wonder about his political future.[23]

Hapgood was so demoralized that he explored the possibility of working for a New Deal agency. He interviewed for jobs with the Indian Bureau and the Federal Emergency Relief Administration (FERA), and for a position as a senior industrial economist with an unnamed government department. Turned down for the latter post, Hapgood wondered if his "arrest record and undesirable experiences" were being held against him. Besides, he wrote Mary Donovan, "it would be too much to expect the FERA to give me a $250 a month job teaching Socialism to the workers." These doubts notwithstanding, he feared that he was beginning to "feel like a tired radical" whose defection to government service would appear as "an act of defeat" to colleagues in the Socialist Party and the labor movement. Still, he mused, having a good job would benefit his family, which in addition to his daughter now included an adopted son, Donovan.[24]

In spite of a flurry of New Deal legislation in summer 1935, Powers Hapgood refused to serve a government whose liberalism he continued to doubt. Moreover, to relinquish his identification as a Socialist would have been a bitter acknowledgement of personal defeat and political failure. Yet at age thirty-six and after fifteen years in public life, he had few options. He had not worked in the mines for more than five years and was isolated from the segment of the working class that for him personified the labor movement's most sterling virtues. Insurgency within the UMWA had proven futile, the experience at Columbia Conserve had soured him on small-scale attempts to build industrial democracy, and his work in the Socialist Party had yielded few dividends. As a freelance agitator, his contacts with the working class in Mayfield and Worcester had proven unavailing. In such places as Terre Haute and Arkansas, where workers had demonstrated the instincts he valued, he lacked the standing to join their ranks. Meanwhile, the New Deal was speaking with considerable credibility to the basic needs of many working-class Americans, leaving leftists on the outskirts of political life. As a lone wolf crying in the wilderness, Powers Hapgood had reached the low point of his political career. His redemption came from a most unlikely source—his archenemy now turned crusading labor leader—the redoubtable John L. Lewis.

Chapter Nine

"An Effectiveness That Few of Us Could Muster"

> I desire, as always, the complete emancipation of
> the working class from wage slavery, but I do think
> that we have to use institutions, which, because
> composed of human beings, are not perfect.
> —Powers Hapgood to Jack Battuello,
> December 31, 1935

Having rebuilt the UMWA with stunning alacrity, John L. Lewis next turned his attention to the larger task of organizing workers in America's mass production industries. Throughout 1934 and the first half of 1935, he challenged the AFL to rethink its narrow conception of craft unionism and organize workers along industrial lines. Nonetheless, AFL president William Green, who had witnessed repeated suppression of labor militancy during the 1920s, responded cautiously to the UMWA president's call for aggressive action. He was particularly uncomfortable with rubber, steel, and auto workers whose frustration with employer opposition and the law's ineffectuality led them to demand a more militant approach. Fearing that a historic opportunity was being squandered by the timidity of Green and other AFL leaders, Lewis's criticism grew more pointed as the AFL convention approached in October 1935.

Powers Hapgood had observed John L. Lewis's efforts to prod the AFL to organize mass production workers with a mixture of curiosity and skepticism. Lewis's hiring of such dissidents as John Brophy and Adolph Germer suggested at the very least some change in the UMWA president's attitude toward his old foes. Hapgood also noted that many on the left had begun to speak approvingly of Lewis's initiatives. As he mused in July 1935, "It's surprising how many radicals think I ought to see Lewis, saying it's much less of a compromise to make peace with him and stay in the labor movement than it is to get a government job and cease to be active in the class struggle." Yet he remained doubtful about the prospects for reconciliation: "I don't know whether it will do any good. I couldn't say anything to him different than I always have."[1]

Nonetheless, with the encouragement of John Brophy and the behind-the-scenes intercession of Daniel Donovan, Hapgood attended the AFL convention at Atlantic City in October 1935. There he witnessed John L. Lewis's blow to the jaw of Carpenters' Union president William Hutcheson and the birth of the CIO. According to Gardner Jackson, Hapgood was "completely swept up by this episode" and became convinced of Lewis's commitment to build an industrial union movement. Hapgood gave a similarly starry-eyed account to Lewis biographer Saul Alinsky more than a decade later, describing his decision to join the CIO as a conversion experience: it was "as though everything I had dreamed of had finally come to pass." The reality was far less an epiphany than this wide-eyed recollection suggested. In making peace with John L. Lewis, Powers Hapgood's enthusiasm over his official return to grace was accompanied by considerable personal misgivings and substantial revision of some of his most cherished political assumptions.[2]

To be sure, the symbolic haymaker that Lewis landed on Hutcheson's jaw appealed to Hapgood's romantic attraction to high political drama. But the most important consideration driving his decision to join Lewis reflected the impact of his decade-long sojourn in political exile and his realization that large institutions, both corporate and governmental, had dramatically expanded their control over political and economic decision making. Throughout his career, Powers Hapgood had clung to a nineteenth-century political vision that sought to create small-scale alternatives to dominant structures of power. The participatory spirit of local unionism, the communal attachments of small mining towns, and the workers' management and ownership his father had crafted at Columbia Conserve were all examples of arrangements that attempted to instill a cooperative spirit, preserve democratic values, and convert workers into industrial citizens. More recently, Hapgood had turned to the Socialist Party, the Progressive Miners of America, and the Southern Tenant Farmers Union as institutions whose civic cultures contrasted with the centralized, bureaucratic model so prevalent in

American public life. Each of these alternatives, however, had been defeated by larger entities—the PMA and the UMWA local union by John L. Lewis's centralized rule, Columbia Conserve by chain stores and large corporations, the Socialist Party by New Deal Democrats, the STFU by big farming interests. This string of setbacks led Powers Hapgood to reconsider his faith in small institutions and conclude that a large, disciplined organization was needed to combat the "capitalist machine." He now saw the CIO as that vehicle and John L. Lewis as its "engineer."[3]

This sentiment came across clearly in Hapgood's first assignment for Lewis. In November 1935, the UMWA chief sent him to Illinois with instructions to help broker a settlement between the PMA and the UMWA. Lewis's purpose was twofold: to eliminate an ongoing source of internal opposition and to test Hapgood's loyalty. By late 1935, conservative elements had taken control of the Progressive Miners, and the once-promising organization had degenerated into red-baiting and violent fratricidal warfare. The new leaders of the PMA, who had supplanted his political allies, denounced Hapgood as a "silk-stocked reformer and Harvard coal digger," employing precisely the kind of language that John L. Lewis had once used against him. Speaking by radio to Illinois miners in January 1935 on "The Necessity for Unity in the Coal Fields," Hapgood urged PMA members to "come back to the main stream of the organized labor movement and forget the little futile eddy outside the main stream." John L. Lewis, he added, "sports an effectiveness that few of us could muster." In contrast to the PMA's failures, Lewis had demonstrated "the ability and courage to fight effectively for his convictions," restored the UMWA to a position of respect, and was now pressing for the formation of industrial unions. To his friends on the left, Hapgood's message was clear. As he explained in a December 31, 1935, letter to Jack Battuello, a PMA leader who remained critical of Lewis, "the people in charge because of their power and fighting ability are more likely to make a success than the average 'class-conscious thinker' who unfortunately usually is a lone wolf crying futilly [sic] in the wilderness."[4]

What Hapgood did not acknowledge were the terms John L. Lewis had imposed as the price for his political rehabilitation. In order to regain his membership in the UMWA, Hapgood agreed to abide by union policies and surrendered his right to run for elective office, concessions that curtailed the freedom of expression for which he had fought so persistently. These concessions paralleled important shifts in his political priorities that brought him much closer to a brand of unionism he had once denounced as "pure and simple." In words that would have met Samuel Gompers's approval, he told PMA members that the UMWA had fulfilled the two major tests of a labor union: the ability to secure improvements in wages and working conditions and to organize its jurisdiction effectively. These functions, he averred, were "even more desirable than democracy." Indeed, Hapgood reportedly told Tom Tippett that the fight for autonomy within the UMWA had produced unnecessary friction and turmoil: "The union was rebuilt on a non-democratic basis," he observed, "and the results speak for themselves."[5]

Hapgood appeared to have endorsed John L. Lewis's oft-repeated contention that trade union democracy should yield to organizational necessity. This changed sense of priorities was poignantly illustrated when Hapgood received a letter in February 1936 from Saverio Beninato, one of the anthracite insurgents whom he had defended in Wilkes-Barre. Beninato had just completed a six-year jail sentence for "devotion to the cause of anthracite coal diggers." Now laid off from the mines and running a small restaurant in a mining town, Beninato denounced local UMWA officials as "do-nothing" and asked Hapgood to return to aid the miners. Although there is no record of Hapgood's response, the terms of his deal with John L. Lewis compelled him to reject Beninato's request. Sympathy for his old comrades' continuing fight for local and district autonomy was now subordinated to the discipline and unity that Lewis demanded as a price for Hapgood's rehabilitation.[6]

Many liberals hailed Lewis's acceptance of Hapgood, Brophy, and other former foes as evidence of the UMWA chief's newfound accessibility and generosity. Some of his old colleagues, however, felt betrayed by Hapgood's reconciliation with Lewis, noting with particular dismay his apparent personal embrace of the CIO leader. Tom Tippett recounted that when he met Hapgood at a February 1936 UMWA convention, the former dissident spoke of his old antagonist "in a voice filled with reverence and adoration." Ed Wieck feared that Hapgood and others in the Lewis camp were allowing "worship of success and boldness to sway their judgments," forgetting the UMWA president's continuing suppression of dissidents and his discouragement of rank-and-file participation. Even Mary Donovan questioned her husband's praise of Lewis in a radio speech aimed at PMA members. But Hapgood defended his remarks, hailing the CIO chief as "outstanding" and "courageous." He claimed that such language was appropriate because he was comparing Lewis only to other AFL leaders.[7]

Hapgood's view of Lewis was complex. He maintained that his political aims remained consistent, telling Jack Battuello that he continued to seek the complete emancipation of the working class from wage slavery, but felt that he had to work through existing institutions, however imperfect. Hapgood also attempted to delineate the terms of his loyalty: "My service is not to an individual but to an organization, the U. M. W. of A., and through it, I hope, to the Committee for Industrial Organization." Nonetheless, Hapgood was surely aware that this distinction between personal and institutional loyalty was unacceptable to Lewis and could provoke conflict if put to the test.[8]

How, then, did Hapgood ultimately regard Lewis? Although his critics exaggerated his "adoration" of Lewis, Hapgood was attracted to the CIO chief's new persona, which tapped deep personal and political chords. When Lewis asserted that the labor movement's "fundamental obligation is to organize people," he was speaking the language of responsibility and commitment that Hapgood associated with personal character and political vision. He was also impressed with Lewis's new willingness to "fight," which embodied the martial spirit Hapgood continually sought to inject into politics. It was this fighting spirit that led Hapgood, along with many others on the left, to suspend judgment and offer the CIO president their provisional loyalty. "If I turn out to be wrong," he told Jack Battuello, "there is no harm done. We will at least have climbed a few flights of steps in the long struggle from the depths. From there we can go on better than from the bottom even if some in whom I now have hope do not continue the climb after a certain point."[9]

Barely two months after his exchange with Battuello, Hapgood received his baptism in the CIO. The sit-down strike by Akron rubber workers in February 1936 provided John L. Lewis with his first opportunity to demonstrate the credibility of the new organization and illuminated the dimensions of Powers Hapgood's new role. The conflict in Akron was especially crucial for the fortunes of the CIO because the AFL had devoted considerable attention to organizing the rubber workers. But its cautious strategy of seeking union recognition under NRA procedures proved unsuccessful, opening the way for the CIO to assist the strikers in developing a more aggressive approach.[10]

Many of the Akron rubber workers were transplanted Southerners from Appalachia, mostly from farming backgrounds. Some, however, had been miners. As was frequently the case, these union stalwarts stood in the vanguard of CIO organizing. In contrast to the clothing workers Hapgood had encountered in Kentucky, the migrants to Akron had been socialized by years of shop-floor conflict. At Goodyear, they had been exposed to "one of the most durable American company unions," the Industrial Assembly. Dissatisfaction with this body's ineffectuality, along with changes in hours and fears of wage cuts, had inspired the workers to seek independent representation. In Akron, Hapgood did not have "to argue with the workers," as he had lamented in Worcester. Although rubber workers did not possess a union culture as highly developed as the UMWA's, by 1936, labor in Akron had attained respectability in the community. When conditions in the rubber factories worsened, the fierce anti-authoritarianism of Appalachian migrants grew more militant and erupted in a series of sit-down strikes that raised the specter of violent confrontation.[11]

Along with Hapgood, Lewis dispatched other veteran organizers to assist the rubber workers, including Leo Krzycki, Adolph Germer, and Rose Pesotta. Krzycki was a Socialist Party leader and an organizer for the Amalgamated Clothing Workers. Germer, a longtime Socialist, had been a prominent UMWA dissident before he reconciled with Lewis. Pesotta was an anarchist, a crack organizer, and a vice president of the International Ladies' Garment Workers' Union (ILGWU) whom Hapgood had met at rallies protesting the impending execution of Sacco and Vanzetti. The group dubbed itself the "Four Musketeers" in an assertion of camaraderie and derring-do. The Musketeers moved to coordinate the strikers' efforts. Hapgood vividly portrayed the atmosphere of the strike, describing "a parlor full of guards, with guns and clubs in every corner, people coming and going at all hours, telephone ringing late and early, constant conferences in smoke-filled rooms, making the rounds of packed shanties in snow and rain, and added to it all the worry as to how it would turn out."[12]

The upsurge of worker militancy in the early CIO period required a delicate balancing act: ensuring that militancy did not degenerate into violence, staving off police intervention, attempting to maintain public sympathy, and defining union objectives in limited terms. The Four Musketeers made an especially valuable contribution in the all-important fight for public opinion. Hapgood and his fellow organizers spoke frequently before civic groups in Akron, casting the strike as pitting "democracy" versus "dictatorship" and appealing for community support "in this fight for democratic privileges." These appeals recalled Hapgood's language in Somerset, but he now had new tools available to reinforce his rhetoric and employed the potent symbolism of industrial unionism and the New Deal to inspire workers and help enlist the public as a partner.[13]

Hapgood assumed several additional roles during the strike. He

The "Four Musketeers" in Akron, Ohio, 1936. John L. Lewis dispatched these veteran organizers to assist the militant but inexperienced rubber workers during their sit-down strike. Seated from left: Leo Krzycki of the Amalgamated Clothing Workers and United Mine Workers of America dissident Adolph Germer. Standing: Rose Pesotta, vice president of the International Ladies' Garment Workers' Union, and Powers Hapgood. (Courtesy Martin P. Catherwood Library, Cornell University)

advised local leaders on strategic matters, helped to maintain the strikers' morale via daily visits to picket lines, and explained the tortuous progress of negotiations at mass meetings. Along with his fellow Musketeers, he also helped the strike leaders navigate the nuances of high-stakes negotiations and instructed the workers on the absolute necessity of maintaining tight discipline. Fears that the Akron standoff might degenerate into a violent conflagration were well founded, with the local sheriff spoiling for a fight and the emergence of a Law and Order League that threatened vigilante justice. Well aware that the outcome in Akron would influence the future success of the CIO, Hapgood was forced to reconcile the encouragement of militancy with the broader responsibilities of leadership.[14]

A restrained approach to confrontation was a far cry from the militant rhetoric that Hapgood had espoused just a few months earlier. Yet he clearly understood that public opinion would not countenance uncontrolled class conflict. Hapgood's moderation was also displayed when he and his colleagues encouraged the rubber workers to accept a bare-bones settlement, one that contained company concessions on key union demands but did not include formal recognition. When old leftist colleagues, such as Brookwood Labor College's A. J. Muste, and local communists attacked the settlement, Hapgood defended the rationale for moderation. When the Goodyear strike began, the union had only 167 members out of a potential membership of 14,000. If the union had been stronger, he explained, it would have "held out for more." Hapgood extended this caution in his post-strike advice, warning workers not to overplay the sit-down tactic even though the company had engaged in "bad behavior," for fear of alienating public support.[15]

Despite the moderate settlement, Hapgood was comforted by other implications of the strike. In its first concerted campaign to build industrial unions, the CIO's tactics of disciplined militancy had proven far more effective than the AFL's strategy of passive legalism. Workers who a decade earlier had been susceptible to the appeals of the Ku Klux Klan now embraced the unifying banner of class solidarity and the quest for democracy over the divisive cultural symbolism of the hooded robe. Finally, the eclipse of Goodyear's vaunted Industrial Assembly signaled a resounding triumph over paternalism, providing the impetus for robust, democratic unionism and working-class independence. With the emerging CIO machine flexing its muscles, the industrial union movement might conceivably make more radical demands once its initial gains were consolidated.[16]

The settlement of the rubber workers' strike in March 1936 was a dramatic personal triumph for Hapgood and established him as one of John L. Lewis's trusted lieutenants and a coolheaded operative who could handle the intense demands of labor conflict. Henry Kraus, an auto worker militant, conveyed the meaning of Hapgood's new status in recalling a United Auto Workers' convention shortly after the CIO victory in Akron. Looking "nothing like the burly old AFL piecards," Hapgood received thunderous applause from the delegates during his speech. Exulting in the Akron triumph, he recounted the UMWA's historic commitment to industrial unionism and urged auto workers to accelerate their efforts with CIO help. In the space of a year, Hapgood had undergone a remarkable transformation, moving from being red-baited by leaders of the United Textile Workers to honored status at the convention of the union destined to become the most powerful in the CIO. Yet just as Hapgood's reputation was flourishing, Akron marked the surfacing of personal troubles that influenced the rest of his career. During the rubber workers' strike his descent into alcoholism became especially pronounced, and he began a relationship with fellow organizer Rose Pesotta, a liaison that plunged both his marriage and his psyche into turmoil.[17]

It is difficult to pinpoint the beginnings of Powers Hapgood's problems with alcohol. By the time he began working for the CIO, it was clear that he was unable to control his drinking and he was subject to periodic binges that incapacitated him for days at a time. John Brophy attributed his drinking to a desire "to be able to be like the rest of the miners." Hapgood cited the pressures of his CIO responsibilities and months of work without respite in an atmosphere that he described as "almost war." He resisted suggestions that he abstain from drinking or seek help, insisting that he could learn to control his excesses. Reflecting his almost obsessive belief in the virtue of being a "producer," Hapgood invariably asserted that a period of vigorous physical labor would enable him to curb his drinking and restore his health. Although this prescription enabled him to rationalize his illness, its rehabilitative effects proved minimal.[18]

Given the importance that sobriety and personal discipline played in both his familial legacy and his conception of character, Hapgood's alcoholism represented a major blow to his carefully crafted self-image. While he tended to blame overwork for his problem, there were clearly other factors. Certainly Hapgood had been demoralized by his lonely years on the political margins and the string of disappointments he had encountered. His deteriorating relationship with his parents was another source of anguish. Finally, the constant pressure of living up to his stringent personal code must have led to powerful feelings of insecurity and self-doubt, sentiments that he sought to soothe with alcohol.

Hapgood's relationship with Rose Pesotta presented another stern challenge to his insistence on rectitude in both private and public behavior. Soon after Akron and at Hapgood's initiative, his friendship with Pesotta blossomed into a love affair. In Pesotta, an anarchist, labor leader, and daughter of the working class, Hapgood saw a woman who embodied all the personal virtues he prized—courage, commitment, sacrifice—and who was more vigorous and passionate than his wife. Like Hapgood, she was faced with the constant need to prove herself in the labor movement, explaining that "the name 'young lady' has been my curse as much as the pedigree 'Harvard graduate' has been to you." Pesotta was also adapting her politics to the institutional demands of the CIO, and Hapgood found in her a trusted confidant who shared his faith in and ambivalences toward the working class. In Powers Hapgood's eyes, Rose Pesotta was the ideal woman who could act as both his comrade and lover, allowing him to combine political commitment and sexual passion in ways that his "comradely" relationship with Mary Donovan apparently did not.[19]

After a brief affair, Pesotta resisted further sexual involvement with Hapgood and was angered when he discussed their relationship with both his wife and his parents. The fact that he would involve his parents in such a delicate personal matter underscored Hapgood's continuing dependence on their guidance and approval, even though he was a man of thirty-six with a family of his own. Ironically, it was Hapgood, the Victorian moralist, who spoke approvingly of open relationships, was "disappointed" over Donovan's "jealous" reaction to his honesty, and described his mother's views as "less modern" than those of his father. Meanwhile, Pesotta, the anarchist, prayed for atonement on Yom Kippur and bemoaned being perceived as a "home wrecker."[20]

Pesotta soon realized that Hapgood had no intention of leaving his wife ("I couldn't walk out on a comrade," he told Pesotta) and accused him of selfishness for continuing to woo her. Citing a book written by his Uncle Hutch that advocated free love, she charged that "it is in the blood of the Hapgood tribe to want everything regardless of whether others suffer by that." This allegation wounded Hapgood deeply. He had continued to insist that there was nothing wrong in his actions. Since he was being honest with all involved, loving someone as "noble" as Pesotta hardly constituted disloyalty to his wife. Hapgood also declared that he had always thought of himself as generous, because he had shunned "wealth, comfort, and privilege" in order "to submerge my interests with those of the masses." Now, in addition to the loss of self-control associated with his drinking, Hapgood's generosity and selflessness were being challenged. His tortured arguments defending the morality of his position seemed both naive and self-indulgent, diminishing his stature in the eyes of both his wife and his lover.[21]

Eventually, a modus vivendi was reached that allowed Hapgood and

Rose Pesotta and Hapgood, late 1930s or early 1940s. In Pesotta, an anarchist, labor leader, and daughter of the working class, Hapgood saw a woman who embodied all the personal virtues he prized—courage, commitment, sacrifice. Hapgood's relationship with Pesotta led to turmoil within his marriage. (Courtesy Martin P. Catherwood Library, Cornell University)

Pesotta to maintain an apparently platonic friendship with Donovan's grudging acquiescence. Hapgood continued, however, to pursue Pesotta. Although maintaining her distance, Pesotta, too, was reluctant to sever their relationship. Hapgood contended that this arrangement allowed all parties to be moderately happy, but the reality was far more painful. His relationship with Pesotta was marked by constant recrimination over his drinking and the distressing knowledge that their romance had no future. Also, Hapgood's marriage became strained even as it survived his infidelity.[22]

Mary Donovan accumulated her own set of grievances. An unpublished essay entitled "Why Do Intelligent Women Marry?" suggested the depth of her discontent. On several occasions she complained that she wanted to do political work "beside wash diapers and cook food." Hapgood does not seem to have questioned his wife's assumption of domestic responsibilities and the subordination of her own political career. Socialized in the masculine culture of the UMWA, he, like most male unionists of his time, gave scant attention to the status or role of women. He was certainly aware of the importance of women's activity in support of the miners, and this experience may well have shaped his perceptions on sex roles. Consistently, Hapgood portrayed Donovan as a loyal comrade and helpmate—"participating in labor struggles, sharing jails with me, keeping house and having a baby on coal miner's wages"—but did not acknowledge her wish to become a political activist in her own right. And while he praised Rose Pesotta's courage and sympathized with her criticism of bureaucratic inertia within the ILGWU, he ignored her complaints about being marginalized within a male-dominated hierarchy. For all his egalitarian commitments, Hapgood was too preoccupied with pursuing his own career and affirming his acceptance within a masculine labor culture to consider gender issues seriously.[23]

Mary Donovan returned to Worcester in 1937 to work for the Textile Workers Organizing Committee but was subjected to merciless red-baiting by followers of Father Charles Coughlin and suffered a breakdown. Hapgood contended that Donovan was hypersensitive to such criticism and expressed the hope that she would not work again. This blasé response to Donovan's anguish illustrated the distance that had grown between Hapgood and his wife and revealed his tendency toward self-indulgence. The triangular relationship that bound Hapgood, Pesotta, and Donovan left each party wounded, and in Hapgood's case encouraged drinking as a source of solace and release.[24]

After a brief stint with the fledgling Steel Workers Organizing

Committee (SWOC), Hapgood was dispatched by John L. Lewis to Camden, New Jersey, in July 1936. There he assisted the United Electrical Workers (UE) in their bid to organize Radio Corporation of America (RCA). The local press described Hapgood as a "lieutenant" of John L. Lewis and a "national labor leader," labels that confirmed his new stature. In Camden, Hapgood found circumstances that resembled Akron. A militant minority of "300 union people with courage" were confronting approximately 6,000 scabs, most of them inspired by the contending AFL union, the International Brotherhood of Electrical Workers (IBEW). Hapgood oversaw the UE picket lines, headed the defense committee for strikers who were arrested by local police, and negotiated with Hugh Johnson, the former National Recovery Act administrator who was now a top adviser to RCA. Hapgood was arrested several times on the picket line, but his bail was reduced by a sympathetic federal judge who accused local authorities of attempting to break the strike. At a hearing the judge captured the buoyant spirit of democratic citizenship animating the workers' quest, recounting the story of a striker who was arrested while reading the Declaration of Independence. When the striker protested to the arresting officer that "he was just saying what Thomas Jefferson said," the cop replied: "Never mind that Jefferson now. We will get him later."[25]

As had been the case in Akron, the CIO helped to broker a moderate settlement following a lopsided union victory in a National Labor Relations Board election. Hapgood candidly attributed this moderation to the union's weakness. Without picket-line help from the UE's Philco local in Philadelphia and the Industrial Union of Marine and Ship-building Workers of America, who had successfully struck Camden shipyards two years earlier, the strike might well have failed. Nevertheless, the Akron formula had again resulted in a clear, if limited, victory for the workers. Under CIO tutelage, a militant minority had triumphed over fierce opposition from one of the nation's largest corporations, and, most significant, the victory gave the UE the credibility it needed to take on other electrical industry giants. Federal courts had thwarted attempts by local authorities to deny workers the right to organize. At the same time, community leaders and the local press lent the union substantial support, encouraging workers to reject RCA's company-inspired union and opt for independent representation. Hapgood also observed that during negotiations, John L. Lewis had "fought like a tiger" to prevent scabs hired during the strike from being retained. Meeting Lewis to discuss strike strategy, Hapgood basked in the CIO chief's praise of his performance, marveling that "it seems almost incredible after the fights of old."[26]

Powers Hapgood faced more sobering circumstances with the approach of the 1936 election. In an effort to reelect Franklin Roosevelt, produce a class-based realignment of American politics, and fashion a more favorable atmosphere for union organizing, the CIO launched Labor's Non-Partisan League (LNPL), which poured massive amounts of money and manpower into the Democratic Party. The CIO suspended organizing drives during the last week of the campaign, an indication of the profound importance it attached to ensuring a Democratic victory. This unprecedented labor initiative on behalf of the Democrats placed the Socialist Party in an awkward position. Many of the party's labor supporters lined up behind LNPL and FDR. Nonetheless, SP leader Norman Thomas decided to run for the presidency, fearing that the party would surrender its raison d'être by failing to oppose the New Deal electorally. This stance further isolated the Socialists from the obvious political thrust of both the labor movement and the American working class. Thomas's decision left Hapgood uncomfortably suspended between his loyalties to the Socialist Party and the CIO. He now had to face questions about his political identity that had been submerged amid the euphoria of his early CIO triumphs.[27]

In a speech before an April 1936 National Association for the Advancement of Colored People (NAACP) banquet in Cleveland, Hapgood had linked the inclusive vision of industrial unionism to the need for an independent labor party capable of representing working-class political concerns. He hoped that the CIO might veer in the direction of independent politics and avoid an entangling alliance with the New Deal. Once LNPL was formed and the CIO threw its full support behind FDR and the Democratic ticket, Hapgood attempted to maintain his personal distance from the campaign. Speaking before a Hosiery Workers' Union picnic in August 1936, he confined his remarks to the CIO and the RCA organizing drive without mentioning Roosevelt and the Democrats. When John L. Lewis spoke on FDR's behalf at a Camden rally, Hapgood appeared late and shunned the reception committee for Lewis, which he felt "would be interpreted as going along with FDR." These actions underscored the importance he attached to maintaining his political independence and his identification as a Socialist.[28]

Hapgood attempted to persuade Norman Thomas to moderate his campaign against Roosevelt, so as "not to cut ourselves off from the labor movement." Hapgood was more fortunate than his fellow Musketeer Leo Krzycki, a Socialist and Amalgamated Clothing Workers' organizer, who was forced against his will by union president Sidney Hillman to campaign publicly for FDR. Because Krzycki was the titular national chairman of the Socialist Party, his defection was an especially cruel blow and signified the stark choice that confronted many socialists within the CIO. Powers Hapgood was able to avoid such humiliation, but he was compelled to relegate his socialism to the realm of private gesture. As he clearly understood, muting his public identification as a Socialist was a decision fraught with profound implications.[29]

For Powers Hapgood, identification as a Socialist provided a public vehicle for dramatizing his moral protest against American capitalism. His experiences in labor conflict left him unconvinced that liberalism could fully humanize or tame corporate power. He continued to regard capitalism as a system that, in his father's words, "hurt human beings" and embodied values—acquisitiveness, individualism, inequality, bureaucratization—that subverted the ideals of fraternity, democracy, and cooperation. On a deeper level Hapgood was acknowledging the degeneration of yet another pillar of his faith. The debacle at Columbia Conserve had distanced him from his family and his belief in cooperative alternatives to large institutions. Now he was forced to conceal the socialist identity that had given his politics their moral distinctiveness.

Flushed with his new status in the CIO, Hapgood's personal assertions of political independence reassured him that his socialist commitment remained intact. Tacitly he knew that his actions were devoid of public meaning; it was the price he had to pay to remain part of the industrial union movement. Rather than actively engage New Deal liberalism as other radicals had done, he began looking for a moral equivalent of socialism that might embody and revive his muted radical commitments. In Hapgood's eyes industrial unionism with its rallying message of inclusiveness, popular participation, and working-class power represented the kernels of a larger program that might yet be directed toward social transformation.[30]

The potential of industrial unionism reached its apex during the 1937 sit-down strike by auto workers at General Motors in Flint, Michigan, a defining moment for the CIO. In a mythic struggle that riveted the nation's attention, workers wrested union recognition from the corporation that symbolized modern American capitalism. Sent to Flint on January 13, 1937, immediately after the police assault later immortalized as the "Battle of the Running Bulls," Hapgood was reunited with Rose Pesotta, who worked with him in maintaining morale, disciplining militancy, and building public support for the strikers during their long siege. His willingness to support aggressive tactics won him the favor of local leaders. Hapgood noted familiar elements that helped lead GM workers to victory: "A courageous minority" backed by "the sympathy of the great mass of workers" had maintained "perfect discipline" in occupying the plants. State and federal officials stayed the hand of local authorities and exerted pressure on GM to settle with the union. The CIO's recipe for success had again proven successful, this time against the most powerful corporation in America.[31]

The thrilling outcome in Flint stimulated Hapgood's romantic impulses. At a crucial point in the strike, Hapgood helped devise the tactic that shifted the balance of power in the union's favor. Along with Roy Reuther, a fellow Socialist and future UAW leader, he helped to create the diversion at Fisher plant #9 that enabled workers to seize the crucial Fisher plant #4 and exert additional pressure on General Motors. Later, he joined future UAW president Walter Reuther in crossing National Guard lines and persuaded authorities to maintain electricity for the sit-downers newly ensconced in Fisher #4. He exulted when the workers occupying Fisher #1 presented him with a "beautiful flak jacket" and marveled when he was greeted upon entering Fisher #2 by workers seated at the mahogany desks of plant officials, briefly achieving the reversal of roles that socialists had long dreamed of. When he informed strikers that injunctions were "mere slips of paper," Hapgood finally found an audience well disposed to receive such a defiant message. The strike also affirmed Hapgood's attraction to Rose Pesotta, whom he claimed to "love even more" after their "wonderful week of comradeship in Flint" as "a fighter for the workers willing to undergo anything."[32]

Beyond these personal ramifications, Hapgood hoped that Flint might be the harbinger of more radical working-class initiatives. Praising the workers' discipline and enthusiasm, he asserted that the "next step is for them to occupy the [factories] to produce for themselves." In Flint, Hapgood experienced the transcendent moment of unity with militant workers for the first time since his glory days in Somerset. At last workers were acting with apparent class consciousness, their leaders were exhibiting a confident assertiveness, and America's corporate titans were forced to capitulate. Hapgood was also inspired by the UAW's membership oath, which thousands took following the triumph in Flint. Members pledged "to subordinate every selfish impulse to the task of elevating the material, intellectual, and moral condition of every worker." This spirit appeared to be shared by the victorious workers and reflected the noble sentiments that had attracted Hapgood to the labor movement nearly two decades earlier. Amid the dizzying events in Flint, such lofty aims affirmed his faith in industrial unionism's potential.[33]

Hapgood's visionary expectations following the victory in Flint were not entirely far-fetched. The initial triumphs of the CIO raised the possibility of democratizing the American workplace and eclipsing both paternalistic and authoritarian forms of managerial control. Roy Reuther likened the scene in Flint "to some description of a country experiencing independence," vividly capturing the spirit of workers who exited the occupied factories waving American flags in affirmation of their newly claimed citizenship rights. As a result of labor's mobilization during the election of 1936, the political order in cities and towns across the nation was being overturned as working-class voters succeeded in ousting entrenched governing elites. Also, the CIO's conscious overtures to ethnic and African-American workers promoted an inclusive, egalitarian spirit that might well be extended beyond the workplace to transform the larger political landscape.[34]

Yet amid this euphoria were disquieting facts that suggested less cause for optimism. Hapgood acknowledged that many workers had sat on the sidelines during the strike, because they were afraid. Although the egalitarian rhetoric of the CIO was stirring and sincere, it masked a serious gulf between the labor movement and black workers. Recounting the strike seven years later, Rose Pesotta cited a letter from an African-American worker at the Chevrolet foundry who expressed pro-union sentiments. The worker lamented, however, that "there is a big coulerd line here," and he had seen no union organizers. Although the state had limited repressive measures against the strikers, public opinion was growing increasingly restive over the continuing prospect of property seizure and potential violence. These obstacles, not readily apparent in the elation that accompanied the triumph over GM, would present the CIO a formidable challenge as it sought to extend industrial unionism to new segments of the American working class.[35]

In the year and a half since he had joined the CIO, Powers Hapgood had moved to the center of working-class struggle and American public life. Stirred by the events in Flint, he asked his old friend John Brophy, who was now the CIO's organizing director, to assign him to Indiana so that he could return to Terre Haute and fight martial law with "the CIO behind him." Instead Brophy requested that his protege return to an earlier task, the organization of shoe workers in New England. There Hapgood met unexpected challenges as he attempted to extend industrial unionism to another segment of the American working class.[36]

Chapter Ten

"The Duty of Every Patriot"

Are the manufacturers here Americans? If they
are, they will obey the law. If they don't, then they
are lawbreakers. If you [manufacturers] want to
play your part in America, it is up to you to obey
the law. If you don't we are going to make you.
—Powers Hapgood, Lewiston, Maine,
April 19, 1937

In chronicling the struggles that shaped the early CIO, scholars have
focused on conflicts waged in integral sectors of the American economy
(auto, steel, rubber) where powerful corporations were subdued by the
new industrial unions. Understandably, the more marginal shoe industry, where Powers Hapgood spent nearly three years as the director of
the Shoe Workers Organizing Committee, has received limited attention. Yet in spring 1937, Hapgood led a strike among Maine shoe
workers that in its drama and militancy rivaled the epic confrontations
in Akron and Flint. For more than three months, thousands of shoe
workers, many of them women and most of French-Canadian descent,
battled manufacturers, courts, police, the press, and the Catholic
Church in their quest for union recognition.

As coordinator of the strike and the fledgling shoe workers' union's
official link to the national CIO, Powers Hapgood was no longer simply
a personal representative of John L. Lewis but a leader invested with
full responsibility for the fate of an organization. This role exposed him
to pressures and challenges that he had not encountered during his
years as a freelance agitator. In Maine, he also faced the familiar

tension between his universalistic, secular political vision and the insular, religious loyalties of ethnic workers. With some success, Hapgood and his comrades found political language that reconciled these conflicting frames of reference. But he also confronted the powerful opposition of entrenched local institutions and learned the limits of the CIO formula that he had employed so successfully in Akron, Camden, and Flint.

Shoemaking had been among the first industries to consolidate operations in centralized factories, mechanize production, and divide labor into discrete functions. Throughout the eighteenth and nineteenth centuries, shoe workers stood in the forefront of attempts to resist industrialism's assault on their artisan traditions. Massachusetts, where Hapgood began his association with the shoe workers, led the way, spawning the fabled Knights of St. Crispin and later lending enthusiastic support to the Knights of Labor. In spite of this long tradition of organizing, employer resistance and continual feuding among contending unions left the industry largely unorganized. By the 1930s, shoe workers were represented by several independent unions and an AFL craft union, the Boot and Shoe Workers. The total membership of these organizations, however, comprised only about 25 percent of the industry's approximately 200,000 workers.[1]

Organizing shoe workers represented a formidable challenge, especially in New England, where the initial demands for CIO assistance arose. In contrast to the centralized manufacturing operations that Hapgood had encountered in earlier CIO campaigns, the New England shoe industry was not located at the hub of mass production. Instead, shoe factories tended to be small and scattered, with more than 60 percent of the plants employing fewer than 100 workers. The industry was characterized by low profits, substandard wages, seasonal fluctuation, and intense competition. Minimal technological requirements and easy duplication of operations encouraged manufacturers to close facilities rather than accept unionization. Inspired by the CIO's successes elsewhere, several of the independent shoe workers' unions based in New England approached John L. Lewis late in 1936 seeking organizational support. Upon learning that her husband was being assigned to help these unionists, Mary Donovan, a shoemaker's daughter who knew the industry well, told Hapgood that shoe workers had been disappointed by labor "fakirs" in the past and awaited a "new messiah" to rescue them from their disillusionment.[2]

Hapgood hardly felt like a new messiah after his initial meetings with the shoe workers. He characterized them as "poor and pathetic," a far cry from the ebullient spirit he had encountered in Akron, Camden, Flint, or among the miners. His first task was to unify the contending unions who had long been separated by petty jealousy and jurisdictional conflicts. Armed with the prestige of being John L. Lewis's personal representative and his own diplomatic skills, Hapgood was invited to help draft a constitution for a proposed Shoe Workers' Organizing Committee. His success in winning the confidence of all factions was affirmed in a February 1937 letter that shoe worker leader Thomas Burns wrote John Brophy while Hapgood was occupied in Flint. Urgently requesting Hapgood's return to settle disputes that had flared among the merging unions, Burns explained that his "usefulness in New England is paramount." Hapgood proved his usefulness by launching a series of "quickie" strikes, mostly in Massachusetts. These militant demands for union recognition resulted in the organization of 5,200 shoe workers during the early months of 1937.[3]

According to the journalist Benjamin Stolberg, the shoe workers fought both reactionary employers and hostile local governments in Massachusetts and had "done wonders" in a relatively short period. Testifying to his new political legitimacy, Hapgood weathered attacks that in pre-CIO days might have proven fatal. Charges by the governor of Massachusetts that he was a Communist scarcely affected his ability to function. After threatening a libel suit, Hapgood received a retraction from a Worcester-area newspaper that had accused him of abandoning workers after the 1934 textile strike. It became apparent, though, that the key to maintaining the union's momentum lay in organizing shoe workers in Maine, where Massachusetts manufacturers had fled to escape the threat of organization. There, employers paid shoe workers 15 percent to 25 percent less than their counterparts in Massachusetts. This differential weakened the union's negotiating position in its newly organized Massachusetts shops and led the ever-recalcitrant shoe workers in Worcester to urge organizers to "Get Maine First" before they would consider joining.[4]

In contrast to Massachusetts, shoe production in Maine was far more concentrated, most notably in the neighboring cities of Lewiston and Auburn, where nineteen factories employed nearly 6,000 workers. Hapgood noted in a telegram to John Brophy: "This district is to the shoe industry what [the] Pittsburgh district is to the steel industry. Victory means sweeping organizational results in all non-union shoe centres." Hapgood went on to explain that 7,000 textile workers in the Lewiston-Auburn area had joined the shoe workers in requesting CIO assistance. If the shoe workers could be organized, he concluded, textile workers would soon follow. Although Hapgood perhaps exaggerated the campaign's significance, the future of the CIO in Maine hinged upon a successful effort among the shoe workers of Lewiston-Auburn. Also, a victory in this shoemaking stronghold would spur the union's ability to expand organization throughout the industry. The stakes were high, then, as Hapgood and his fellow organizers launched their offensive early in 1937.[5]

Most of the shoe workers in Lewiston and Auburn were of French-Canadian descent. They had migrated to Maine during the latter half of the nineteenth century, taking jobs in the textile and shoe industries after agriculture had declined north of the border. Family, church, and *la survivance*—the maintenance of French customs and traditions—dominated the worldview of most French-Canadian immigrants, who gradually relinquished their hopes of returning to Canada and accepted permanent residence in the United States. Rose Pesotta, who was attempting to organize French-Canadian garment workers in Montreal at the same time, declared that these "Catholic girls" were "handicapped by church, family, and traditions" and torn between their loyalties to the "shop and the church." Consequently, throughout the nineteenth century and well into the twentieth, inward-looking French-Canadian workers demonstrated limited interest in unions. This orientation was reinforced by their priests, many of whom saw unions as subversive of proper attitudes toward authority and social place. The beginning of the organizing drive also coincided with a budding public backlash against the CIO, which in the aftermath of the GM sit-down strike was increasingly denounced as a threat to property rights and social order.[6]

The attitudes of French-Canadian workers had begun to change by the 1930s. Earlier disputes over church control of local parishes led to questioning of clerical authority and an erosion of social deference. Although most French-Canadian workers in Lewiston and Auburn remained loyal to the church (indeed, they raised $800,000 in 1937 to construct the second largest church in New England), they were less willing to grant their priests unconditional obedience. As the second generation began to perceive itself as more Franco-American than French-Canadian, it chafed under its second-class status in the shoe factories, especially as CIO organizers explained the disparity between their working conditions and those enjoyed by unionized workers in Massachusetts. In addition, the failure of an earlier strike in 1932 had demonstrated the futility of a local effort unaided by outside support.

All of these factors made success in Lewiston and Auburn appear imminent to Powers Hapgood and his fellow organizers.[7]

Hapgood arrived in Lewiston on March 12, 1937, to assume overall coordination of the strike. William Mackesy, a veteran shoe worker from Lynn, led the effort on a day-to-day basis. Emboldened by the CIO's successes in auto, rubber, and steel, Hapgood confidently addressed a meeting of more than three thousand people at Lewiston's city hall, where he mocked the manufacturers as "little fellows." Cockily, he asserted that organizing shoe workers would be "child's play" compared to the more protracted struggles in heavy industry. Hapgood did, however, attempt to allay fears that a distant, menacing CIO bureaucracy would subvert local labor relations, assuring the gathering that control of newly organized unions would remain in local hands. Although the English-language *Lewiston Evening Journal* was generally hostile to the union cause, it was charmed by the Harvard graduate turned CIO leader, describing him as "not at all the usual agitator." In a March 27, 1937, editorial the *Journal* noted, "Mr. Hapgood . . . has an especially winsome style of speech and is seemingly sincere." Hapgood's demeanor won both him and the union credibility in an environment distrustful of outside influences that threatened to overturn local traditions.[8]

Even before Hapgood's arrival, the union had worked diligently to overcome local suspicion of outside agitators, bringing in French-speaking organizers and encouraging French-Canadian workers to assume positions of leadership. For example, Alexina LeClair, a French-speaking stitcher, became noted for her oratory and singing and was dubbed the "sweetheart of the CIO." The union mounted a special appeal to women, who complained about suffering sexual harassment at the hands of their supervisors. As LeClair noted at a union meeting, she was given good work until she "refused the attention of the boss." LeClair eloquently summarized the mood of the strikers in declaring: "We will earn a living and not simply an existence." This argument elevated the workers' cause into a noble quest to obtain respect from their employers and allow French-Canadian workers, long denigrated by the Yankee power structure in Lewiston and Auburn, to gain full acceptance as first-class citizens. By establishing an independent institution, the union, as "the agency through which they could get justice," shoe workers were challenging deeply rooted patterns of power and authority in their community, a fact that the manufacturers did not ignore. Here was a battle that embodied Powers Hapgood's deepest aspirations for industrial unionism. The inspiring rhetoric of Alexina LeClair and others allowed the workers to claim moral legitimacy in the face of powerful opposition that quickly began to form.[9]

A week after his arrival in Lewiston, Hapgood concluded that the union had gained sufficient support to petition the shoe manufacturers' association for recognition. The manufacturers offered no official response, prompting the union to call a strike, which commenced on March 24. Similar to events in Akron, Camden, and Flint, the strike attracted widespread support from skilled workers whose absence crippled production and induced others to walk off their jobs. By early April, approximately four to five thousand workers were out on strike, effectively shutting down shoe production in Lewiston and Auburn. Regular union meetings held at city hall in Lewiston attracted hundreds of workers, underscoring the depth of support for the union, support that was perhaps broader than Hapgood had witnessed in earlier CIO struggles.[10]

Resistance to the union now began in earnest. As Hapgood and other shoe worker leaders noted in a telegram to John L. Lewis, the union's opponents "openly boasted [that] Maine will be [the] first state to keep out [the] CIO." The *Lewiston Daily Sun* echoed and personalized this sentiment in an April 3, 1937, editorial: "The people of these two cities ought to get together and give notice that they are not going to be bullied by any Hapgood nor any Lewis nor any CIO." The stage was now set for a fierce struggle. Both sides recognized that the outcome would decide not only the union status of the shoe industry in Lewiston and Auburn but also the fate of the CIO in Maine.[11]

In an effort to undercut support for the CIO, the manufacturers granted the shoe workers a 10-percent wage increase shortly after the strike began but refused to recognize the union. Their stance was supported by virtually the entire social apparatus of Lewiston and Auburn, including the English-speaking press, local politicians, clergy, and community leaders. Picketing was severely restricted by court order. On March 30, police in Auburn arrested and fined forty strikers for engaging in what a local judge described as a "concentrated effort to break the peace of the community." While professing sympathy for the plight of the workers, the mayors of both Lewiston and Auburn denounced the CIO as "outside agitators" and supported a plan for an "Industrial Board" to settle the strike. The proposed board, which Hapgood denounced as a "dummyboard," was to be chaired by Father Edouard Nadeau, a prominent local priest. As a kind of community-sponsored company union, the Industrial Board would hear the shoe workers' grievances, but in return, they would not be allowed to join an outside organization. Father Nadeau was joined by other priests in opposing the CIO, which they regarded as tainted by its association with Communists, whose materialism violated the sanctity of property, family, and faith in God.[12]

The anti-union campaign of Lewiston's and Auburn's civic leaders climaxed on April 20 when Maine Supreme Court justice Harry Manser granted the manufacturers an injunction declaring the strike illegal. In a ruling that distorted the meaning of the Wagner Act, which had been upheld by the U.S. Supreme Court just a week earlier, Manser held that the union was required to represent a majority of workers before it could legally seek recognition from the employers. Although the act required demonstration of majority status to obtain exclusive representation, it explicitly allowed unions to strike in order to gain majority support and recognition from employers. A National Lawyers' Guild report subsequently noted that Manser's ruling amounted to a "judicial nullification" of the Wagner Act. Faced with this phalanx of community opposition, Hapgood and other union leaders sought new ways to dramatize the legitimacy of the workers' cause.[13]

The manufacturers and their allies charged that the CIO was an outside, alien force bent on subverting social order. They linked this argument to a virulent attack on the patriotism of the strikers. According to one local judge, "in my opinion any man who strikes against his employer cannot be a good American citizen." To blunt these charges, Hapgood invoked the language of patriotism, citizenship, and character that he had used fifteen years earlier in Somerset and more recently in Kentucky. In his first address in Lewiston, he asserted that it was "the duty of every patriot" to ensure that wage standards never again sank to depression levels. "The best patriots," he declared, "are those who go out to reform conditions to bring workers those wages they need to keep up prosperity." This argument not only reflected New Deal Keynesianism but also cast the workers' economic aspirations in broader terms, suggesting that a living wage was needed to ensure both citizenship rights and the practice of democracy.[14]

Other union activists invoked citizenship as a unifying identity that justified the strikers' cause. Union attorney Benjamin Arena insisted that the workers were not criminals or trespassers as their critics claimed but citizens. William Dobbs, an organizer from Boston, proclaimed that "we are all Americans, not 'outsiders,' whether we speak French, Polish, or Lithuanian." Hapgood drove the point home with a forceful attack on the employers' Americanism: "Are the manufacturers Americans? If they are, they will obey the law. If they don't, then they are law breakers. . . . If you want to play your part in America, it is up to you to obey the law. If you don't, we are going to make you."[15]

The language of Americanism was familiar terrain on which Powers Hapgood could speak with enormous personal conviction and where he had previously enjoyed his greatest political effectiveness. While the workers were attempting to "play their part in America" by exercising their rights as citizens, the manufacturers were engaging in behavior that violated democratic and constitutional ideals. Under the welcoming umbrella of patriotism and citizenship, Hapgood and his fellow organizers sought to transcend traditions of insularity and deference that had inhibited French-Canadian workers from declaring their allegiance to unions. The influence of their rhetoric is difficult to assess. Workers' loyalties undoubtedly were divided between familiar institutional arrangements and the new aspirations embodied by the CIO. Newspaper reports suggested that the patriotic language of CIO leaders was well received by workers attending mass meetings. The fact that striking war veterans intended to wear their uniforms and carry the American flag during a march in Auburn further attested to the appeal of patriotic imagery. The CIO's legitimacy was also supported, as elsewhere, by the workers' perception that the president and the federal government backed union organization. As an "angry citizen" complained to the *Evening Journal:* "A great many of our workers seem to be under the impression that it [the CIO] is a labor union authorized by government. All the CIO speakers say in their speeches that President Roosevelt is back of it."[16]

The protracted, bitter conflict in Lewiston and Auburn pitted this inclusionary vision of participatory citizenship backed by the federal government against hierarchical traditions of authority sanctioned by employers, the church, and local community leaders. In Akron, Flint, and other locales opposition to the union had not been nearly so monolithic, and workers had found allies from other groups within the community. But in Lewiston and Auburn, beyond favorable coverage from Lewiston's French-language newspaper, *Le Messager,* the "workers' spirit," in Hapgood's words, was their only asset. This spirit was embodied by female strikers, who wanted recognition of their status as skilled workers, a better standard of living for their families, and freedom from sexual harassment. Their militancy, which included physical altercations with scabs and rock-throwing at the police, underscored both the depth of their grievances and a willingness to challenge the boundaries of their traditional social role. Other women, however, who described themselves as "God fearing," denounced the

CIO as "unlawful and depraved" for its alleged slurs against the Church and its charges of sexual harassment. These sharp divisions, which undercut efforts to build a solid community-labor alliance, had not been nearly so evident in Hapgood's previous CIO experiences among predominately male work forces. With community opposition escalating, he and other strike leaders looked to the national CIO to send additional financial support and exert pressure on wavering shoe manufacturers to settle.[17]

John L. Lewis and John Brophy were too preoccupied with the crucial organizational drive in steel to lend the shoe workers much assistance. By late April, a series of events enabled the union's opponents to subvert the strike. Following Judge Manser's injunction, strike leaders decided that a dramatic response was needed to regain the CIO's momentum. On April 21, nearly one thousand workers heeded the union's advice to defy the injunction, marched to the bridge that linked Lewiston to Auburn, and attempted to cross. A melee ensued between police and strikers, with many women involved in the fighting. The incident was reported in the English-language press as "Red Wednesday," an obvious attempt to discredit the strikers and depict such violence as the logical outcome of the CIO's agitation.[18]

Maine Governor Lewis Burrows dispatched National Guard troops to establish order. The strikers, in the words of the *New York Times,* "defied the bayonets." Underscoring their appropriation of patriotic symbols, they sang the "Star Spangled Banner" and hoisted Hapgood on their shoulders as he urged them to maintain their picket lines. Addressing a mass meeting on April 22, an aroused Hapgood returned to the themes of patriotism, constitutionalism, and citizenship: "They are the lawbreakers, not we," he declared to enthusiastic applause. He likened the strike to the fight for liberty embodied in the Revolutionary and Civil Wars and demanded that Maine obey the laws of the nation. Omitting mention of his experiences in the coal fields, he noted that he had encountered many police forces but "had never seen until yesterday in Auburn a place where those officers would not permit citizens to exercise the rights granted them under the Constitution of the United States." Hapgood's bravura performance also included a rare religious reference: he likened the workers to "that great figure of love" [Jesus] and their opponents to Pontius Pilate. Newspaper accounts suggest that his rhetoric, which cast the workers as true patriots, citizens, and Christians and branded their opponents as betrayers of these proud identities, was extremely well received. At last Hapgood appeared to have established the vital connection with ethnic workers that had eluded him in previous encounters.[19]

But Hapgood soon would not be in a position to lift the workers' spirits, for Judge Manser responded decisively to the events of April 21. At a May 6, 1937, hearing he found Hapgood and seven other strike leaders in contempt of his injunction and sentenced them to six-month prison terms. Hapgood accepted his fate with equanimity. In a telling admission, he confided that incarceration was a welcome relief from the responsibilities of leadership. The pressures of maintaining the strikers' morale, managing a fractious union staff, and confronting such obdurate opposition weighed heavily on Hapgood, who had been briefly hospitalized for exhaustion earlier in the strike. Reflecting a sober awareness of his new role, Hapgood did not romanticize his imprisonment and feared that the strike was unraveling in his absence.[20]

Throughout May and June, Hapgood and his fellow organizers languished in jail. As the picket lines began to weaken, the union sought federal intervention to override local resistance, filing numerous unfair labor practice charges with the National Labor Relations Board (NLRB). Following an investigation, the board dismissed many of the union's allegations but it did find the strike for recognition legal and ordered that elections be held to determine the workers' preferences. The manufacturers had other ideas. Even before the NLRB's ruling, they devised an alternative to their rejected Industrial Board, resurrecting the Lewiston-Auburn Shoe Workers Protective Association (LASPA), a company-inspired organization that had surfaced during the abortive 1932 strike. Represented by a prominent local attorney, LASPA had few French-Canadians among its leaders and was widely regarded as a tool of the shoe manufacturers. By late April, the new organization claimed several thousand members, including many strikebreakers. The shoe workers now faced a new obstacle in their struggle for an independent union—a competitor that was officially sanctioned by community leaders.[21]

Faced with implacable opposition from the manufacturers, dwindling funds, and ebbing support from the workers, Hapgood and the union leadership decided to end the strike on June 28, 1937, after thirteen weeks on the picket line. Several days later, Hapgood and his colleagues were released from their six-week stint in jail when the Maine Supreme Court overturned Manser's contempt citation. With the NLRB ordering elections, Hapgood believed that it was the right "psychological moment" to withdraw the picket lines. The union decisively won the balloting in virtually every plant, but LASPA's refusal to participate offered the manufacturers a pretext for avoiding negotiation. In the end, companies either closed their doors for good, reopened their operations under new names, or resisted recognizing the union altogether. The manufacturers learned that they could prolong the board's appeal process to their advantage, and the NLRB proved unable to compel obedience. In spite of the herculean efforts of the workers and the commitment of union leaders, the manufacturers had made good on their boast and halted the advance of the CIO in Maine.[22]

In a postmortem on the strike, Hapgood acknowledged several key miscalculations on the union's part. Like most observers, he had not counted on the Supreme Court upholding the Wagner Act, which might have deterred the union from launching a strike so late in the shoe industry's busy season. Perhaps convinced that the victory over General Motors had blunted corporate opposition, Hapgood also failed to anticipate the determination of the manufacturers and the depth of their support. William Mackesy, the strike leader on the ground, noted the weight of community opposition, especially that of the church: "We were utterly unable to impress the clergy. This was a new experience that I will not try to explain. Suffice it to say it was a heavy liability." Although Hapgood had appropriated the imagery of citizenship and patriotism, he was too much the secular cosmopolitan to craft a religious appeal or develop a strategy to neutralize the clergy. Moreover, some of the leading strike activists displayed a fierce anticlericalism, which damaged their cause among those whose loyalties were perhaps divided between the church and the CIO.[23]

As Hapgood and William Mackesy admitted, the union simply lacked the ingredients in Lewiston and Auburn that were present in the CIO's earlier successes. Without community support and the willingness of the state to restrain local authorities, a militant minority was unable to triumph. Contrary to Hapgood's claim, even if the CIO had poured additional resources into Maine, it is unlikely that the workers could have relied on economic power alone to vanquish their adversaries. Although he had coordinated an effective strike that attracted fervent support, the CIO had been unable to overcome powerful local institutions and fully convert ethnic workers into industrial citizens.[24]

The loss in Maine was Hapgood's first experience with defeat since joining the CIO. His brief hospitalization during the strike foreshadowed physical and psychological problems that were accentuated by his drinking and by the burden of his new responsibilities. The outcome of the strike also contained important implications for both his conception of industrial unionism and his personal role in the CIO. It suggested distinct limits to the CIO formula and underscored the obstacles to developing an enduring culture of unity among working-class ethnics. Indeed, the fierce opposition that Hapgood and the shoe workers faced was but the advance column of a powerful counterattack being orchestrated by the CIO's enemies.

Chapter Eleven

"The Most Responsible Job I've Ever Had"

Sometimes I wish the IWW was still alive. It is so
easy to be idealistic when one doesn't have to be
practical.
—Powers Hapgood to Rose Pesotta, June 10, 1940

In July 1937, John L. Lewis appointed Powers Hapgood as the executive director of the Shoe Workers Organizing Committee. Hapgood
proudly informed his parents that it was the "most responsible job" he
had ever held. He soon discovered the difficulty of reconciling his
commitment to working-class mobilization with the complex demands
of union leadership. Following the Lewiston and Auburn strike, Hapgood encountered a whirlpool of contending forces—aggressive workers, a shaky industry, inadequate labor laws, internal union divisions—
that made him feel more like a harried bureaucrat than a crusader for
the working class. As the industrial union movement's initial dyna-
mism waned, Hapgood began to question the meaning of his role within
the CIO and his place within the New Deal industrial order.[1]

Somewhat ironically for a lifelong advocate of local union autonomy,
after the Maine defeat Hapgood argued that the CIO should exert more
direct influence over the affairs of the Shoe Workers Organizing Committee. In forming the new organization, the shoe workers had united
volatile forces, including Communists and conservative Catholics. Cultural and ideological divisions between these factions had surfaced

repeatedly during the Lewiston-Auburn strike, often preventing Hapgood from taking decisive action. Under these circumstances democracy often abetted obstructionism, and Hapgood saw the value in imposing a tighter rein over the bickering factions. Noting the firm control that the CIO exercised over the Steel Workers Organizing Committee, Hapgood sought similar authority to direct the affairs of the shoe workers.[2]

The state of the shoe industry presented the union with some real constraints. The recovering American economy relapsed in 1937, and the industry was running at only 30 percent of capacity. The shoe workers experienced a severe drop in membership dues that, coupled with the union's hefty expenditures during the Maine strike, left its coffers depleted. Buckling under the weight of the recession, the manufacturers pressed Hapgood to grant wage concessions. They urged him to get John L. Lewis to intercede with Franklin Roosevelt and seek protection against increasing competition from imported shoes. This type of cooperative relationship, well established in other highly competitive industries such as clothing and construction, was much less familiar to Hapgood, whose early years in the fierce class conflict of mining caused him to fear embracing employers too closely.[3]

Hapgood's discomfort was compounded by a rising tide of shop-floor discontent. Increasingly, he was forced to restrain the demands of shoe workers for higher wages and greater power on the shop floor. When women stitchers in one shop revolted against a supervisor and threatened to strike in order to obtain her dismissal, he told them that their actions violated the union contract. The workers bluntly informed Hapgood that the national office had no right to impinge on local authority. Hapgood was discomfited by this assertion. He wound up supporting the workers but feared that their actions jeopardized the union's long-range institutional security. Facing women workers in Lynn, Massachusetts, who sat down instead of employing the contract's arbitration procedures, Hapgood took a tougher stand, insisting that the militants terminate their strike. "These girls were real fighters and I admire them, but I had to fight them," he lamented. Lynn, which once housed fifty-seven shoe factories, was now down to eleven "due primarily to stoppages rather than high labor cost."[4]

Hapgood was now confronted with the limits imposed by volatile economic conditions, contractual obligations, and the new system of industrial relations that sought to divert worker militancy into legalistic and procedural forms of resolution. Although many CIO leaders accepted these constraints and attempted to consolidate union gains,

Powers Hapgood reacted uneasily. To his chagrin, he was becoming what the sociologist C. Wright Mills termed a "manager of discontent" rather than "a new man of power" standing shoulder-to-shoulder with workers facing down their bosses. Yet in a sick industry, unchecked rank-and-file activism offered employers little incentive to deal with the union and threatened to undermine their already shaky economic position. In earlier CIO struggles, Hapgood had justified restraining worker militancy in order to gain union recognition from America's most powerful corporations. Now he was compelled to discourage rank-and-file activism simply to ensure the union's survival. The bureaucratic and managerial overtones of his new role distressed Hapgood. He feared that he was beginning to manipulate rather than mobilize workers, contradicting the democratic commitments that defined his political identity.[5]

Hapgood's headaches mounted throughout late 1938 and 1939 as he became ensnarled in the labyrinthine procedures of the NLRB. The union had targeted the Hamilton-Brown Shoe Company, the industry's second largest, and attempted to organize its workers, many of whom were located in small towns throughout the South and Midwest. In May 1937, the union persuaded spontaneous strikers in one Hamilton-Brown plant to return to work as evidence of good faith. Management's response to this olive branch was to fire one hundred union activists and establish a company union. Later, Hamilton-Brown dissolved the company union and recognized the AFL's Boot and Shoe Workers.[6]

The company refused to comply with NLRB rulings declaring its actions illegal and even closed one plant rather than recognize the CIO. Hapgood threatened to seek enforcement by pressing the NLRB to appeal to the circuit court. He summarized the union's plight in March 1938: "The Board is so slow it is tragic but because of the opposition of the manufacturers and the AF of L, they won't make a decision until they think they have a 100 percent chance before the Supreme Court." The union's restrained use of direct action and its attempt to utilize legal channels had not been rewarded by either the company or the labor board. As a result, the campaign at Hamilton-Brown fizzled. Stymied by the manufacturers' resistance, the NLRB's ineffectuality, and the union's limited resources, Hapgood grew frustrated by the obstacles circumscribing his leadership.[7]

In 1939, Hapgood attempted to reestablish the union's momentum by launching an organizing campaign at one of the shoe industry's leading companies—the Endicott-Johnson Corporation. Speaking before the Shoe Workers' second constitutional convention in October 1939, Hapgood described the organization of Endicott-Johnson as the paramount issue facing the union. The firm employed nearly 18,000 workers in twenty-seven plants, mostly located in upstate New York. Endicott-Johnson prided itself as being an enlightened employer. Its extensive program of welfare capitalism and corporate philanthropy was widely recognized, leading Hapgood and the Shoe Workers to believe that the company might be reluctant to tarnish its reputation by engaging in a bruising clash with the union.[8]

Hoping to cut a deal akin to the one John L. Lewis had reached two years earlier with Myron Taylor of U.S. Steel, Hapgood approached company president George Johnson in early 1938. If Endicott-Johnson recognized the union, he suggested, it could achieve the labor peace that Taylor had gained for his company, along with the additional benefits of eliminating cutthroat competition and assuring price stability. The Johnson family refused to consider Hapgood's offer. They were far more confident of their competitive position than Myron Taylor and recognized that the Shoe Workers lacked the resources the CIO had invested in organizing steel. More important, for nearly fifty years, they had conducted their operations without union involvement and were determined not to let "outsiders" have any say in how they managed their affairs.[9]

Endicott-Johnson had long provided its employees with a host of benefits—profit-sharing, medical services, housing—similar to those offered to Columbia Conserve workers. These benefits, which the company described as the "Square Deal," jibed neatly with another powerful symbol of industrial harmony, the "Happy Family." Both images were repeatedly invoked by Endicott-Johnson. As the Shoe Workers and their AFL rivals, the Boot and Shoe Workers, accelerated their organizing efforts among Endicott-Johnson workers, the company depicted both unions as "strangers" and "outsiders." Management's efforts were augmented by the Triple Cities Civic and Workers' Committee, which rallied community support on the company's behalf. When the NLRB admonished Endicott-Johnson for committing unfair labor practices, some local citizens complained about the government's "Un-American muzzling" of a great, benevolent company. To Endicott-Johnson and its defenders, outside forces (the state and the unions) were conspiring to destroy the Happy Family and replace it with impersonal arrangements based on unfamiliar notions of governmental regulation and collective bargaining. In contrast to the Lewiston-Auburn strike where Powers Hapgood and the CIO had been able to depict their opponents as "un-American," the broad community consensus supporting Endicott-Johnson's Happy Family blunted such arguments, offering a competing set of values that the union found difficult to counter.[10]

Nonetheless, the Shoe Workers waged an aggressive campaign leading up to the representation election in January 1940. In the inclusive spirit of industrial unionism, the union published articles and made radio broadcasts in foreign languages in appealing to ethnic workers who comprised nearly 50 percent of Endicott-Johnson's labor force. A female executive board member depicted the union as a defender of traditional values, arguing that only by obtaining a living wage could women return to their proper role in the home and permit men to reemerge as the principal breadwinners for the family. In a July 6, 1939, radio address, Hapgood sought to assure workers that the CIO would not disturb the cooperative relationship between Endicott-Johnson and its employees. These efforts at easing the workers' fears were undermined not only by the company's well-entrenched paternalism but also by the fierce partisan struggle between the Shoe Workers and their AFL rival, which relentlessly red-baited the CIO union. These charges of Communist domination strengthened Endicott-Johnson's claim that the unions were untrustworthy outsiders principally interested in aggrandizing themselves at the expense of the workers.[11]

Nearly 80 percent of Endicott-Johnson workers voted against the union in the January 1940 election. The local press hailed the vote as a "Victory for America." This characterization was a painful reminder of the union's inability to appropriate cultural symbols and establish its legitimacy. For Hapgood, being defeated so convincingly by a paternalistic employer must have been especially disturbing. Since his encounter nearly twenty years earlier with the Rockefeller Plan, he had viewed paternalism as a means of manipulating rather than empowering workers, substituting dependency and deference for character-building notions of independence and solidarity. Even as the CIO vanquished paternalistic schemes elsewhere, Endicott-Johnson's decisive victory underscored the lingering power of welfare capitalism, especially in workplaces where management succeeded in approximating the family relationship that reassured workers amid prevalent insecurity. Beyond losing the ideological battle with Endicott-Johnson, Hapgood realized that the Shoe Workers had failed in a last-ditch effort to gain a toehold in their industry, making the union's future precarious. He now began to ponder his role in the CIO, which was struggling against a determined political counterattack by its opponents and appeared in danger of forfeiting its initial elan.[12]

Hapgood had submerged his commitments to democracy, socialism, and workers' control upon joining the CIO but now expressed doubts about the "machine" that he had been so instrumental in building. He found the unanimity at the October 1939 CIO convention "dull" and likened it to the "ACWA, ILG, or present day UMW conventions." Rose Pesotta expressed similar criticism of what she called "moral disintegration" within the ILGWU, charging that the union's substitution of "one-man rule for statesmanship" obscured any sense of obligation to the organization's rank and file. In contrast to Pesotta's more analytical stance, Hapgood's thoughts lapsed into nostalgia. He fondly recalled his insurgent days in the miners' union when conventions crackled with the electricity of factional intrigue and debate. Although he overlooked the strong-arm tactics that had often marred these conventions and romanticized their drama, Hapgood did legitimately fear an increasing retrenchment that threatened the potential of industrial unionism.[13]

Several months earlier, Hapgood had expressed regret over his diminishing connections with the Socialist Party as he devoted his full energies to the CIO. Hapgood met with old Socialist colleagues and union organizers Franz Daniel and Philip Van Gelder in a New York hotel room, speaking for nearly five hours—"the first talk of this kind" they had had in years. Hapgood summarized their quandary succinctly: "We are all working for CIO unions but is our work helping socialism or not?" Daniel and Van Gelder had dropped out of the Socialist Party in disgust over being upbraided by unsympathetic SP officials for their reluctance to promote party policies among their union constituents. In a description that included himself, Hapgood noted that "they feel sad, however, at the 'pure and simple' policy of the unions for which they are working." Nothing specific emerged from the discussion, although Hapgood and his comrades agreed to confer more frequently.[14]

Hapgood now questioned his role as a labor leader. The most responsible job he had ever had seemed to him a "long, continuous grind" rather than a boost to socialism or a heroic manifestation of his courage. He told Rose Pesotta that he wished he were fighting alongside the Loyalists in Spain and continued to take target practice in the event a fascist threat should emerge in the United States. "How I long to be there [Spain] to feel that I'm really doing something worthwhile in the class struggle," he mused, continuing to define "worth" as a gallant display of personal bravery. As Nazism began its advance across Europe in late 1939, these feelings of inadequacy intensified. Hapgood lamented that his work at Endicott-Johnson seemed trivial in comparison to the task of fighting fascism overseas. Although this sentiment was probably widespread, it nearly debilitated Hapgood, who longed for a clear-cut fight unfettered by political compromise or moral ambiguity.[15]

Alienated from his work and guilty over his troubled relationships with his wife, his parents, and his lover, Hapgood more frequently sought solace in drinking. Occasionally his binges incapacitated him for prolonged periods. In March 1938, his father was so disturbed that he wrote both John Brophy and John L. Lewis, pleading with them to send his son back to Indiana for rehabilitation. "His unusually bright prospects have become black indeed," confessed William Hapgood to John L. Lewis. Rose Pesotta echoed these concerns. She urged Hapgood to seek help "if you want to retain your position in the labor movement and your name in the REVOLUTIONARY movement."[16]

Hapgood rejected these attempts to get him to seek treatment. He insisted that he could abstain on his own and needed only a stint of hard, productive labor to restore his health. As he informed Pesotta in December 1937, "I have put in some hard work on the farm and sometimes wish I could earn my living as a producer instead of [as] an agitator." The prospect of becoming a bureaucrat terrified Hapgood; it reminded him of the white-collar milieu from which he had perpetually sought to escape. His dreams of transcendent oneness with workers fading, he sought comfort in a simpler past where he was unencumbered by the responsibilities of leadership. Yet he must have sensed the limitations of his fantasized producer identity. Hard work on the farm scarcely relieved his gnawing fear that he could no longer present himself as a moral man in an immoral society. Hapgood now risked retreating into a private sphere that bore little connection to working people's struggles or the political realities of modern corporate capitalism.[17]

Sobered by the difficulties of organizing in the shoe industry, Hapgood contemplated leaving the Shoe Workers but was persuaded to stay by the union's General Executive Board. At the union's second convention in October 1939, he described the proceedings as the "least bitter and acrimonious" in his experience. He also welcomed the praise he received from many delegates for his leadership, taking some credit for "reasoning with the factions" and establishing a semblance of internal unity. Yet he could see little future for himself within the Shoe Workers. Under their constitution he was ineligible to hold elective office because he was not a bona fide worker in the industry. Ironically, Hapgood had gained respect and acceptance as a labor leader—one of his original aims in entering the labor movement—but in a marginal industry and within a union where his status remained impermanent.[18]

By the beginning of 1940, Hapgood prepared to leave the Shoe Workers for the Industrial Union of Marine and Shipbuilding Workers of America (IUMSWA). This union was headed by two Socialist comrades, John Green and Philip Van Gelder, whose members had provided Hapgood with vital picket-line support during the RCA campaign in Camden. Green's and Van Gelder's organizing efforts among shipbuilding workers were just beginning to bear fruit. Between 1939 and 1940, the IUMSWA had doubled its membership from 11,000 to 22,000 and with defense mobilization underway, had the potential to organize thousands more. In a letter to CIO organizing director Allan Haywood, Green requested that Hapgood be appointed as organizing director for the shipbuilders. He explained that unlike shoes, the shipbuilding industry had an assured market, no runaway shops, and a "higher type of worker" with whom the former coal miner would fit in well. Presumably, Hapgood hoped that these more favorable circumstances and work with like-minded colleagues would allow him to revive his faith in the potential of industrial unionism. Yet he was handicapped from the outset by his drinking. One union official praised Hapgood's sincerity and skill but noted that his drinking problem impaired his effectiveness.[19]

Unfortunately, Hapgood's experience in the IUMSWA proved nearly as frustrating as his tenure with the Shoe Workers. Coordinating a shipyard strike in California during summer 1940, he collided with the new wartime apparatus that was emerging to oversee labor-management relations. The strike at the Consolidated Steel shipyard in Long Beach was an enormously complicated affair. While the IUMSWA was attempting to negotiate a contract, the company signed a backdoor deal with the AFL Metal Trades Department. The AFL also won tacit support for its cause from International Longshoremen's and Warehousemen's Union (ILWU) president Harry Bridges, whom Hapgood described as "playing" with the AFL in order to defend his own jurisdiction. Once again, Hapgood was embroiled in a heated internal dispute that exposed serious fissures in the house of labor. In order to press their cause, the CIO shipyard workers decided to strike, committing themselves to a special assessment to fund the walkout and agreeing to fine workers who did not fulfill their picket-line obligations. These commitments to labor solidarity were reinforced by the CIO's strong political base in the area. Bowing to CIO demands, other union employers in the vicinity consented to allow workers to punch in late, thereby freeing them for picket-line activity.[20]

Union leader John Green was sensitive to the political repercussions of a defense industry strike. Both he and Philip Van Gelder recognized the integral role Washington would play in the future of the union, both in terms of awarding shipbuilding contracts and ensuring production in a wartime atmosphere. Although he shared Hapgood's frustrating experience with the NLRB, Green hoped to take advantage of new avenues for resolving industrial disputes. As the strike wore on and threatened to disrupt shipbuilding, it drew the attention of new governmental agencies designed to oversee defense mobilization and ensure labor-management cooperation in maintaining production. Sidney Hillman, the Amalgamated Clothing Workers' president, was now serving as labor's representative on the National Defense Advisory Commission. With the approval of Green and Van Gelder, Hillman requested that Hapgood call off the strike. Hapgood balked at this request and pleaded with Hillman to help resolve the jurisdictional dispute between the AFL and the CIO. To Hapgood's dismay, Hillman refused to intervene, fearing that he might damage his credibility as an honest broker.[21]

When Hapgood reluctantly urged the workers to end their strike and obey the "national policy" of both the CIO and the government, he was rebuffed by union members, who showed no faith in the governmental apparatus established to adjudicate such disputes. As the local union secretary wrote John Green, "this membership believes now and has for a considerable time, that we have been alone in the wilderness on the west coast as the only local that upholds the traditions of industrial organization." Hapgood sympathized with this view, but he found himself squeezed between the militancy of the workers, the demands of the wartime state, and the CIO leadership's increasing hesitation to offend the Roosevelt administration. Eventually, Sidney Hillman helped craft stabilization agreements in shipbuilding that were satisfactory to both CIO and AFL leaders. But once again, Powers Hapgood had faced the unenviable task of discouraging worker militancy, this time in the name of a national policy that he feared was draining the industrial union movement of its democratic, fraternal spirit.[22]

The Long Beach strike also illuminated the dissonance between the moral universe of Hapgood's personal code and the harsh intrusion of political realities. The conflict between the AFL and the CIO had spilled over to the local waitresses' union, many of whose members had left the AFL and formed CIO restaurant unions in protest. Both unions established picket lines in front of the other's restaurants. In contrast to his CIO colleagues, Hapgood refused to cross either picket line out of what he acknowledged was "sentimentality." For Hapgood, picket lines were sacred symbols of commitment and solidarity and not to be crossed even if one disagreed with the motives of those on strike. Conceding that "if all our people did what I did, there would be no CIO," he refused to "blame our men for calling me a sentimental fool." Deeply distressed, he wondered if it were possible to be both practical and idealistic in the political arena and mused how painful it was to stand "alone against the crowd."[23]

Hapgood longed for an unambiguous form of class conflict where he could play a heroic role: "Sometimes I wish the IWW was still alive. It is so easy to be idealistic when one doesn't have to be practical." Anticipating a later generation's rediscovery of the Wobblies, Hapgood sought to justify his growing qualms about bowing to political necessity and bureaucratic imperatives. Yet his chosen exemplar was never as pure or uncompromising as his fond reverie suggested. Indeed, the Wobblies had begun to rethink their fierce syndicalism and anti-organizational bent in the months before their persecution by the government during World War I. Again, Hapgood was groping for an identity that would enable him to reassert his moral integrity and restore a radical flavor to his politics. Although he anticipated the emerging bureaucratic tendencies that undercut the CIO's democratic potential, his search for a usable past remained mired in nostalgia and sentimentality. In fact, the tentative tone of his reminiscences suggests that Hapgood understood the inadequacy of his analysis. Nonetheless, his profound frustration left him powerless to relinquish comforting images that evoked a less complicated time.[24]

Hapgood's musings about the IWW also reflected his diminishing hopes that the industrial union movement might yet move toward the implementation of a larger program. These misgivings were accentuated by the machinations of John L. Lewis prior to the presidential election of 1940 and made him fear that the collapse of the CIO was imminent. Long-simmering tensions among Lewis, Sidney Hillman, and Philip Murray could not be contained after the CIO president shocked most of his colleagues by endorsing Republican Wendell Willkie's bid to prevent Franklin Roosevelt from winning an unprecedented third term. As an "appointed man," Hapgood was instructed by CIO organizing director Allan Haywood to support Lewis's endorsement of Willkie. Hapgood rejected Haywood's request, noting that "John L. will not like my refusal to conform." To be sure, he agreed with Lewis's criticism of FDR's lukewarm support for labor, having never been fully convinced of the New Deal's willingness to use state power to enforce workers' rights. Yet he was also well aware of the depth of working-class support for Roosevelt and worried that a Willkie victory would permit the CIO's opponents to intensify their already powerful attack on the industrial union movement's progress.[25]

As did many others, Hapgood attempted to distinguish between "industrial" and "political" loyalty to Lewis: "If I were not a loyal Socialist, I would agree with Van Bittner's statement. . . . I am 100 percent for John L. Lewis as head of the CIO and also 100 percent for the reelection of Roosevelt." He expressed hope that FDR would win but asserted that "I can't change my loyalty as quickly as others do." Accordingly, he declared that "I will vote for Norman [Thomas], since like Jim Farley, I believe in party loyalty and will vote straight Social-ist." Unable to "bear the thought of missing a vote for the SP," Hapgood even contemplated flying back to Indiana for fear that his absentee ballot might not arrive in time to be counted. Hapgood's profound anxiety at the prospect of "missing a vote for the SP" reflected the heightened psychological needs driving his politics and the persistence of what Irving Howe has called "an old-style Debsian rectitude, morally admirable but not really able to cope with the complexities that Roosevelt was introducing into capitalist society." If he were to deal with these complexities more convincingly, Hapgood would have to consider options besides private expressions of loyalty to a party that had been rendered irrelevant by the New Deal.[26]

Being reminded that he was an appointed man underscored Hap-good's precarious status. If Lewis remained in power, he might again be sent into political exile. Therefore, Hapgood was relieved when Lewis made good on his pledge to resign in the event of Willkie's defeat, and Philip Murray's succession was approved. Yet Hapgood noted with considerable regret that Lewis had "ruined his effectiveness as the leader of a great movement." He had come to admire his old foe's "guts," even if the CIO president lacked "diplomacy" or "idealism." For all his flaws, Lewis had endorsed working-class mobilization, warned about the dangers accompanying detente with the New Deal state, and not ruled out the possibility of an independent political stance for labor. With Lewis no longer at the helm and "the diplomat," Philip Murray, in his place, Hapgood lamented that "the days of '35 and '37 will not return." Hapgood's assessment tended to ignore the hostile political context that was impeding the CIO's momentum—active attempts in Congress to gut the National Labor Relations Act, investigations into the Communist presence in the CIO, fierce competition from the AFL, public opinion that had grown less enamored of labor—and making fights against the "industrial barons" far more difficult to carry out.[27]

After five years with the CIO, Powers Hapgood again felt isolated and adrift. Initially energized by the mantle of leadership, he was nearly overwhelmed by its responsibilities. Late in 1940, he considered quitting the CIO, contending that his discouragement made him a "burden on the workers." Complicating matters further, Hapgood's psychological needs dictated that he be either a producer or a warrior, identities not easily attainable in the new system of industrial relations that was forged during World War II. Still, despite his attraction to these invented identities, Hapgood could not envision severing his ties to the industrial union movement. On the final leg of his political odyssey, he returned to familiar ground, seeking to relieve his restlessness and discover a renewed sense of purpose.[28]

Chapter Twelve

"The Fundamental Principles of the CIO"

We are entering a new era—the era of arbitration
by disinterested individuals, mostly on
governmental payroll, who will consider this some
times an unpleasant duty, while the workers will
remain aloof, the leaders will disclaim any
responsibility, and thus the labor movement will
die a natural death.
　　　　　　　—Rose Pesotta to Powers Hapgood,
　　　　　　　　January 30, 1943

Powers Hapgood's political odyssey ended where it began, in his native Indiana, to which he returned in 1941 as a regional director for the CIO. The final decade of his life was framed by two wars, one a "hot" war against fascism, the other a "cold war" aimed at containing communism. After initial hesitation, Hapgood attempted to enlist in the former but insisted on noncombatant status in the latter, placing himself outside the consensus that governed American politics following World War II. Rejecting cold war liberalism, he attempted to fashion an alternative that, in his words, would uphold the "fundamental principles of the CIO." But his effort was short-circuited by his deteriorating health and more significantly, by the narrowing of political space that accompanied the advent of the cold war. In his final years, Powers Hapgood achieved perhaps his greatest success in harmonizing his personal needs with his political ideals, yet he ended his career as a tragic figure, ostracized from the movement that he loved and had been so instrumental in helping to erect.

Hapgood's search for a niche within the CIO continued after the 1940 convention. During the first half of 1941, he served as a special assistant to CIO organizing director Allan Haywood, working on the successful drive to organize Ford and helping to direct a bitter strike at International Harvester in Chicago. At International Harvester, Hapgood initially relished his role leading picket lines, but his mood quickly changed. As in Long Beach with the shipbuilders, he found himself uneasily wedged among conflicting forces—union factionalism, AFL intervention, the demands of wartime governmental agencies—that led to a settlement without a clear victory or defeat.[1]

An incident during the International Harvester strike highlighted Hapgood's persistent difficulty in comprehending the disparate influences shaping working-class consciousness. He was asked by local officials to deliver a radio address encouraging workers to vote for the union in upcoming representation elections. Reviewing a copy of the speech, which was written by a local union officer, Hapgood dismissed it as "meaningless oratory" and "bunk." He objected especially to the religious references in the text that invoked "humility on Sunday," the Tower of Babel, and Christ's teachings. Despite his reservations, Hapgood left these references in the speech, and to his surprise, it was extremely well received. It is impossible to identify precisely the reasons for this response, but it appears plausible that its familiar biblical imagery connected with an ethnic, working-class audience who perhaps attended church regularly and regarded themselves as believers. Although local unionists recognized that workers frequently used religious symbols and imagery to order their world, Hapgood's unreconstructed secularism prevented him from creatively engaging working-class religiosity.[2]

In September 1941, Hapgood assumed the position that he would occupy for the remainder of his career, agreeing to become a CIO regional director in Indiana. His decision was accompanied by considerable misgivings. He still longed to establish a fuller relationship with Rose Pesotta and even contemplated leaving Mary Donovan but was deterred by the fear that his action would harm his children. Hapgood had hoped to obtain a job nearer Pesotta, but when she discouraged his affections, he opted for the post in Indiana. For her part, Pesotta had wearied of contending with Hapgood's drinking and her role as the other woman. Her repeated insistence that he take a pledge of sobriety strained their relationship further, for he resented her implying that he was unable to control his behavior and "be normal." At her request his letters became less frequent and matter-of-fact, allowing Pesotta to stem her emotional losses. But Hapgood continued to mourn a love that could not be.[3]

On the stump as a CIO regional director in Indiana, a position he accepted in 1941. During the early years of World War II, Hapgood faced a formidable challenge: what alternatives could he offer to the emerging system of workplace contractualism, union consolidation, and domination by professional leadership? (Courtesy Lilly Library, Indiana University)

Lapsing into self-pity, Hapgood lamented being confined to Indiana. Once again, his sense of personal independence was circumscribed by the burden of submitting to his father's authority. In fact, his decision to return to Indiana was at least partially triggered by family considerations. William Hapgood was going blind, and Eleanor Hapgood's health had grown more delicate. Given his parents' physical deterioration, Hapgood felt obligated to assume the responsibility of overseeing the family farm outside of Indianapolis. His action was not wholly self-sacrificial; the farm provided him with the opportunity to reclaim his identity as a producer and prove that he was not succumbing to the softness of bureaucratic routine. Still, being near to his parents placed new pressures on Hapgood and continually reminded him of their strained relationship. Torn between his sense of obligation and his resentment over increasing parental demands on his time, Hapgood sought to sublimate these tensions by renewing his sense of political commitment.[4]

Soon after his arrival in Indiana, Hapgood sought alternatives to what he regarded as the pallid world of mature labor relations. He squirmed in his role as a member of wartime joint labor-management committees, telling Rose Pesotta in January 1942 that "I'll be glad when the necessity for these things is past." For radicals like Hapgood, the dense, legalistic system of industrial relations that was being cemented during World War II threatened to erode the participatory, activist orientation of the early industrial union movement. The unhappy result was a shift in the locus of working-class activity from the shop floor and the streets to the hearing room and the voting booth, environments far less conducive to promoting class solidarity and rank-and-file activism. Yet, as Hapgood understood, the CIO under the tight control of John L. Lewis had been no model of democratic, decentralized unionism. Moreover, for many union leaders, World War II offered a rare historical opportunity to translate increased membership and enhanced bargaining power into an unprecedented degree of social legitimacy and political influence. In light of these attitudes, Hapgood faced a formidable challenge: what alternatives could he offer to the emerging system of workplace contractualism, union consolidation, and domination by professional leadership?[5]

His concern over the direction of the CIO led Hapgood to seek a dramatic escape from the clutches of bureaucratic routine. Like most of his fellow leftists, he had observed the growth of European fascism with alarm. Yet he remained reluctant to embrace Franklin Roosevelt's defense buildup, despite his escalating fears. Referring to an argument with a left-wing colleague, he noted: "My reason tells me he is right but memories of Gene Debs and what we all said tell me he is wrong." Hapgood was recalling Debs's warning that World War I would only serve to enrich capitalist elites at the expense of the working class. Perhaps, too, he remembered his contacts with European workers two decades earlier and their pledges of international working-class solidarity in the event of another war.[6]

But as the Nazis overran Europe, Hapgood, fearing the consequences of fascism for European trade unionists and ethnic minorities, dropped his opposition to American involvement. In a speech before an Indiana State Industrial Union Council convention in September 1942, he told the delegates about Hitler's destruction of the German labor movement and noted that one of his old mining comrades had been imprisoned in a concentration camp. These personal memories spurred him to seek a more direct role in the war effort once the United States became an official combatant. As he explained to Allan Haywood, "at the present time I feel that the picket lines are on the battle fields of Europe and Asia."[7]

In contrast to the world of compromise and constraint that he inhabited as a labor official, Hapgood saw World War II as a morally unambiguous cause aimed at defending democratic values and workers' rights. Despite his age (forty-two) and his family obligations, he attempted to enlist, just as he had twenty years earlier. Hapgood's consuming need to demonstrate his selflessness and character coincided with the political imperative to fight fascism, offering him an irresistible opportunity to integrate private belief and public behavior. War would also allow him to escape the morass of family relationships that had grown more tangled following his return to Indiana. As a young man, Hapgood had sought to overcome parental opposition to his enlistment. Now, as an adult, he lobbied government bureaucrats for a commission, seeking to enter either the Army Air Corps, Combat Intelligence, or even Public Relations if the first two options were foreclosed.[8]

Hapgood enlisted such old colleagues as Heber Blankenhorn and Gardner Jackson, now associated with wartime planning agencies, to help speed his acceptance, but their efforts and those of other influential friends proved unavailing. He did get as far as taking a physical in May 1942 but suspected that his lengthy arrest record and labor activities made military authorities loath to approve his commission. What he did not know was that the FBI had placed him under surveillance in 1940 and branded him as a security risk unsuitable for military service.[9]

According to data collected by FBI agents and informants, Hapgood's associations left no doubt that he was a Communist. Reports submitted to high-ranking FBI officials, including bureau director J. Edgar Hoover, noted his 1935 advocacy of a united front between the Socialist and Communist Parties and his affiliation with the Columbia Conserve Company, described by an overzealous informant as a "communistic" organization. His activities during the war—speeches to the NAACP, criticism of government rationing programs, defending the political rights of the Communist Party—confirmed his unreliability in the eyes of the FBI and led to the following conclusion in October 1941: "It is recommended that this individual be considered for custodial detention in the event of a national emergency." In spite of assurances from a friend on the Wartime Manpower Commission that "Powers is extremely devoted to our form of government and is in no way tainted with anything that could be called radicalism," Hapgood was deemed a subversive at the moment he was attempting to act as a patriot. To his deep chagrin, he again had to find moral equivalents for war in lieu of service on the front lines.[10]

Assuaging his disappointment, Hapgood approached his duties as CIO regional director with renewed energy. His participation in joint labor-management committees supporting the war effort brought him closer to mainstream liberal politics, as did his warming relations with the Democratic Party and his role as a lobbyist on behalf of the CIO's legislative agenda. Although Hapgood retained his membership in the Socialist Party (by 1942, he and Mary Donovan comprised half of the SP's membership in Indianapolis!), he understood that in order to be politically relevant, he would have to travel in Democratic Party circles. As his Shipbuilding Workers' Union comrade Philip Van Gelder had recognized nearly a decade earlier, "when your union was 100 per cent behind Roosevelt, it just didn't make sense to say, hell, that's ok for you guys, but I'm for Norman Thomas." Moreover, in an extremely conservative state where the American Legion enjoyed what amounted to third-party status and the New Deal impulse was weak, attempting to nurture liberalism within the Democratic Party made eminent political sense. Hapgood's loyalty was conditional, however, and he sought to fashion a more aggressive political role for labor. Along with state CIO secretary-treasurer Walter Frisbie, he led a group of non-Communist liberals who shared his convictions and prodded the Democratic Party to be more vigorous in defending workers' rights and combating racial discrimination.[11]

Hapgood also expressed concern that if the CIO were not sufficiently vigilant, it risked squandering its wartime gains, as had happened following World War I. In order to ensure that labor could sustain its advances and press for a revitalized liberalism, he undertook several initiatives. Although he dutifully presented CIO president Philip Murray's plan for industry councils that would administer wartime production and allow labor to exercise its influence more independently, he showed less enthusiasm for such arrangements than did his old mentor John Brophy, who became a vocal advocate of tripartite planning. As an avowed secularist, Hapgood was not attuned to the corporatist, catholic social doctrine that inspired Brophy's and Murray's conception of shared governance. Hapgood offered no direct criticism of industry councils and recognized that labor could not avoid engagement with the administrative apparatus of the wartime state. The thrust of his own activities reflected a more voluntaristic tradition that sought to enhance labor's internal strength, reinforce its political independence, and support activism at the local level. His aim was to revive the spirit of John Brophy's larger program, which he feared was being undermined by the constraints of routine union work and the wartime state's micromanagement of industrial conflict.[12]

In seeking to surmount the enervation of bureaucratic routine and spur working-class mobilization, Hapgood rededicated himself to the task of organizing. He noted that workers from smaller, nonunion shops in industries marked by substandard wages were seeking CIO assistance, which he eagerly provided. Hapgood acknowledged the salutary impact of state intervention, observing that the War Labor Board's oversight made "the life of an organizer a little less tough." Whenever possible, however, he opted to bypass official channels, capitalizing on the exigencies of wartime and the impetus of worker militancy to obtain first contracts without becoming entangled in legalistic proceedings. In instances where companies refused to obey government edicts to bargain in good faith, Hapgood abandoned the CIO's no-strike pledge and encouraged direct action, as was the case in a strike of African-American cannery workers in Indianapolis in October 1942. While Hapgood by no means adopted a wholly voluntaristic approach, he seized upon every possible opportunity to employ worker mobilization as both a political tool and a character-building device. By mid-1944, he reported that Indianapolis, long a bastion of the open shop, was nearly 80 percent organized. Although his numbers may

Doing the desk work that he abhorred, possibly in Indiana as regional
director. As American involvement in World War II became imminent,
Hapgood sought a dramatic escape from the clutches of bureaucratic
routine, attempting to enlist despite his age and family responsibilities.
(Courtesy Lilly Library, Indiana University)

have been exaggerated, Hapgood had done much to fortify the CIO's
institutional strength in Indiana, which he recognized as essential to
labor's ability to advance a larger program.[13]

Hapgood attempted through his organizing efforts to encourage an
inclusive vision of industrial unionism that would permit fresh, new
voices to be heard in labor's chorus. Attending a 1943 convention of the
Food and Tobacco Workers Union where he served as a CIO representative, he hailed the presence of African-American, Latino, and Filipino
delegates, many of whom were women. He was especially vigorous in

assisting African-American workers, aiding movie operators in black
theaters and red caps at the Indianapolis railroad station in organizing
and collective bargaining. Nor did Hapgood confine his efforts to the
blue-collar workers who had been the principal objects of the CIO's
attention. In January 1944, he urged the president of the United Office
and Professional Workers Association to be more aggressive in honoring the requests of clerical workers in Indianapolis seeking to be
organized. Hapgood's willingness to extend CIO assistance to African-
Americans, white-collar workers, and small nonunion operations was
well within the boundaries of official CIO policy. But the intensity of his
efforts underscored his commitment to ensuring that the CIO could
credibly present itself as a spokesperson for broad segments of the
American working class.[14]

Hapgood's advocacy of an inclusive, egalitarian industrial unionism
was perhaps most vividly reflected in his passionate commitment to
eradicating racial discrimination. This emphasis was rather new for
Hapgood, whose belief in a transcendent class loyalty had made him
reluctant to acknowledge racial conflict within the working class or to
grant race any special status in his political analysis. He had, however,
encountered the use of African-Americans to break coal miners' strikes
and, as recently as the Ford strike in 1941, had observed numerous
"colored scabs" crossing union picket lines. These were disturbing
realities, which by the mid-1940s he was no longer willing to overlook.[15]

Hapgood was alarmed by the rising tensions that had marked the
entry of African-Americans into wartime defense industries. In response, he sought to implement a program to combat racial conflict
similar to that launched by UAW president R. J. Thomas after the
shocking 1943 race riot in Detroit. This program included antidiscrimi-
nation measures in employment and housing and the establishment of
a biracial commission to oversee race relations. On numerous occasions
Hapgood spoke out against racist practices, which struck close to home
when "ignorant, stupid, cruel white neighbors" threatened Jamaican
contract workers employed on his family's farm. In another instance he
defended an African-American red cap who had protested a white
passenger's use of racial slurs. And, in an act that attracted widespread
local publicity, he defied the Indianapolis police chief's attempt to ban
a CIO interracial dance and sought a restraining order barring such
intervention.[16]

But Hapgood did not spare the CIO from his criticism and became a
freelance agitator for racial justice within the house of labor. Speaking

before the Indiana State Industrial Union Council (IUC) convention in 1945, he praised the delegates for holding an integrated gathering but implored them not to condone segregated private clubs run by local unions. Hapgood urged the delegates to pass a resolution against racial discrimination because "it calls upon us to put into action one of the most fundamental principles of the CIO." Of course, passing resolutions was one thing; enforcing them was another matter. Refusing to relax his efforts, Hapgood sought in 1947 to squash a proposed union social club in Kokomo that was linked to corrupt politicians and the Ku Klux Klan. If the CIO were to rediscover its vitality and justify its claim to speak on behalf of all working people, he insisted, it needed to embrace an unabashed policy targeting racism and implement it at the local level. By challenging trade unionists to assume personal responsibility for ridding labor's ranks of racism, Hapgood found an issue that enabled him to speak with moral authority and transcend the bureaucratic constraints of his leadership role. Given the Hoosier State's virulently racist past, his actions took special courage and established Hapgood as one of Indiana's leading liberal voices during a time of growing political retrenchment.[17]

During the war years Hapgood also revisited a commitment that he had subordinated upon joining the CIO—the practice of democracy within the trade union movement. He regarded the undemocratic circling of the CIO wagons darkly, especially as he observed events in the UMWA. His Somerset buddy Faber McCloskey had emerged as a leading dissident in District 2 and complained that his attempt to win elective office was unfairly defeated by the Lewis machine. During his initial years in the CIO, Hapgood had ignored such reports from old comrades, accepting John L. Lewis's argument that "when the full strength of this Union was pitted against the opposition of the financial, political, and the thoughtless element of our citizenship . . . I did not have time" to think about autonomy. Now, in a less turbulent period, Hapgood had time to reflect on his experience in the CIO and concluded that the price for his concession had been too high. By 1944, he quietly began to aid a budding autonomy movement for "decency and justice" within the UMWA.[18]

District 2 was one of the centers of the autonomy movement, which sought to return to the district level the control over local union affairs that John L. Lewis had expropriated. The rhetoric of the autonomy advocates stirred Hapgood's deepest impulses, recalling his youthful vision of the local union as an incubator of fraternity and democracy. As the insurgents declared in an August 1944 editorial, "the movement for autonomy and self-government in the United Mine Workers of America is the miners' modern Declaration of Independence." The leaders of the movement "pledge their loyalty, willingness of self-sacrifice and their very lives . . . to the UMWA." The editorial's title articulated a theme that Hapgood had himself used in pressing for racial justice: "Our Boys at the Front Die for Democracy . . . Let's Have It in the UMWA." Here was yet another fight for fundamental principles couched in the imagery of patriotism and sacrifice that might revive the moral commitments Hapgood viewed as essential to the health of industrial unionism.[19]

The most that Hapgood could do to aid the autonomy movement, however, was to contribute money and privately urge others to lend their support. As he explained to the movement's leader, Ray Edmondson, "If there is anything I can do without subjecting myself to the accusation that I am not obeying the democratic discipline of the CIO, you can count on me to do it." But Hapgood knew all too well that the discipline of the CIO might not conform to democratic standards; union leaders understandably frowned upon supporting insurgencies that might provoke similar challenges in their own backyards. These boundaries confined his actions to the realm of the private gesture, enabling him to atone personally for excusing John L. Lewis's highhandedness but lacking practical impact on the UMWA's political direction.[20]

The autonomy movement itself was beset by serious limitations, some familiar and others of more recent vintage, that enabled John L. Lewis to vanquish his opponents. Like many in Lewis's long line of rivals, the movement's leader, Ray Edmondson, was motivated more by personal animus than political conviction. Although the miners still possessed some semblance of a union culture, several decades of authoritarian rule by John Brophy's successors had eroded the democratic ethos of District 2. Hapgood's old comrades were now a lonely band of insurgents who lacked a substantial base within the union. Unfortunately for them, the once-venerable tradition of union autonomy was largely unfamiliar to a new generation of miners who had benefited materially from Lewis's centralized leadership and were unattuned to the issues raised by the insurgents.[21]

Hapgood distinguished between his admiration for Lewis's willingness to use direct action and disapproval of his autocratic rule. This distinction underscored a nagging contradiction in his thought that defied easy resolution. Throughout his career he had struggled with what Michael Walzer has called the central problem of the modern age, "the connection of specialists and commoners, elite and mass." As he had long ago conceded, labor needed a disciplined, powerful machine capable of contending with the centralized structures of corporate and governmental authority that were amassing even more power during the war. Yet the discipline, obedience, and professional expertise demanded by this machine seemed incompatible with the rank-and-file activism and local union autonomy that Hapgood aimed to resuscitate. The possibilities for sustaining small-scale alternatives and democratic enclaves, already circumscribed by the rise of modern bureaucracy, appeared dimmer with the growing centralization of authority under the wartime state. His attachment to the miners notwithstanding, Hapgood would have to seek other avenues to press his renewed commitment to democratic values and civic participation.[22]

In spite of the futility of his support for democracy within the UMWA, Hapgood could take comfort in his solid record of achievement as a CIO regional director. Joseph Shepard of the Indianapolis Newspaper Guild commented in 1948 that "he is one of this city's top citizens, and is so regarded by the clergy, by educators, social workers, city and state officials." Hapgood's generous support for other unions, his studious avoidance of factional infighting, his commitment to organizing, and his principled stand against racism won him a loyal following. Anchored in his native state, buoyed by his status as a CIO leader, and more willing to engage the political mainstream, he appeared to have overcome his old antipathy toward liberals. Within the hostile environment of Indiana's conservative political culture, Hapgood seemed positioned to help labor and liberals forge a closer alliance.[23]

Yet Hapgood remained restless and dissatisfied, tormented by old demons and doubts. He regretted not participating directly in the war and strained to demonstrate his commitment, spending more than 30 percent of his salary on war bonds, donating blood on over a dozen occasions, and raising hundreds of baby chicks to help overcome domestic shortages of food. Farm labor, Hapgood observed, offered the "satisfaction that desk or conference work will never give me." He tended toward overwork, however, declaring that he couldn't be "a driver of workers in the morning and a bargainer for workers in the afternoon" unless he was willing to toil as hard as those he employed. Anxious that he was not fulfilling the perfectionist demands of his personal code, Hapgood drove himself to the point of physical breakdown.[24]

Hapgood's woes were exacerbated by ongoing disputes with his parents. He was embarrassed in 1942 when workers at Columbia Conserve struck for higher wages and refused his father's request to accompany him across the picket lines. As William Hapgood's health deteriorated, Powers felt increasingly obligated to manage the family farm. He resented his father's second-guessing of his decisions, however, and the fact that he was compelled to divert much of his salary to meet mortgage payments on the land. These pressures aggravated Hapgood's drinking. His binges grew more frequent and intense, leading him to request a leave from his CIO activities early in 1945 so that he could engage in "hard manual labor" to restore his health. Once again, this solution failed. Late in 1945 and early in 1946, Hapgood was arrested for drunk driving. Although he was acquitted of the charges and the CIO stood by him, his stature within the labor movement suffered. Allan Haywood issued a pointed warning after his second arrest: "I cannot impress upon you too strongly the necessity for avoiding what everybody who knows you and thinks a lot of you, knows to be true."[25]

Rose Pesotta urged Hapgood "to rest and write" in order to regain his health. This was the course that she had followed, publishing a memoir of her organizing activities (*Bread upon the Waters*), which embodied the basic outline of Hapgood's critique of the CIO. He rejected her advice, claiming that he was too young to leave the CIO and anticipated "big things" for the labor movement with the end of World War II. He resisted severing his ties to the working class, explaining "I would never forsake that because I love the cause even though I do not have the hope of my youth anymore that I would live to see the cooperative commonwealth." Hapgood may have relinquished his youthful dream, but his reference to nineteenth-century imagery reflected the enduring difficulties he had in adapting to the terrain of modern American politics. Dissatisfied with cold war liberalism and workplace contractualism, he continued to long for an ideal that possessed the appeal of nineteenth-century challenges to corporate capitalism or even the stirring overtones of John Brophy's larger program. More modestly, Hapgood hoped that the labor movement could at least function as a principled critic of the emerging cold war consensus. After the war he learned just how difficult achieving even this limited aim would be.[26]

The wave of strikes following World War II and labor's determination to extend its wartime gains created tensions in the CIO's relations with the Democratic Party, now led by Harry Truman. Hapgood continued to press the Democrats to remain loyal to the legacy of the New Deal. In November 1945, he was part of a delegation of one hundred Indiana labor leaders who sought to retain their state party chairman as a "symbol of liberalism." A year later, he wrote a scathing letter to Judge T. Alan Goldsborough, who had granted the Truman administration an injunction against a controversial nationwide UMWA strike. Quoting from James Russell Lowell's "Stanzas on Freedom," Hapgood likened Goldsborough to a "slave who fear[s] to speak/For the fallen and the weak." He concluded with a blistering attack on the Democratic Party: "I have supported the New Deal and its candidates except in the 1940 election when I voted for Norman Thomas, but at the present time, I fail to see the difference between the party of Goldsborough, Truman, Bilbo, and Rankin and the party of Taft and Dewey."[27]

While Hapgood's equation of Goldsborough and Truman with the archconservatives Bilbo and Rankin was hyperbolic, he accurately identified divisions within the Democratic Party that even in Franklin Roosevelt's day had blunted its reformist initiatives. These divisions were accentuated by a rising political backlash against the labor movement and the beginnings of a postwar crusade against communism that would have a chilling effect on American liberalism. At the very least, Hapgood hoped to keep Democrats from diluting the commitments that had gained them working-class loyalty and status as a quasi-social democratic party.

The issue that most marked Hapgood's postwar political initiatives occurred along the fault line that indelibly shaped the future of the industrial union movement: the CIO's relation with communism. Tensions between the CIO and Communists within its ranks emerged with a vengeance following World War II. As the Truman administration rallied support to contain the Soviet Union and appeared to relax its commitment to extending New Deal reforms, Communists quarreled with official CIO policy, which supported the Marshall Plan to aid Western Europe and opposed the establishment of a third party. Powers Hapgood supported the CIO leadership with few reservations. He was well aware of the suffering in war-torn Europe, and his repeated attempts to recast the Democratic Party suggest that he had serious doubts about the viability of a third-party effort.[28]

Yet in contrast to John Brophy, Allan Haywood, Adolph Germer, and other CIO colleagues who actively undermined the Communist Party, Powers Hapgood championed the rights of the CP. In 1946, he joined a group of academics and civil libertarians in petitioning the governor of Indiana to allow the Communists to remain on a statewide ballot. Later, he demanded that the CIO oppose national legislation seeking to outlaw the party. Earlier, in 1942, he and Walter Frisbie had charged the Indianapolis police chief with using vagrancy arrests to harass CP officials. As was the case with his stand against racism, Hapgood's visible public actions on behalf of the Communists required special fortitude. With the staunchly anti-Communist American Legion head-quartered in Indianapolis and the ultraconservative Eugene Pulliam editing the leading newspapers in the state, Indiana was at the fore-front of anti-Communist sentiment rising across the country. In this charged political atmosphere, Hapgood touched a raw nerve.[29]

What prompted Hapgood's staunch defense of the Communist Party's right to exist? He was certainly not naive about the CP. He had long been repelled by the revelations about Stalin's crimes and the CP's willingness to subordinate trade union interests when the party line changed. Nonetheless, in contrast to most anti-Communist liberals, he harbored grave doubts about acquiescing in the party's demise.

Hapgood had long been a committed civil libertarian; his memory of unchecked authority in the coal fields and his years as a freelance agitator had made him keenly aware of how easily the rights of citizens could be abrogated. Also, he had not forgotten the stultifying effect on the UMWA's democratic traditions incurred by John L. Lewis's disre-gard for freedom of expression. In part, too, his attitude was prompted by his own experience with red-baiting. Throughout his career he had been unfairly and inaccurately tagged with that label, most recently in 1939 when both Communist renegade Benjamin Gitlow and AFL leader John Frey identified him as a Communist before the House Committee on Un-American Activities (HUAC). Although the CIO had supported him during these attacks, he well understood the devastating impact that red-baiting could have on an activist's political legitimacy. Hap-good prophetically feared that a new red scare would discredit all forces on the left, non-Communist and Communist alike, resulting in political sterility and conformism. As he explained in a 1947 letter to Humphrey Bogart and Lauren Bacall that praised the actors for denouncing HUAC's investigation of Hollywood, if the committee had its way, "even [the] most truthful criticisms of plantation owners, employers, bank-ers, and others will be labeled 'communistic.'" Closer to home, he worried that denying the CP a role within the CIO would have a disastrous effect on labor unity and serve to stifle debate, inflicting yet another blow against the possibilities for union democracy.[30]

Hapgood began to express these concerns publicly as internal strife raged within the Indiana CIO. Throughout the 1940s, Communists and their liberal allies had fought bitterly with more conservative elements, and these debates intensified with the advent of the cold war. By then, the Indiana CIO was contradicting national policy by urging more militant action against racial discrimination, praising Henry Wallace's criticism of Harry Truman, and endorsing the possibility of a third political party. At the 1947 state CIO convention, an opposition slate emerged to challenge incumbent president James McEwan and secretary-treasurer Walter Frisbie, Hapgood's close political ally. Although neither McEwan nor Frisbie were Communists, their willingness to cooperate with CP elements prompted conservatives to seek their ouster. The opposition slate was apparently sanctioned by top CIO operatives; circumstantial evidence suggests that both John Brophy and Allan Haywood approved the insurgents' campaign. The challengers pressured Hapgood to abandon the incumbents and support their attempted coup. Hapgood refused, explaining that it had always been his policy to back incumbent leaders who were capably performing their duties. Clearly, too, he understood that the ouster of McEwan and Frisbie would jettison his efforts to reshape the CIO and make him a marginal figure in the state labor movement.[31]

Hapgood spoke on the convention floor against a resolution blaming the CIO's setbacks in the 1946 elections on the Communist Party. The resolution was tabled, but Frisbie and McEwan were not so fortunate, losing a close election to their opponents. Quite possibly under the direction of John Brophy, the new leadership succeeded in expelling Communists from the state executive board in 1948, preceding a similar move by the national CIO. The *Indianapolis Star* described this action as a purge, noting that it was "believed to be the first of its kind in the nation." To pave the way for this move, the victorious forces in 1947 turned their fire on Hapgood, pressing for his ouster shortly after they assumed power.[32]

In a carefully orchestrated smear campaign, Hapgood's opponents, led by James Robb, a conservative UMWA veteran who had been his predecessor as regional director, began to question his leadership. A Michigan CIO newspaper editor wrote CIO secretary-treasurer James Carey to repeat a charge made by another of Hapgood's antagonists: "Powers Hapgood has developed into a very strange person during the last year, having moved clear over to the other side and down the line constantly with certain people out there." James Pascoe, an anti-Communist UE official, referred to a "certain CIO director" who "should be straightened out or put out." Marcus Deardorff, whose attempt to form a segregated union social club in Kokomo had earned him Hapgood's ire, accused his antagonist of neglecting his duties as a regional director. In this case and perhaps in others, Hapgood's forthright opposition to racism served to activate his enemies. Even before this loud whispering campaign, his political position within the CIO had been eroded by his drinking. In fact, he had previously proposed a plan to Allan Haywood for a reduced work schedule that would allow him more time on the farm. Haywood now insisted upon accelerating this arrangement, and replaced Hapgood as regional director without notifying him.[33]

Hapgood offered his own version of events in Indiana. All his efforts had been designed to uphold national CIO policy and maintain unity between the contending factions. He argued that he was simply attempting to duplicate at the state level the balancing act that Philip Murray was engaged in nationally. It was the personal humiliation and lack of consideration from old union comrades that most distressed him. His abrupt departure would signify to his opponents that he was leaving under fire. "I can just see their smug smiles when they see me," Hapgood explained. Imploring Haywood to help salvage his dignity, he reminded him that he was the "third one put on the CIO staff" and deserved a better fate.[34]

Hapgood's local supporters lobbied to prevent his ouster. Writing Haywood in January 1948, Joseph Shepard declared: "There is a strong feeling here that it would be a bitter and tragic thing, and a grave mistake as well, were Powers Hapgood to be relieved here as regional director. . . . In these times of red scares, red smears, and general red hysteria, we feel that if Powers were to be relieved at this time, the impression would be held within and without the CIO, that Powers had been 'purged.'"[35]

Haywood denied Shepard's plea, and Hapgood's resignation from the CIO became official in March 1948. Although his forced departure was facilitated by his alcoholism, there was an inescapable political dimension to Hapgood's removal from the CIO. His ouster marked the unsuccessful culmination of his attempt to reshape industrial unionism and test the boundaries of postwar American liberalism. Hapgood's fervent beliefs in nonsectarianism, union democracy, and political independence, and his militant opposition to racism were considered inappropriate as the cold war grew hot within the house of labor.

It was one thing to use the language of patriotism and citizenship to justify working-class mobilization but quite another to employ such imagery in defending Communists or pressing for strong measures to oppose racial discrimination. In this context Powers Hapgood was no match for those who appropriated the language of patriotism, citizenship, and character in order to buttress a cold war consensus. His purging illustrated just how narrowly the postwar CIO leadership defined the parameters of acceptable dissent. In an atmosphere where labor leaders feared for their survival, even a staunch non-Communist radical like Powers Hapgood was deemed expendable. Once again, he was sent into exile; his long journey from college to the ranks of labor was over, leaving him deeply disillusioned as he retired to the family farm.[36]

Allan Haywood offered to retain Hapgood as a special assistant but proposed an initial assignment that added insult to injury, suggesting that he go to Mayfield, Kentucky, to lead an organizing drive for the Amalgamated Clothing Workers. Whether or not Haywood intended to humiliate Hapgood is unclear. Not surprisingly, Hapgood refused the offer to revisit a political cul-de-sac and devoted himself to full-time management of the farm. Throughout 1948, he attended gatherings of the Socialist Party, Americans for Democratic Action, and the UMWA, attempting to maintain some feel for the liberal political pulse in America. Perhaps seeking to rediscover the spirit that had first attracted him to the labor movement, he made a pilgrimage to Somerset, where he visited Mike Demchak, an old ally from his days as a UMWA insurgent, who was continuing the lonely fight for union autonomy. He also contemplated a political comeback by running for statewide office as a Democrat, a quest that was never fulfilled. Driving back to the farm from Indianapolis, Powers Hapgood died of a heart attack on February 4, 1949, ten months short of his fiftieth birthday.[37]

A memorial service for Hapgood at the Amalgamated Clothing Workers' hall in Indianapolis brought together both elite and mass. Among the mourners were the governor of Indiana; red caps and other workers whom he had helped to organize; UMWA colleagues; and a host of political, labor, and civic leaders. John Brophy suppressed whatever misgivings he had had about Hapgood's course and read the simple miners' burial rites, honoring his protege by recalling the identity that had given him his deepest and most enduring pleasure. Hapgood's death prompted an outpouring of emotion from across the political spectrum. Mary Donovan recalled that one of the people "so instrumental in having Powers thrown out of the CIO job" was weeping uncontrollably in the rear of the union hall. John L. Lewis saluted his old foe for having "the moral strength to acknowledge error when such acknowledgment was constructive or dictated by the equities of relationships between men." The archconservative *Indianapolis Star*, which believed that "the Socialist theories espoused by Mr. Hapgood will destroy America," nonetheless praised him as a "good, loyal American." Tragically, these tributes came too late to acknowledge the legitimacy of Powers Hapgood's dissent or to salvage his career. As Rose Pesotta observed, his death symbolized the passing of a certain vision of trade unionism, one that would not be easily revived.[38]

Indeed, it was Rose Pesotta who most acutely grasped the disappointments and unresolved tensions of Hapgood's life. Although their contact had virtually ceased following the war, she never relinquished her loyalty to the man she called her "pal." She knew the painful family conflicts that clouded his final years, the devastation exacted by his alcoholism, his frustrations with the working class and the CIO, and the depth of his unrequited love for her. Learning of Hapgood's death over the radio, Pesotta rushed to Indianapolis. Publicly, she eulogized her pal as "an idealist of the purest, rarest quality, which has become an extinct species." She also noted that he had taken pride "in doing the type of work most labor leaders would shun away from."[39] Privately, she was deeply anguished: "He had no other alternative but to choose the farm as his duty but his heart was in the labor movement, once he severed his active connections there his heart was gone out of him and a man can not be sustained by duty alone . . . it was not what Powers deserved. . . . Few really understood what an unhappy man he was."[40] Pesotta concluded her public eulogy with an elegiac reflection that captured both the promise and pathos of Powers Hapgood's odyssey: "And he died as he lived—at the wheel—driving, driving into the dark unknown, alone and unafraid."[41]

Epilogue

The industrial union edifice that Powers Hapgood helped erect endured for nearly four decades. Buoyed by a cold war economy and America's dominant role in an increasingly global marketplace, unionized workers reaped the benefits of collective bargaining. Strong industrial unions led the way in negotiating an impressive array of benefits akin to those that William Hapgood had provided Columbia Conserve workers. Union contracts offered protection against abuses on the shop floor, while labor's prominent role within the Democratic Party enabled workers to defend their bargaining table gains in the political arena. These achievements would have pleased Powers Hapgood, for they marked the emergence of a legitimacy for the labor movement, something he had fought to establish throughout his career.

Hapgood's pleasure in these accomplishments would surely be tempered by other developments. In his beloved UMWA, the corrosive effects of John L. Lewis's autocratic reign culminated with the union's near total descent into corruption and thuggery. The rigid cold-war consensus embraced by most labor leaders perpetuated a self-congratulatory, uncritical vision that left unions ill prepared to respond to the challenges posed by a changing political climate and the rise of a global economy. The post–World War II era was also marked by a diminished commitment to organizing and a cautious approach to fighting racial discrimination that resulted in the perception, however unfair, that labor was a special interest more concerned with defending the status quo than with extending democratic and egalitarian values. The support for the Vietnam War by the AFL-CIO leadership confirmed this perception for many middle-class liberals, intellectuals, and youthful radicals and led to their estrangement from the labor movement. Although some New Left and civil rights movement veterans found their way into union jobs, most did not regard the labor movement with the reverence and hope that had inspired Powers Hapgood and his circle several generations earlier.

But there are clear signs that the strained relationship among labor, intellectuals, and young people is on the mend. The expansion of multinational corporations and the advent of fierce international competition have triggered convulsive changes in America's economic and social structure, prompting a growing debate over what rules should govern corporate behavior in the new global marketplace. Although many working- and middle-class Americans have benefited from the current economic boom, they have begun to question the growing maldistribution of wealth and income, the erosion of job security, and the stresses involved in balancing the demands of work and family life. Young people are also expressing concern about their economic futures and their status in the twenty-first-century workplace. Moreover, there is a growing awareness on college campuses and elsewhere of the reemergence of sweatshops and the appalling conditions under which articles of clothing and other goods purchased by middle-class consumers are often produced.

Simultaneously, the labor movement appears more prepared than at any time within the last three decades to respond to these concerns. The election of John Sweeney as AFL-CIO president in 1995 signaled labor's willingness to adopt a more thoughtful and aggressive approach toward reversing its declining membership, overcoming its political marginalization, and reestablishing its status as a spokesperson for American workers. Equally important, Sweeney, an Irish Catholic whose moral sensibilities recall John Brophy's faith-based politics, has called upon labor to engage in an extended process of reflection and self-criticism as an integral part of developing a strategy for its revitalization. Powers Hapgood would certainly have endorsed this approach, which bears more than a passing resemblance to the "larger program" that he and Brophy had proposed for resuscitating the UMWA.

The new AFL-CIO leadership has made a special effort to reach out to liberals, intellectuals, and the young. Even before Sweeney's election, the AFL-CIO had established an Organizing Institute charged with recruiting and training young people from both college and rank-and-file backgrounds to become union organizers. The institute's resources have been increased under the current AFL-CIO leadership, attracting hundreds of college students to unions and bringing labor into much closer contact with academia. This unprecedented attempt to recruit young people reflects not only labor's profound need for capable organizers but also a serious attempt to forge new ties among unionists, academics, and the middle class. The AFL-CIO has also consciously sought a rapprochement with potential liberal allies, sponsoring numerous gatherings aimed at reinvigorating the lapsed alliances between labor and elements of the middle class that were so important to Powers Hapgood and his generation.[1]

Powers Hapgood's career provides valuable insights for a labor movement attempting to revitalize itself and for liberal intellectuals and young people seeking to support its efforts. Hapgood understood that labor was most effective when it articulated a moral argument and reminded Americans that treating workers as a commodity was one of the surest ways to undermine the nation's democratic ideals. His recognition that civic participation in both workplace and society was a necessary antidote to bureaucracy and elitism is especially relevant at a time when new configurations of wealth and power threaten to overwhelm possibilities for democratic control and assertions of the public good.

Hapgood's advocacy of an aggressive approach to eradicating racial discrimination should be a priority for a movement that must contend with significant demographic changes in the working class. His ability to wage political fights without succumbing to bitterness or demonizing his opponents reflected an awareness that has dwindled in contemporary politics and diminished the educational possibilities of vigorous public debate. Finally, Hapgood's willingness to explore, investigate, and reveal the working-class world to a middle-class audience identified a vital task that deserves greater attention today. By examining crucial changes in the workplace and the employment relationship, intellectuals, journalists, and social observers have the opportunity to spur public debate and prompt action on issues long neglected in our social policy and political discourse.

Powers Hapgood's experience also offers some cautionary notes, especially to middle-class liberals and intellectuals seeking a closer relationship with the labor movement. He reminds us of the dangers of romanticizing the working class and embracing nostalgia over critical analysis. His life illustrates the limits of a universal, secular vision that fails to appreciate the cultural affinities, local attachments, and multiple identities that often shape and define working-class lives. His example also reveals the risks involved when political action is guided excessively by personal need. In the wake of the New Left's disintegration and the rise of what has come to be called "identity politics," the historic tendency of middle-class radicals to obscure distinctions between their personal needs and the complex demands of public life has become even more pronounced. If these activists are to contribute to a revitalized liberal-labor alliance, they need to move beyond the politics of personal identity and commit themselves to finding common ground with working people.

But Powers Hapgood's greatest legacy may lie in the realm of spirit and sensibility. Whether enjoying victory or experiencing defeat, Hapgood remained a passionate searcher, unwilling to relax his ethical commitments and or to surrender his visionary dreams. This spirit was eloquently expressed in a Christmas greeting sent out by his CIO office in 1943. More than fifty years later, his message retains the power to motivate and inspire: "Whereas, Productive work, not for the snatched profit, but for the common good and for the planned destiny of mankind is our ultimate purpose; now, therefore be it resolved, That we practice patience with those who wait restlessly for this, and hope to those who have ceased to believe that it will come."[2]

Notes

Introduction

1. Kurt Vonnegut, *Jailbird* (New York, 1979), 13, 18.

Chapter 1. "A Sincere, Consuming Quest for a Faith"

1. Hutchins Hapgood and Neith Boyce, "The Story of an American Family," manuscript, 112–13, Powers Hapgood Papers, Lilly Library, Indiana University (hereafter PH Papers); Gerold Baumann, "Powers Hapgood: Profile of a Hoosier Radical" (master's thesis, Butler University, 1964); "Biographical Sketch of the Late Seth Hapgood," Norman and Elizabeth Reynolds Hapgood Papers, Manuscript Division, Library of Congress; Norman Hapgood, *The Changing Years: Reminiscences of Norman Hapgood* (New York, 1930), 23–24.

2. Michael Marcaccio, *The Hapgoods: Three Earnest Brothers* (Charlottesville, 1971), 1–7, 214–18; Hutchins Hapgood, *A Victorian in the Modern World* (Seattle, 1972), 17, 41, 55, 256, 431–32; Moses Rischin, introduction to Hutchins Hapgood, *The Spirit of the Ghetto* (Cambridge, 1967), xi; Norman Hapgood, *Changing Years,* 11–12, 41. On nineteenth-century middle-class values, see Janet Fishburn, *The Fatherhood of God and the Victorian Family: The Social Gospel in America* (Philadelphia, 1981), 12–20.

3. Hutchins Hapgood, *Victorian in the Modern World,* 17, 41, 55, 256, 431–32; Rischin, *Spirit of the Ghetto,* xi; Norman Hapgood, *Changing Years,* 6.

4. Marcaccio, *Hapgoods,* 18–19; Hutchins Hapgood, *Victorian in the Modern World,* 55, 66; Rischin, *Spirit of the Ghetto,* xii.

5. Marcaccio, *Hapgoods,* 73–86, 116–40; Christopher Lasch, *The New Radicalism in America, 1889–1963: The Intellectual as a Social Type* (New York, 1965), 165.

6. Marcaccio, *Hapgoods,* 18–19; Hutchins Hapgood, *Victorian in the Modern World,* 128, 204–6, 331; John P. Diggins, *The American Left in the Twentieth Century* (New York,

1973), 78; Christopher Lasch, *The True and Only Heaven: Progress and Its Critics* (New York, 1991), 38.

7. Marcaccio, *Hapgoods,* 165–67; Hutchins Hapgood, *Victorian in the Modern World,* 24–27, 255–57; Powers Hapgood (hereafter PH) to Father, December 25, 1925, PH Papers.

8. Hutchins Hapgood, *Victorian in the Modern World,* 256; Marcaccio, *Hapgoods,* 165–67; John Bartlow Martin, *Indiana: An Interpretation* (Bloomington, 1992), 159–60; Boyd Gurley, "Business Without a Boss," *Indiana Times,* February 13, 1930; Louis Filler, introduction to William P. Hapgood, *The Columbia Conserve Company: An Experiment in Workers' Management and Ownership* (Philadelphia, 1975); and Russell E. Vance, Jr., "An Unsuccessful Experiment in Industrial Democracy: The Columbia Conserve Company" (Ph.D. diss., Indiana University, 1956), 21. Powers Hapgood's daughter, Barta Monro, recalled that the family frequently referred to the individual forays of its members as "another great Hapgood experiment," suggesting that risk-taking occupied an honored if ironic family status. Author's interview with Barta Monro, April 14, 1990.

9. William P. Hapgood, *Columbia Conserve Company,* 44, 46; *Information Service,* Department of Research and Education, Federal Council of Churches of Christ in America, October 31, 1931.

10. Baumann, "Profile of a Hoosier Radical," 3; Edward A. Leary, *Indianapolis: The Story of a City* (Indianapolis, 1971), 135–37; Clifton J. Phillips, *Indiana in Transition* (Bloomington, 1968), 366; James H. Madison, *The Indiana Way* (Bloomington, 1986), 177–78; Martin, *Indiana,* 89–100.

11. Madison, *Indiana,* 168, 186, 227–28, 291.

12. Ibid., 166.

13. PH Diary, January 6, 27, 1915, March 25, 1915, April 23, 1915, August 29, 1915, PH Papers.

14. PH Diary, January 24, 1915, March 9, 14, 15, 24, 1915, April 1, 6, 10, 27, 1915, May 10, 1915, PH Papers; John Brophy, interview with John Hall, undated, box A5–39, reel 10, 94, John Brophy Papers, Department of Archives and Manuscripts, Catholic University of America, Washington, D.C. (hereafter Brophy Papers).

15. PH Diary, February 14, 1915, April 7, 8, 27, 1915, PH to Mother and Father, March 21, 1918, PH to Mother, April 3, 1918, October 19, 1920, PH to Mother and Father, November 14, 1920, PH to Father, November 15, 1920, Father to Lad, October 15, 1923, PH Papers. On neurasthenia, see E. Anthony Rotundo, *American Manhood: Transformations in Masculinity from the Revolution to the Modern Era* (New York, 1993), 185–87; and Tom Lutz, *American Nervousness, 1903: An Anecdotal History* (Ithaca, 1991), 32–33.

16. Peter Filene, *Him / Her / Self: Sex Roles in Modern America* (Baltimore, 1986), 76; PH to Uncle Hutch (Hutchins Hapgood), February 7, 1929, PH Diary, February 25, 1917, PH Papers.

17. PH Diary, January 8, 11, 1915, notes at conclusion of 1915 diary on Hill Club, PH Papers.

18. Fishburn, *Fatherhood of God,* 158–60; Henry May, *The End of American Innocence* (New York, 1959), 9; Lasch, *True and Only Heaven,* 166, and *New Radicalism in America,* 110–11; PH to Mother, April 3, 1918, PH to Mother and Father, March 21, 1919, PH Papers; Warren I. Susman, *Culture as History: The Transformation of American Society in the Twentieth Century* (New York, 1984), xix–xxx.

19. PH Diary, December 31, 1916, January 4, 20, 1917, March 2, 1917, PH to Aunt Yaya (Alice Page Converse), April 29, 1917, PH to Mother, November 18, 1917, PH Papers.

20. PH to Mother and Father, November 29, 1917, December 2, 10, 12, 1917, January 3, 20, 23, 27, 1918, March 6, 1918, PH Papers.

21. "The Reminiscences of Gardner Jackson," Columbia University Oral History Collection, New York, 1955, 75–104; David M. Kennedy, *Over Here: The First World War and American Society* (Oxford, 1980), 178–85.

22. Nick Salvatore, *Eugene V. Debs: Citizen and Socialist* (Urbana, 1982), 46–47.

23. PH Diary, December 28, 1916, March 17, 1918, January 7, 1920, PH to Mother and Father, December 17, 1917, PH Papers; Joseph Freeman, *An American Testament: A Narrative of Rebels and Romantics* (London, 1938), 142; Rotundo, *American Manhood,* 224–36, 279–83.

24. Leslie Fishbein, *Rebels in Bohemia: The Radicals of the Masses, 1911–1917* (Chapel Hill, 1982), 154–55. On PH's reaction to his Uncle Hutch, see PH to Mother and Father, April 6, 1920, June 6, 1920, PH to Uncle Hutch, January 28, 1929, February 27, 1929, and Hutchins Hapgood to PH, February 4, 1929, PH Papers. The 1929 letters were an especially searing exchange, where PH expressed stern disapproval of what he regarded as his uncle's dissolute life. Hutchins's psychological woes were accentuated by the death of his son during the influenza epidemic of 1919. See *Victorian in the Modern World,* 432–33.

25. PH Diary, February 12, 1917, PH to Aunt Yaya, April 29, 1917, PH to Mother, November 18, 1917, PH Papers.

26. PH to Mother and Father, January 20, 1918, April 3, 1918, September 24, 1918, October 4, 1918, November 5, 10, 19, 1918, PH Papers.

27. PH to Mother and Father, February 2, 1918, PH to Mother, February 6, 1918, PH Papers; Hugh G. J. Aitken, *Taylorism at Watertown Arsenal: Scientific Management in Action, 1908–1915* (Cambridge, 1960), 149–54, 323–24.

28. PH to Mother and Father, April 14, 15, 18, 21, 1918, PH Papers.

29. PH to Mother and Father, February 9, 19, 1919, March 9, 15, 1919, PH Papers.

30. PH to Mother and Father, October 19, 1919, February 22, 1920, October 11, 1920, PH Papers.

31. PH to Mother and Father, March 5, 1919, PH Diary, March 1, 1920, PH Papers.

32. PH to Father, November 28, 1918, PH to Mother and Father, December 8, 1918, April 30, 1919, PH Diary, January 6, 1920, PH Papers.

33. PH to Mother and Father, December 8, 1918, March 5, 1919, November 9, 1919, PH to Aunt Yaya, March 14, 1920, PH Diary, March 1, 10, 1920, PH Papers; Carleton H. Parker, *The Casual Laborer and Other Essays* (Seattle, 1982), 4–7, 26, 59, 111, 164; Cornelia Stratton Parker, *An American Idyll: The Life of Carleton H. Parker* (Boston, 1919).

34. Freeman, *American Testament,* 170–71.

35. PH Diary, March 10, 1920, PH to Mother and Father, March 10, 1920, PH Papers. On J. T. "Red" Doran, see Joyce L. Kornbluh, ed., *Rebel Voices: An IWW Anthology* (Ann Arbor, 1964), 61–63.

36. PH Diary, March 10, 1920, PH Papers.

37. PH Diary, January 7, 1917, PH to Mother and Father, April 6, 1919, Gordon W. Allport to PH, April 30, 1919, PH to Mother, May 3, 1919, PH to Mother and Father, October 16, 1919, PH Papers; Raymond W. Albright, *Focus on Infinity: A Life of Phillips Brooks* (New York, 1961), 397.

38. PH to Mother, June 28, 1919, PH Papers.

39. PH Diary, December 31, 1919, January 2, 1920, March 28, 1920, PH Papers.

40. May, *End of American Innocence,* 311; Fishburn, *Fatherhood of God,* 117, 123–25; Timothy L. Smith, *Revivalism and Social Reform: American Protestantism on the Eve of the Civil War* (Gloucester, 1976); John L. Thomas, *Alternative America: Henry George, Edward Bellamy, Henry Demarest Lloyd and the Adversary Tradition* (Cambridge, 1983); Donald Meyer, *The Protestant Search for Political Realism, 1919–1941* (Middletown, 1988), 130; PH to Mother and Father, January 19, 1922, PH Papers; and Kurt Vonnegut, *Jailbird* (New York, 1979), 19–20. Vonnegut recalled a dialogue between Hapgood and an Indianapolis judge during a post–World War II court case. When the judge asked him why he had chosen to devote his life to the betterment of the working class, Hapgood reportedly replied: "Because of the Sermon on the Mount, sir."

41. PH to Mother, November 25, 1918, PH to Mother and Father, February 11, 1920, William P. Hapgood to PH, April 12, 1920, PH to Gilbert Grosvenor, March 22, 1920, PH Diary, January 5, 1920, PH Papers; Martin, *Indiana,* 164.

42. Marcaccio, *Hapgoods,* 167–69; Kim McQuaid, "Industry and the Cooperative Commonwealth: William P. Hapgood and the Columbia Conserve Company, 1917–1943," *Labor History* 17, no. 4 (fall 1976): 512–13; PH, "Railroad Ownership," March 17, 1919, and "The Life and Doctrines of Louis Blanc," January 4, 1920, PH Papers.

43. PH, "Democratic Government in Industry," April 14, 1919, "The Works Council Movement in the United States," May 1, 1920, PH Papers.

44. PH, "Democratic Government in Industry," "Works Council Movement"; Richard Edwards, *Contested Terrain: The Transformation of the Workplace in the Twentieth Century* (New York, 1979); 91–97; Lizabeth Cohen, *Making a New Deal: Industrial Workers in Chicago, 1919–1939* (Cambridge, 1990), 47, 171–73.

45. PH Diary, March 14, 1920, PH to Mother and Father, May 20, 1919, PH to Gilbert Grosvenor, March 22, 1920, PH, "From College to the Ranks of Labor," *The World Tomorrow* 6, no. 2 (February 1923): 49–50, PH Papers. The impulse to "bum" was not confined to Powers Hapgood and his friends. Gardner Jackson recalled that Robert Frost, who taught him at Amherst, encouraged his young student to leave school and "go on the bum" in order to experience life beyond the campus. See Jackson, "Reminiscences," 70.

2. *From College to the Ranks of Labor*

1. Warren Harding, quoted in William E. Leuchtenburg, *The Perils of Prosperity, 1914–1932* (Chicago, 1958), 89.

2. PH Journal, October 16, 1920, PH to Mother and Father, November 14, 1920, PH to Father, November 15, 1920, PH Papers.

3. PH Journal, October 6, 7, 12, 1920, PH to Mother and Father, October 6, 11, 1920, PH Papers; Carleton H. Parker, "Understanding Labor Unrest," in *The Casual Laborer and Other Essays* (Seattle, 1972), 27–55.

4. For other experiences with the IWW, see Len DeCaux to Hapgood, September 7, 1921, PH Papers; Peggy Lamson, *Roger Baldwin: Founder of the American Civil Liberties Union* (Boston, 1976), 92; and Joseph Maier and Richard W. Weatherhead, *Frank Tannenbaum: A Biographical Essay* (New York, 1974), 3–7.

5. PH Journal, October 16, 1920, PH to Mother and Father, November 14, 1920, PH to Father, November 15, 1920, PH Papers.

6. Carter Goodrich, *The Miner's Freedom* (Boston, 1925), 15, 22, 24, 41; John Brophy, *A Miner's Life* (Madison, 1964), 39; "The Reminiscences of John Brophy," Columbia University Oral History Collection, New York, 1972, 30–45; David Brody, *Workers in Industrial America: Essays on the Twentieth Century Struggle* (New York, 1980), 3–5; Ewa Morawska, "'For Bread with Butter': Life Worlds of Peasant Immigrants from East Central Europe, 1880–1914," *Journal of Social History* 17, no. 3 (spring 1984): 313–14; Robert H. Zieger, *John L. Lewis: Labor Leader* (Boston, 1988), 9–10; Whiting Williams, *What's on the Worker's Mind* (New York, 1920), 94, 123–25; and Christopher Lasch, *The True and Only Heaven: Progress and Its Critics* (New York, 1991), 300–303.

7. "Making Labor Pay," *The Nation* 114, no. 2960 (March 29, 1922): 360; PH Diary, October 1, 6, 26, 1920; "Why I Choose to be a Coal Miner," undated, PH Papers.

8. PH Journal, October 22, 26, 1920, PH Papers; J. L. Hutchinson to John Brophy, July 19, 1923, box 29, folder 6, Milhard B. Hanson to John L. Lewis, box 54, March 11, 1928, District 2 Papers, United Mine Workers of America Archives, Stapleton Library, Indiana University of Pennsylvania (hereafter District 2 Papers); Wilson Carey McWilliams, *The Idea of Fraternity in America* (Berkeley, 1973), 543; David Montgomery, *The Fall of the House of Labor: The Workplace, the State, and American Labor Activism, 1865–1925* (Cambridge, 1987), 338; and Alan Derickson, *Workers' Health, Workers' Democracy: The Western Miners' Struggle, 1891–1925* (Ithaca, 1988), 57–85.

9. "Prologue," PH Papers; "Reminiscences of John Brophy," 187; PH to Rose Pesotta, June 20, 1937, Rose Pesotta Papers, New York Public Library (hereafter RP Papers, NYPL).

10. PH to Mother and Father, October 21, 1920, November 11, 1920, PH Papers; Zieger, *John L. Lewis,* 10.

11. PH to Mother and Father, November 11, 1920, PH Papers; Melvyn Dubofsky and Warren Van Tine, *John L. Lewis: A Biography* (New York, 1977), 64; Nick Salvatore, ed., *Introduction to Seventy Years of Life and Labor: An Autobiography of Samuel Gompers* (Ithaca, 1984), xl–xli.

12. PH Journal, November 6, 1920, January 7, 1920, PH Papers.

13. Warren I. Susman, *Culture as History: The Transformation of American Society in the Twentieth Century* (New York, 1984), 271–85; Loren Baritz, *The Good Life: The Meaning of Success for the American Middle Class* (New York, 1989), chap. 2, esp. 56–83; Lasch, *True and Only Heaven,* 301; Henry May, *The End of American Innocence* (New York, 1959), 9; Joseph Freeman, *An American Testament: A Narrative of Rebels and Romantics* (London, 1938), 170; Michael Walzer, *The Company of Critics: Social Criticism and Political Commitment in the Twentieth Century* (New York, 1988), 21–22.

14. John P. Diggins, *Up from Communism: Conservative Odysseys in American Intellectual History* (New York, 1975), 80–81; John Dos Passos, quoted in Freeman, *American Testament,* 342.

15. PH, "Paternalism vs. Unionism in Mining Camps," *The Nation* 112, no. 2913 (May 4, 1921): 661–62; PH to Mother, December 7, 1920, PH Papers; Brody, *Workers in Industrial America,* 55; Donald Meyer, *The Protestant Search for Political Realism, 1919–1941* (Middletown, 1988), 63–64.

16. PH, "Paternalism vs. Unionism."

17. David M. Kennedy, *Over Here: The First World War and American Society* (Oxford, 1980), 92, 292–94; Leuchtenburg, *Perils of Prosperity,* 140–57; Peter Filene, *Him/Her/Self: Sex Roles in Modern America* (Baltimore, 1986), 122–23, 133–34, 140; Loren Baritz, introduction to *The Culture of the Twenties* (Indianapolis, 1970); Susman, *Culture as History,* 105–21, 271–85.

18. Meyer, *Protestant Search for Political Realism,* 55–106; Steve Fraser, *Labor Will Rule: Sidney Hillman and the Rise of American Labor* (New York, 1991), 160–61; Leuchtenburg, *Perils of Prosperity,* 130–39; Kennedy, *Over Here,* 293–95.

19. PH to Mother, January 23, 1921, PH Diary, February 10, 1921, PH Papers.

20. PH Diary, March 26, 1921, PH Papers; Susman, *Culture as History,* 89, 96.

21. PH Diary, February 15, 17, 1921, March 21, 1921, PH Papers.

22. Maier and Weatherhead, *Frank Tannenbaum,* 4–6; Freeman, *American Testament,* 68–70; May, *End of American Innocence,* 302; PH Diary, June 16, 1921, PH Papers; Louis Filler, *Vanguards and Followers: Youth in the American Tradition* (Chicago, 1978), 56.

23. Frank Tannenbaum, quoted in Maier and Weatherhead, *Frank Tannenbaum,* 8; PH Diary, February 24, 1921, June 10, 16, 1921; PH to Mother and Father, June 28, 1921, PH Papers; Susman, *Culture as History,* 76.

24. PH Diary, February 24, 1921, June 10, 16, 1921, PH to Mother and Father, June 28, 1921, PH Papers; Freeman, *American Testament,* 375.

25. Lamson, *Roger Baldwin,* 12, 17–19, 46, 110–11, 118; Freeman, *American Testament,* 292–94.

26. PH Diary, March 16, 1921, June 14, 19, 1921, PH Papers; John A. Saltmarsh, *Scott Nearing: An Intellectual Biography* (Philadelphia, 1991), 34, 50, 52.

27. PH Diary, February 20, 1921, March 3, 7, 8, 1921; PH Papers; Brophy, *Miner's Life,* 184; Elizabeth Cocke Ricketts, "'Our Battle for Industrial Freedom': Radical Politics in the Coal Fields of Central Pennsylvania, 1916–1920" (Ph.D. diss., Emory University, 1996), 375–76; Sanford M. Jacoby, *Employing Bureaucracy: Managers, Unions, and the Transformation of Work in American Industry, 1900–1945* (New York, 1985), 102–3.

28. John Brophy, interview with John Hall, box A5–39, reel 10, 93–94, Brophy Papers; "Reminiscences of John Brophy," 24; Brophy, *Miner's Life,* 3–14, 24; Brody, *Workers in Industrial America,* 3–5.

29. "Reminiscences of John Brophy," 189–251; Brophy, *Miner's Life,* 122; L. A. O'Donnell, *Irish Voice and Organized Labor in America: A Biographical Study* (Westport, 1997), 163–77; Report of President John Brophy to the 28th Consecutive and 5th Biennial Convention, District No. 2, United Mine Workers of America, March 1922, box 316, District 2 Papers, 19; Ricketts: "'Battle for Industrial Freedom,'" 372–77.

30. Report of President John Brophy, 18.

31. Brophy, interview with John Hall, box A5–39, reel 10, 94–95, Brophy Papers; PH Diary, March 26, 1921, July 5, 10, 1921, PH Papers; Antonio Gramsci, quoted in Michael Walzer, *The Company of Critics: Social Criticism and Political Commitment in the Twentieth Century* (New York, 1988), 91, and "Fascist Reaction and Communist Strategy, 1924–1926," in *An Antonio Gramsci Reader: Selected Writings, 1916–1935,* ed. David Forgacs (New York, 1988), 184–85.

32. PH Diary, March 23, 24, 30, 1921, PH Papers.

33. PH, "Car-Pushing in the Mines," *Survey* 46, no. 10 (June 4, 1921): 310–11; "Report on Compensation Investigation Among the Coal Miners of District No. 2, UMWA," undated, 1921; PH Diary, July 6, 8, 9, 1921, PH Papers; Report of President John Brophy, 26–27.

34. PH, "In Non-Union Mines: The Diary of a Coal Digger" (New York, 1921).

35. PH, "Journal of My Trip to the Non-Union Coal Fields in Pennsylvania," August 8, 24, 31, 1921, PH Papers; PH, "In Non-Union Mines," 46. An advertisement for Hapgood's journal in the April 12, 1922, issue of the *New Republic* was subtitled "Daily Record of the

Human Side of Getting Coal in Central Pennsylvania," a description that underscored his determination to arouse the conscience of his readers.

36. PH, "In Non-Union Mines," 28, 30, 40, 46, Mildred Allen Beik, *The Miners of Windber: The Struggles of New Immigrants for Unionization, 1890s–1930s* (University Park, 1996), 256–57.

37. PH, "In Non-Union Mines," 30–31.

38. Ibid., 7, 48.

39. Ibid., 48.

40. PH to Mother and Father, January 19, 1922, PH Papers.

41. Ibid.

42. Ibid.

43. Ibid.; E. Anthony Rotundo, *American Manhood: Transformations in Masculinity from the Revolution to the Modern Era* (New York, 1993), 226–31.

44. Mother and Father to Powers, January 21, 1922, PH Papers.

45. PH to Mother and Father, January 19, 1922, PH Papers.

46. Christopher Lasch, *The New Radicalism in America, 1889–1963: The Intellectual as a Social Type* (New York, 1965), 227, and *True and Only Heaven,* 301; Hutchins Hapgood, *The Spirit of Labor* (New York, 1907) 215; May, *End of American Innocence,* 302; John Patrick Diggins, *The American Left in the Twentieth Century* (New York, 1973), 78; Leslie Fishbein, *Rebels in Bohemia: The Radicals of the Masses, 1911–1917* (Chapel Hill, 1982), 4, 6, 111; Richard Davis Gillam, "C. Wright Mills: An Intellectual Biography" (Ph.D. diss., Stanford University, 1972), 46, 87, 180, 209; and Todd Gitlin, *The Sixties: Years of Hope, Days of Rage* (New York, 1987), 362–76, 424–27. For memoirs of radicals attesting to the personal motives that spurred political commitment, see Len DeCaux, *Labor Radical, From the Wobblies to the CIO, A Personal History* (Boston, 1970); George Charney, *A Long Journey* (Chicago, 1968); Freeman, *American Testament;* and Junius Scales and Richard Nickson, *Cause at Heart: A Former Communist Remembers* (Athens, 1987). For contrasting views of radicals with working-class origins, see Steve Nelson, James R. Barrett, and Rob Ruck, *Steve Nelson: American Radical* (Pittsburgh, 1981); and Wyndham Mortimer, *Organize! My Life as a Union Man* (Boston, 1971).

47. PH, "Why I Choose to Be a Coal Miner," undated; "On Being a Manual Worker (An Appeal to Young Progressives)," *New Student* 12, no. 17 (May 19, 1923): 5; "From College to the Ranks of Labor," *The World Tomorrow* 6, no. 2 (February 1923): 49–50, PH Papers.

48. PH, "On Being a Manual Worker," "Why I Choose to Be a Coal Miner;" Daniel T. Rodgers, *The Work Ethic in Industrial America, 1850–1920* (Chicago, 1978), 211–19; Rotundo, *American Manhood,* 234.

49. PH, "Why I Choose to Be a Coal Miner." On labor's plight in the 1920s, see Brody, *Workers in Industrial America,* 45; Leuchtenburg, *Perils of Prosperity,* 124–27, 140–45; Irving Bernstein, *The Lean Years: A History of the American Worker, 1920–1933* (Baltimore, 1966); and Loren Baritz, *The Good Life: The Meaning of Success for the American Middle Class* (New York, 1990), 106, 116.

50. Hank Costigan to PH, June 2, 1921, Horace B. Davis to PH, July 9, 1921, April 28, 1922, PH to Mother, August 19, 1921, PH Diary, June 13, 1921, Len DeCaux to PH, February 25, 1922, August 8, 1922, PH to Mother and Father, July 30, 1922, Alice Kimball to PH, February 19, 1923, PH to Mother, June 12, 1924, PH Papers; PH, "From College to the Ranks of Labor," 49–50; Clarke A. Chambers, *Seedtime of Reform: American Social Service and Social Action, 1918–1933* (Ann Arbor, 1967), 110–11; Freeman, *American Testament,* 371–80; Filler, *Vanguards and Followers,* 56; Nancy Schrom Dye, *As Equals and Sisters: Feminism, the Labor Movement, and the Women's*

Trade Union League of New York (Columbia, 1980), 36–44; Clarence Darrow, quoted in Lamson, *Roger Baldwin,* 120.

51. PH Diary, June 14, 1921, PH to Roger Baldwin, February 23, 1922, PH Papers.

52. Lamson, *Roger Baldwin,* 92; PH to Rose Pesotta, September 1936, RP Papers, NYPL; Eloise to Powers, December 21, 1921, March 11, 1922, PH Diary, June 13, 1921, PH Papers.

53. Bernard K. Johnpoll, *The Impossible Dream: The Rise and Demise of the American Left* (Westport, 1981), 18, 21, 29.

54. PH to Mother and Father, January 19, 1922, PH Papers.

3. *The Somerset Strike*

1. PH to Mother, March 9, 1922, PH Papers.

2. Melvyn Dubofsky and Warren Van Tine, *John L. Lewis: A Biography* (New York, 1977), 75–76; Robert H. Zieger, *John L. Lewis: Labor Leader* (Boston, 1988), 26–27; John Brophy, *A Miner's Life* (Madison, 1964); 178–80.

3. Dubofsky and Van Tine, *John L. Lewis,* 78–80; Philip Murray to John L. Lewis, August 11, 1921, John L. Lewis to Philip Murray, August 12, 1921, box 27.5a, United Mine Workers of America Papers, Historical Collections and Labor Archives, Pennsylvania State University (hereafter UMWA Papers).

4. Brophy, *Miner's Life,* 180; Heber Blankenhorn, *The Strike for Union* (New York, 1924), 10.

5. Dubofsky and Van Tine, *John L. Lewis,* 76; Mildred Allen Beik, *The Miners of Windber: The Struggles of New Immigrants for Unionization, 1890s-1930s* (University Park, 1996), xxii; Blankenhorn, *Strike for Union,* 8; "Questions for Coal Barons," *New Republic* 31, no. 390 (May 24, 1922): 360–61; Murray to Lewis, August 11, 1921, Lewis to Murray, August 12, 1921, box 27.5a, UMWA Papers.

6. PH to Mother, April 10, 1922, PH to Mother and Father, April 23, 1922; PH, "Why I Choose to Be a Miner," PH Papers.

7. Brophy, *Miner's Life,* 176, 184; Dubofsky and Van Tine, *John L. Lewis,* 82.

8. Blankenhorn, *Strike for Union,* 14, 68; Beik, *Miners of Windber,* 261–62. For examples of requests for organizing before the strike, see Michael J. Musilek, et al. to John Brophy, February 14, 1919, Charles Burke to John Brophy, February 18, 1919, Joseph Seidel to John Brophy, March 18, 1920, E. J. Gaentz to John Brophy, March 28, 1919, box 33, Edward J. Robinson to John Brophy, May 13, 1918, box 38, District 2 Papers.

9. Blankenhorn, *Strike for Union,* 46; Local 3084, District 2, United Mine Workers of America, "To All Organized Labor of America and Canada," January 20, 1922, box 27.5a, UMWA Papers; Consolidation Coal miners petition, October 9, 1922, box 29, District 2 Papers. On the meaning of industrial democracy during World War I, see Joseph A. McCartin, "'An American Feeling': Workers, Managers, and the Struggle over Industrial Democracy in the World War I Era," in *Industrial Democracy in America: The Ambiguous Promise,* ed. Nelson Lichtenstein and Howell John Harris (Cambridge, 1993), 67–86.

10. Blankenhorn, *Strike for Union,* 134, and "Liberty and Union in the Coal Fields," *The Nation* 114, no. 2967 (May 17, 1922): 594–96; Elizabeth Cocke Ricketts, "'Our Battle for Industrial Freedom': Radical Politics in the Coal Fields of Central Pennsylvania,

1916–1920" (Ph.D. diss., Emory University, 1996), 465; PH to Mother and Father, June 26, 28, 1922, PH Papers.

11. Blankenhorn, *Strike for Union,* 39, 121, 135; Ricketts, "'Battle for Industrial Freedom,'" 461–62; PH to Mother and Father, July 22, 1922, PH Papers.

12. Blankenhorn, *Strike for Union,* 80–81; Len DeCaux, *Labor Radical: From the Wobblies to the CIO, A Personal History* (Boston, 1970), 94; PH to Mother and Father, June 28, 1922, Maude McCreary to PH, August, 1922, PH Papers; *Johnstown (Pa.) Herald,* May 1, 1922, July 25, 1922; *Johnstown (Pa.) Ledger,* May 2, 1922.

13. Blankenhorn, *Strike for Union,* 80–81; Beik, *Miners of Windber,* 306–7.

14. PH to Mother and Father, November 12, 1923, PH Papers; *Quemahoning Coal Company vs. John Brophy, et al.,* box 29, file 10, 61, 91–92, District 2 Papers.

15. Blankenhorn, *Strike for Union,* 39, 46, 182–84, 187, 233; PH to Mother and Father, December 12, 1922, PH Papers; John Kerr to John Brophy, September 27, 1922, box 30, file 6, John Brophy to J. G. Brown, March 22, 1922, box 29, file 3, J. L. Hutchinson to John Brophy, July 19, 1923, box 29, file 6, District 2 Papers.

16. John Brophy, Report on Civil Liberties to John Hays Hammond and Members of U.S. Coal Commission, May 28, 1923; PH to Mother and Father, May 21, 1922, unsigned letter to PH, November 7, 1922, PH Papers; Blankenhorn, *Strike for Union,* 133; Beik, *Miners of Windber,* 284–85, 292–93; Arthur Taylor to John Brophy, June 28, 1922, box 30, file 11, District 2 Papers.

17. Dubofsky and Van Tine, *John L. Lewis,* 86–87; PH to Mother and Father, August 16, 1922, PH to Mother, September 3, 1922, PH Papers; Brophy, *Miner's Life,* 194–99.

18. Brophy, *Miner's Life,* 190–92; John Dushaw and John Mitchell to John L. Lewis, September 17, 1922, box 27.5a, UMWA Papers. For correspondence on the Revloc issue, see John Brophy to John L. Lewis, September 21, 1922, L. G. Ball to John L. Lewis, September 5, 1922, J. H. Weaver to John L. Lewis, September 5, 26, 1922, box 27.5a, UMWA Papers.

19. Dubofsky and Van Tine, *John L. Lewis,* 87, 122; PH to Mother and Father, August 16, 1922, PH Papers.

20. PH to Mother and Father, August 16, 1922, PH Papers. A perceptive account of Lewis's philosophy is found in Dubofsky and Van Tine, *John L. Lewis,* 29, 80, 299. Compare John Brophy's assessment in "The Reminiscences of John Brophy," Columbia University Oral History Collection, New York, 1972, 602–28.

21. Colin J. Davis, *Power at Odds: The 1922 Railroad Shopmen's Strike* (Urbana, 1997), 130–32; Zieger, *John L. Lewis,* 5; David Brody, *In Labor's Cause: Main Themes on the History of the American Worker* (New York, 1993), 149; Alan J. Singer, "'Something of a Man': John L. Lewis, the UMWA, and the CIO, 1919–1943," in *The United Mine Workers of America: A Model of Industrial Solidarity?* ed. John H. M. Laslett (University Park, 1996), 110–13; John L. Lewis, "The Futility of Union Democracy," in *Unions, Management, and the Public,* ed. E. Wight Bakke, Clark Kerr, and Charles W. Anrod, (New York, 1967), 178–80.

22. Brophy, *Miner's Life,* 192–93; PH to Mother and Father, June 6, 14, 19, 1922, July 4, 11, 18, 1922, October 18, 1922, William P. Hapgood to PH, June 14, 1922, PH to Uncle Norman, August 20, 1922, Elizabeth Brandeis to PH, October 10, 1922, PH Papers; Roger Baldwin to John Brophy, July 29, 1922, September 23, 1922, John Brophy to Roger Baldwin, September 30, 1922, box 31, file 2, District 2 Papers; PH to Norman Hapgood, June 13, 1922, Norman and Elizabeth Reynolds Hapgood Papers, Library of Congress; Elizabeth Gilman to editor, *The Nation* 114, no. 2967 (May 17, 1922): 344.

23. PH, "Coal and Men," Mary Donovan Hapgood Papers, Lilly Library, Indiana University, Bloomington (hereafter MDH Papers).

24. Blank (Heber Blankenhorn) to Jim (James Mark), September 20, 1922, box 32, District 2 Papers.

25. Memorandum of Delegation of Miners in New York and Washington, September 30, 1922, PH Papers; "The Case of the Somerset Miners," "Memorandum for Powers Hapgood on Things to Be Done in District No. 2," Miners' Committee of Somerset and Cambria County, Pennsylvania Strikers to His Honor Mayor Hylan and the Board of Estimate, box 49, District 2 Papers; Blankenhorn, *Strike for Union,* 174–75; Eileen Mountjoy Cooper, "That Magnificent Fight for Unionism," *Pennsylvania Heritage* 17, no.4 (fall 1991): 12–17; PH, "The Coal Strike Continues," *New Republic* 32, no. 409 (October 4, 1922): 147; McAlister Coleman, *Men and Coal* (New York, 1943), 86–87.

26. Draft, Statement of Miners to Mayor Hylan, *Penn Central News,* September 23, 1922, box 27.5a, UMWA Papers; Edward J. Berwind to William W. Woodin, September 27, 1922, box 49; Miners Delegation news release, September 29, 30, 1922, box 31, Delegation of Pennsylvania Miners to Honorable Charles Craig, box 29, "The Case of the Somerset Miners," District 2 Papers; Albert (Armstrong) to PH, October 8, 1922, PH to Mother and Father, November 19, 1922, December 10, 1922, Mary Blankenhorn to PH, December 12, 1922, PH Papers; Brophy, *Miner's Life,* 198.

27. "Statement of Facts and Summary of Committee Appointed by Honorable John F. Hylan to Investigate the Labor Conditions at the Berwind-White Company's Coal Mines in Somerset and Other Counties, Pennsylvania," December 1922, box 45, Heber Blankenhorn Papers, Archives of Industrial Society, Hillman Library, University of Pittsburgh; Mary Blankenhorn to PH, December 12, 1922, PH Papers; Brophy, *Miner's Life,* 194.

28. PH to Mother and Father, April 23, 1922, July 22, 1922, Allison to PH, May 15, 1924, PH Papers; "Making Labor Pay," *The Nation* 114, no. 2960 (March 29, 1922): 360; Daniel Horowitz, *The Morality of Spending: Attitudes Towards the Consumer Society in America* (Baltimore, 1985), 125–27; David M. Kennedy, *Over Here: The First World War and American Society* (New York, 1980), 288–92.

29. Brophy, *Miner's Life,* 195–96; PH to Mother and Father, January 25, 1923, PH Papers; Charles S. Davidson to editor, *Penn Central News,* February 14, 1923, District 2 Papers; Resolutions on Back Pay Issue, Local 3408 (February 12, 1923), Local 570 (February 12, 1923), Local 1995 (February 9, 1923), Local 176 (February 6, 1923), Local 1924 (February 7, 1923), Local 476 (January 29, 1923), Local 842 (January 17, 1923), Local 1056 (undated), box 32, District 2 Papers; Minutes of the Proceedings of Special Convention of UMWA, District 2, April 17, 1923, box 329, District 2 Papers.

30. Brophy, *Miner's Life,* 196–97; PH to Mother and Father, April 1, 1923, PH to Somerset County Officers and Members, May 23, 1923, PH Papers; Frank Hefferly to John L. Lewis, June 7, 1923, box 27.5a, UMWA Papers.

31. Minutes of Special Convention, April 17, 1923; PH to Mother and Father, April 14, 1923, PH Papers.

32. Minutes of Special Convention, April 17, 1923, PH Papers.

33. John Brophy to Arthur Gleason, July 12, 1923, Brophy Papers; Edward P. Johanningsmeier, *Forging American Communism: The Life of William Z. Foster* (Princeton, 1994), 186.

34. Minutes of the Progressive International Conference of the UMWA, June 2, 1923, John L. Lewis to John Brophy, July 11, 1923, PH to Mother, February 6, 11, 1923, PH Papers; Dubofsky and Van Tine, *John L. Lewis,* 122–24.

35. For criticism of PH by Lewis partisans, see PH to Mother, April 23, 1923, PH to Mother and Father, December 30, 1923, January 10, 1924, PH Papers.

36. PH to Mother and Father, July 20, 1923, District 2, UMWA, to Local Unions, August 14, 1923, PH Papers; Beik, *Miners of Windber,* 306–9.

37. Frank Tannenbaum to PH, May 20, 1922, J. J. Doran to Anna N. Davis, May 21, 1922, Mary Blankenhorn to Eleanor Page Hapgood, September 30, 1922, PH Papers; PH, "Coal Strike Continues," 147.

38. PH to Mother and Father, April 23, 1922, July 22, 1922, September 5, 1922, William Hapgood to PH, October 9, 1923, PH Papers; PH, "Coal Strike Continues," 147.

39. PH to Mother and Father, September 5, 1922; PH Papers; PH, "Coal Strike Continues," 147; Christopher Lasch, *The True and Only Heaven: Progress and Its Critics* (New York, 1991), 377–78.

40. PH "Coal Strike Continues," 147.

41. PH to Mother and Father, October 19, 1923, Mother to Powers, October 19, November 9, 1923, Father to Lad, October 26, 1923, November 1, 1923, Father to Powers, December 19, 1923, PH Papers; Dubofsky and Van Tine, *John L. Lewis,* 124.

42. Father to Lad, October 26, 1923, November 1, 1923, PH Papers.

43. Milton Derber, *The Idea of Industrial Democracy in America, 1865–1965,* (Urbana, 1970), 19–20; *Gary Gerstle, Working-Class Americanism: The Politics of Labor in a Textile City, 1914–1960* (New York, 1989), 331; PH to Mother and Father, May 21, 1922, October 18, 1923, PH Papers. The quote on the Greenwich miners is taken from PH, "Greenwich Number Three," *Locomotive Engineers Journal* 58 (March 1924): 173–74, 230.

44. PH to Mother and Father, November 28, 1923, PH Papers.

45. John Brophy, interview with John Hall, box A5–39, reel 13, 79–80, Brophy Papers; Eloise to Powers, August 14, 1922, Betty Houghton to Powers, November 2, 11, 1922, Alma Littel to Eleanor Page Hapgood, February 3, 1923, Horace Davis to PH, April 28, 1922, PH Papers.

46. Earl C. Lindsey to PH, November 29, 1922, David McCord to PH, February 15, 1923, Mother to PH, March 28, 1923, PH to Mother, June 25, 1923, Paul Furnas to PH, July 26, 1923, PH Papers; Freeman, *American Testament,* 331.

47. PH to Mother and Father, June 10, 1923, October 22, 24, 1923, PH to Mother and Father, November 28, 1923, December 19, 1923, PH Papers.

4: "'Round the World Underground"

1. Melvyn Dubofsky and Warren Van Tine, *John L. Lewis: A Biography* (New York, 1977), 124–25.

2. Mother to PH, October 8, 15, 1923, November 9, 1923, William P. Hapgood to PH, October 15, 1923, April 8, 1924, PH Papers.

3. William P. Hapgood to Lad, October 15, 27, 1923, Emmet McCabe to PH, October 12, 1924, Charles Ghizzoni to PH, July 10, 1925, PH Papers.

4. William Price to Sister and Brother, March 12, 1924, Elizabeth Mallon to PH, March 14, 1924, John Kerr to Harry Ward, March 17, 1924, PH Journal, July 7, 12, 15, 20, 1924, PH to Mother and Father, September 21, 1924, PH to Norman Hapgood, October 10, 1924, PH Papers; Hywel Francis and David Smith, *The Fed: A History of the South Wales Miners in the Twentieth Century* (London, 1980), 34.

5. PH Journal, July 9, 10, 24, 1924, November 9, 1924, PH Papers; Alan Fox, *History and Heritage: The Social Origins of the British Industrial Relations System* (London, 1985), 303, 330–33.

6. PH, "In the British Pits," *New Masses* 1, no. 5 (September 1926): 23.

7. PH Journal, September 13, 1924, PH to Mother and Father, September 21, 1924, November 16, 1924, PH Papers.

8. PH, *New York Herald Tribune,* May 9, 1926.

9. Francis and Smith, *Fed,* 34, 37, 42, 54; K. O. Morgan, quoted in Fox, *History and Heritage,* 258; Roger Fagge, *Power, Culture and Conflict in the Coalfields: West Virginia and South Wales, 1900–1922* (Manchester, 1996), 77, 83–86, 168, 237–54.

10. Robert Smillie, *My Life for Labour* (London, 1924), 150; Francis and Smith, *Fed,* 7; Fox, *History and Heritage,* 124–25, 144, 157–58, 164–65, 261, 331–33; Standish Meacham, *A Life Apart: The English Working Class, 1890–1914* (Cambridge, 1977), 27; Fagge, *Power, Culture and Conflict,* 50–51, 64, 237.

11. Jack Evans to PH, May 24, 1925, June 7, 1925, PH Papers.

12. PH to Mother and Father, June 17, 1925, PH Papers.

13. Beatrice Carew, "From a Miner's Wife," *New Republic* 30, no. 388 (May 10, 1922): 305–6.

14. PH Journal, May 8, 15, 17, 22, 1925, June 4, 7, 1925, PH to Mother and Father, December 7, 14, 1924, PH to Mother (Ella Reeve) Bloor, September 28, 1928, PH Papers. On the French labor movement during this period, see Gary Cross, "Redefining Workers' Control: Rationalization, Labor Time, and Union Politics in France, 1900–1928," in *Work, Community, and Power: The Experience of Labor in Europe and America, 1900–1925,* ed. James E. Cronin and Carmen Sirianni (Philadelphia, 1983), 143–65; and Roger MaGraw, *A History of the French Working Class,* vol. 2 (Oxford, 1992), 229–35.

15. PH Journal, December 10, 12, 19, 24, 25, 26, 29, 30, 1924, January 10, 1925, PH to Mother and Father, December 7, 14, 1924, PH Papers.

16. PH Journal, December 19, 20, 1924, May 22, 1925, PH to John Henck, December 21, 1924, PH Papers.

17. Meacham, *Life Apart,* 148; Christopher Lasch, *The True and Only Heaven: Progress and Its Critics* (New York, 1991), 36; Michael Walzer, *The Company of Critics: Social Criticism and Political Commitment in the Twentieth Century* (New York, 1988), 225–27.

18. Emma Goldman to PH, October 10, 1924, November 21, 1924, December 27, 1924, January 19, 1925, March 5, 1925, April 13, 1925, PH Papers.

19. William Green to PH, July 1, 1925, PH to Mother and Father, October 12, 1924, PH Journal, October 26, 1924, PH Papers.

20. PH Journal, September 13, 28, 1924, PH Papers.

21. Joseph Freeman, *An American Testament: A Narrative of Rebels and Romantics* (London, 1938), 494–96; John P. Diggins, *The American Left in the Twentieth Century* (New York, 1973), 78; Janet Fishburn, *The Fatherhood of God and the Victorian Family: The Social Gospel in America* (Philadelphia, 1981), 162; William P. Hapgood to Leslie Hopkinson, August 31, 1927, PH to Louis Budenz, June 6, 1947, PH Papers.

22. Evelyn Preston to PH, July 24, 1924, PH Journal, July 18, 1925, PH Papers.

23. PH to Mother, July 16, 1925, PH to Mother and Father, July 18, 27, 1925, PH to Auntie, July 23, 1925, PH Journal, July 18, 27, 1925, PH Papers.

24. PH to Mother and Father, August 26, 1925, PH Papers; Peggy Lamson, *Roger Baldwin: Founder of the American Civil Liberties Union* (Boston, 1976), 180–81.

25. PH Journal, August 5, 12, 16, 1925, September 13, 1925, October 10, 20, 1925, PH to Mother and Father, October 20, 26, 1925, PH Papers; Freeman, *American Testament,* 320–33.

26. PH Journal, October 11, 1925, PH Papers; Freeman, *American Testament,* 331.

27. Roger Baldwin to PH, October 22, 1925, February 18, 1926, PH to Mother and Father, July 18, 1925, PH Papers; Lamson, *Roger Baldwin,* 184–87; Freeman, *American Testament,* 332.

28. Sherwood Eddy, quoted in Donald Meyer, *The Protestant Search for Political Realism, 1919–1941* (Middletown, 1988), 193. Compare Hapgood's impressions of the Soviet Union with the more cautious reaction of John Brophy in *A Miner's Life,* 220–23, and the favorable impressions of Walter and Victor Reuther in Nelson Lichtenstein, *The Most Dangerous Man in Detroit: Walter Reuther and the Fate of American Labor* (New York, 1995), 40–46. Somewhat less starry-eyed than Hapgood nearly a decade earlier, the Reuthers were nonetheless moved by evidence of the "genuine proletarian democracy" they observed during their tenure at the Gorky Auto Works.

29. Eva to Happy, May 3, 1926, Ida to Happy, November 10, 1925, December 2, 1925, May 3, 1928, PH Papers.

30. Ida to Happy, November 10, 1925, PH Papers.

31. PH Journal, December 7, 17, 25, 1925, January 8, 21, 1926, PH to Father, December 25, 1925, January 4, 1926, PH to Mother, January 8, 1926, PH Papers.

32. PH to Father, January 4, 1926, PH Journal, January 21, 1926, PH Papers. On anti-Asian sentiment in the United States, see Gwendolyn Mink, *Old Labor and New Immigrants in American Political Development: Union Party, and State, 1875–1920* (Ithaca, 1986), 97–112; and Alexander Saxton, *The Indispensable Enemy: Labor and the Anti-Chinese Movement in California* (Berkeley, 1971).

33. PH to Mother and Father, December 17, 1925, Notations at end of PH Journal, 1924, PH Papers.

34. PH to Mother and Father, September 6, 1924, PH to Aunt Yaya, September 13, 1924, PH Papers.

35. PH to Mother and Father, September 24, 1924, PH to Aunt Yaya, September 13, 1924, PH to Mother, January 8, 1926, PH to Father, January 29, 1926, PH Papers.

36. John L. Thomas, *Alternative America: Henry George, Edward Bellamy, Henry Demarest Lloyd and the Adversary Tradition* (Cambridge, 1983) 258–59; Lawrence W. Levine, "Progress and Nostalgia: The Self-Image of the Nineteen Twenties," in *The American Novel in the Twentieth Century,* ed. Malcolm Bradbury and David Palmer (London, 1971); William E. Leuchtenburg, *The Perils of Prosperity, 1914–1932* (Chicago, 1958), 204–24; Lasch, *True and Only Heaven,* 320–21; Loren Baritz, introduction to *The Culture of the Twenties* (Indianapolis, 1970).

37. John Kerr to PH, April 20, 1924, January 8, 1925, U. S. G. Gallagher to PH, October 19, 1924, Isabelle Williams to PH, October 21, 1924, George Gregory to PH, undated, 1924, PH Papers; Alan J. Singer, "Class-Conscious Coal Miners: Nanty Glo Versus the Open Shop in the Post World War I Era," *Labor History* 29, no. 1 (winter 1988): 60–63; Elizabeth Cocke Ricketts, "'Our Battle for Industrial Freedom': Radical Politics in the Coal Fields of Central Pennsylvania, 1916–1920" (Ph.D. diss., Emory University, 1996), 496–510; Mildred Allen Beik, *The Miners of Windber: The Struggles of New Immigrants for Unionization, 1890s–1930s* (University Park, 1996), 311–16. Significantly, in his memoirs, John Brophy also neglected to mention the rise of ethnic and racial antagonism in District 2. Brophy's silence on this subject suggests that Hapgood was

by no means alone in his reluctance to acknowledge these barriers to working-class solidarity.

5. Save the Union

1. John Brophy to PH, June 6, 1925, March 10, 1926, John Kerr to PH, April 20, 1924, September 29, 1924, January 8, 1925, July 8, 1925, Dennis Bolger to PH, November 23, 1924, U. S. G. Gallagher to PH, Faber McCloskey to PH, January 1, 1925, Charles Ghizzoni to PH, February 2, 1925, PH Papers; Melvyn Dubofsky and Warren Van Tine, *John L. Lewis: A Biography* (New York, 1977), 103, 106–7, 133–35, 143; Carl Meyerhuber, *Less Than Forever: The Rise and Decline of Union Solidarity in Western Pennsylvania, 1914–1948* (Selinsgrove, 1987), 66–67; David Brody, *In Labor's Cause: Main Themes on the History of the American Worker* (New York, 1993), 150; Bulletin, District 2, Clearfield, Pennsylvania, June 26, 1926, July 14, 1926, box 27.5a, UMWA Papers; Report of John Brophy to the Membership of District No. 2, United Mine Workers of America, March 1927, box 49, District 2 Papers.

2. Elizabeth Cocke Ricketts, "'Our Battle for Industrial Freedom': Radical Politics in the Coal Fields of Central Pennsylvania, 1916–1920" (Ph.D. diss., Emory University, 1996), 521–34; Alan Singer, "John Brophy's 'Miners' Program': Workers' Education in UMWA District 2 during the 1920s," *Labor Studies Journal* 13, no. 4 (winter 1988): 59–61.

3. On the LaFollette-Wheeler campaign, see Isabelle to PH, October 21, 1924, John Kerr to PH, August 4, 1924, September 29, 1924, Faber McCloskey to PH, January 1, 1925, U. S. G. Gallagher to PH, October 19, 1924, Emmet McCabe to PH, October 12, 1924, PH Papers. On the Ku Klux Klan, see Alan J. Singer, "Class-Conscious Coal Miners: Nanty-Glo Versus the Open Shop in the Post World War I Era," *Labor History* 29, no. 1 (winter 1988): 56–65; Mildred A. Beik, *The Miners of Windber: The Struggles of New Immigrants for Unionization, 1890s-1930s* (University Park, 1996), 311–16; Neal J. Ferry to John L. Lewis, November 1, 1924, John J. Mates and Neal J. Ferry to John L. Lewis, March 14, 1925, John Watson to John L. Lewis, February 16, 1925, and Patrick Devitt to John Ghizzoni, February 24, 1931, box 27.5a, UMWA Papers. For an account of a far more timid response to the Klan among Illinois miners, see David Thoreau Wieck, *Woman from Spillertown: A Memoir of Agnes Burns Wieck,* (Carbondale, 1992), 94–97.

4. District 2 Bulletins, June 26, 1926 and July 14, 1926, UMWA Papers; Devitt to Ghizzoni, February 24, 1931, box 27.5a, UMWA Papers; Singer, "Class-Conscious Coal Miners," 62–63; Paul Fuller to John Brophy, January 2, 1925, Paul Fuller to PH, January 15, 1925, John Kerr to PH, March 7, 1926, PH Papers.

5. Evelyn (Preston) to PH, May 11, 1925, March 26, 1926, PH to Mother and Father, March 25, 1923, August 20, 1924, Betty Houghton to PH, November 2, 1922, Ida to Happy, December 2, 1925, May 3, 1928, PH Journal, January 17, 1922, Boston Psychopathic Hospital case record folder no. 12200–27472, August 22, 1927, PH Papers; PH, "Coal and Men," MDH Papers.

6. PH Journal, August 15, 20, 1924, Evelyn to PH, March 26, 1926, PH Papers; Wieck, *Woman from Spillertown,* 256.

7. PH to Mother, December 18, 1924, April 20, 1926, PH to Mother and Father, December 3, 1925, PH Papers.

8. Hapgood was especially disapproving of consumer culture, which he viewed as self-aggrandizing and artificial. See PH, "Journal of My Trip to the Non-Union Coal Fields in Pennsylvania," September 1, 1921, and PH to Mary Donovan, May 21, 1930, PH Papers.

9. Report of John Brophy to Membership of District 2, March 1927, District 2 Papers.

10. PH to Mother, April 20, 1926, PH Papers.

11. Ibid.

12. Ibid.

13. Nick Salvatore, *Eugene V. Debs: Citizen and Socialist* (Urbana, 1982), 270–71; Herbert G. Gutman, *Work, Culture and Society in Industrializing America* (New York, 1977), 78–117; and Christopher Lasch, *The True and Only Heaven: Progress and Its Critics* (New York, 1991), 215–17.

14. Roger Baldwin to PH, February 26, 1926, PH Papers.

15. Ibid.

16. Mary Blankenhorn to PH, October 29, 1925, Fred A. Moore to PH, March 2, 10, 1926, "Instructions," March 16, 1926, Eleanor Copenhaver to PH, May 30, 1926, Kirby Page to PH, April 20, 1926, Edgar Williams to PH, May 9, 10, 1926, PH to Mother and Father, May 13, 1926, PH Papers.

17. Whiting Williams to PH, March 13, 1926, Anne Johnston to PH, March 19, 1926, G. P. Putnam to PH, April 7, 1926, G. H. Doran to PH, April 16, 1926, PH to Mother and Father, June 13, 1926, July 26, 1926, D. C. Chambers to PH, July 19, 1926, PH Papers; PH, "Coal and Men," MDH Papers. The fact that Alice Hamilton, a pioneering public health specialist and staunch liberal, diligently attempted to find a publisher for Hapgood's journal two years later attests to his continuing desire to see his exploits gain public recognition. See Edward Weeks to Alice Hamilton, May 15, 1928, Alfred A. Knopf to Alice Hamilton, June 19, 1928, PH Papers.

18. PH to Mother, June 1, 1926, PH Papers; Dubofsky and Van Tine, *John L. Lewis,* 127.

19. PH to Mother and Father, July 26, 1926, PH Papers.

20. John Brophy, interview with John Hall, box A5–39, reel 8, 51–52, Brophy Papers; Dubofsky and Van Tine, *John L. Lewis,* 127; John Brophy, *A Miner's Life* (Madison, 1964), 213–14; Meyerhuber, *Less Than Forever,* 97; Zieger, *John L. Lewis,* 41.

21. John Brophy, "A Larger Program for the Miners Union," Clearfield, Pennsylvania, November 8, 1926, box 49, District 2 Papers; Brophy, *Miner's Life,* 214–15; and John Brophy, "Elements of a Progressive Union Policy," in *American Labor Dynamics,* ed. J. B. S. Hardman (New York, 1928), 191.

22. PH to Mother and Father, July 10, 26, 1926, PH Papers; Edward Johannings-meier, *Forging American Communism: The Life of William Z. Foster* (Princeton, 1994), 236–37; Dubofsky and Van Tine, *John L. Lewis,* 127; Meyerhuber, *Less Than Forever,* 95–97.

23. PH to Pat McDermott, September 21, 1926, PH Papers.

24. Johanningsmeier, *Forging American Communism,* xiv, 236, 400n48, and letter to author, October 28, 1995; Benjamin Gitlow, *I Confess: The Truth About American Communism* (Freeport, 1939), 383; PH to Norman Thomas, January 1, 1940, Norman Thomas Papers, New York Public Library (hereafter NT Papers); John Bartlow Martin, *Indiana: An Interpretation* (Bloomington, 1992) 165; Mary Donovan to PH, September 20, 1927, PH to Ray, March 10, 1934, PH Papers.

25. PH to Mother and Father, July 26, 1926, PH to Officers and Members of District

2, October 20, 1926, PH Papers. Even Hapgood's future wife, Mary Donovan, wondered if he was a secret Communist. See Mary Donovan to PH, September 29, 1927, PH Papers.

26. Dubofsky and Van Tine, *John L. Lewis,* 127–28; Albert Coyle to PH, September 3, 1926, PH Papers. The text of the Coyle-Hapgood correspondence was published in the *New York Times,* October 13, 1926.

27. PH to Officers and Members of District 2, October 20, 1926, PH to William Green, October 15, 1926, PH Papers; *UMWA Journal,* November 1, 1926.

28. William Green to PH, November 16, 1926, PH Papers.

29. Brophy, *Miner's Life,* 219; PH to "Friend Jack" (John Kerr), November 17, 1926, Stephen Ely to John Kerr, November 24, 1926, Thomas Kennedy to PH, November 30, 1926, PH to David McKee, December 1, 1926, PH Papers.

30. "Trial of Powers Hapgood," December 2, 1926, PH to Mother, December 3, 12, 1926, PH Papers.

31. Brophy, *Miner's Life,* 217–18; Ricketts, "'Our Battle for Industrial Freedom,'" 546–48; "John Brophy Appeals to International Executive Board for Honesty and a Square Deal," May 28, 1927, PH Papers.

32. Alan Singer, "Communists and Coal Miners: Rank-and-File Organizing in the UMWA During the 1920s," *Science and Society* 55, no. 2 (summer 1991): 144–45.

33. PH to Mother and Father, May 1, 1927, PH Papers.

34. *Indianapolis News,* January 27, 1927; Tom Tippett, *Federated Press,* January 29, 1927; Martin, *Indiana,* 165–66.

35. "Proceedings of the Thirtieth Consecutive Constitutional Convention of the UMWA," January 2–February 2, 1927, vol. 1, 231–34; Dubofsky and Van Tine, *John L. Lewis,* 129; PH, "Gangsterism Rules the Mines," *New Masses* 2, no. 5 (March 1927): 19–20.

36. PH, "Gangsterism Rules the Mines."

37. Ibid.

38. PH to Mother and Father, April 10, 20, 1927, PH Papers; James Mark to John L. Lewis, April 13, 1927, John L. Lewis to James Mark, April 20, 1927, box 28, "Conference of the Progressive Miners," April 30, 1927, PH to James Mark, April 11, 1927, box 49, District 2 Papers; Beik, *Miners of Windber,* 321–24.

39. PH to Mother and Father, April 20, 1927, PH Papers; PH, "Company Dishonesty Exposed," April 1927, box 49, District 2 Papers; Beik, *Miners of Windber,* 323.

40. PH to Mother, April 25, 1927, PH Papers; William Parks to James Mark, June 12, 1927, box 52, District 2 Papers.

41. Jack Evans to PH, undated, 1926, June 6, 1926, November 26, 1926, September 7, 1927, Edwin Jenkins to Comrade, January 31, 1927, PH Papers; Hywel Francis and David Smith, *The Fed: A History of the South Wales Miners in the Twentieth Century* (London, 1980), 52–69; Alan Fox, *History and Heritage: The Social Origins of the British Industrial Relations System* (London, 1985), 329–36. Evans's September 1927 letter to Hapgood described the miners' refusal to concede defeat as "criminal folly," suggesting just how much his own attitude toward rank-and-file militancy had changed.

42. On Norman Thomas and the changing character of the Socialist Party, see Irving Howe, *Socialism and America* (New York, 1985), 49–50; and Daniel Bell, "Marxian Socialism in the United States," in *Socialism and American Life,* vol. 1, ed. Donald Drew Egbert and Stow Persons (Princeton, 1952), 370–80.

43. PH to Evelyn, May 2, 1927, William P. Hapgood to Jack, November 8, 1927, PH to Mary, December 23, 1927, PH Papers.

44. PH to Evelyn, May 2, 1927, PH Papers; John Patrick Diggins, *The Rise and Fall of the American Left* (New York, 1992), 165. On masculinity and Communism, see Richard Hofstadter, *Anti-Intellectualism in American Life* (New York, 1962), 293–94.

45. PH to Mother and Father, March 20, May 8, July 10, 25, 1927, PH to Evelyn, May 2, 1927, Eleanor Roosevelt to PH, July 21, 1927, Adolph Germer to PH, February 21, 1927, PH Papers.

6. Exile at Home

1. On the concept of agitation, see Richard Hofstadter, *The American Political Tradition and the Men Who Made It* (New York, 1974), 175–210.

2. William E. Leuchtenburg, *The Perils of Prosperity, 1914–1932* (Chicago, 1958), 82–83; John P. Diggins, *The American Left in the Twentieth Century* (New York, 1973), 143; Roberta Strauss Feuerlicht, *Justice Crucified: The Story of Sacco and Vanzetti* (New York, 1977), 382–83; PH to Mother and Father, August 20, 1927, PH Papers.

3. PH to Mother and Father, undated, August 1927, August 5, 12, 23, 1927, Father to PH, August 14, 1927, PH to Alvan T. Fuller, August 14, 1927, PH Papers.

4. PH, "In a Boston Insane Asylum," *The Nation* 125, no. 3244 (September 7, 1927): 226; "The Reminiscences of Gardner Jackson," Columbia University Oral History Collection, 1955, 218; Boston Psychopathic Hospital case record folder no. 12200–27472, William P. Hapgood to PH, August 14, 1927, PH Papers. Jackson, who was integrally involved in the Sacco-Vanzetti defense committee, claimed that Hapgood was near hysterics when he was arrested. Hapgood's demeanor during his confinement belied this assessment. Both his public behavior and private reflections, however, suggest that he was having great difficulty keeping his emotions under control.

5. PH, "In a Boston Insane Asylum"; PH to Mother and Father, August 5, 13, 1927, PH Papers.

6. Mary Donovan Hapgood, "No Tears for My Youth," MDH Papers; PH to Mother and Father, September 4, 1927, PH to John Beffel, March 1, 1944, PH Papers.

7. Mary Donovan Hapgood, "No Tears for My Youth," MDH Papers; PH to Mother and Father, September 4, 1927, PH Papers. Hapgood's parents were not the only ones to express doubts about Mary Donovan. For other reservations, see "Reminiscences of Gardner Jackson," 200–225; and John Brophy, interview with John Hall, box A5–39, reel 10, 96, Brophy Papers. Donovan, in turn, resented the "attitude of Powers's parents towards me," claiming that they dominated him and exercised "absolute control" over his life. See "No Tears for My Youth," 6–8.

8. PH to Rose Pesotta, undated, 1936, RP Papers, NYPL.

9. Mary Donovan to PH, September 9, 17, 19, 20, 21, 26, 1927, PH Papers.

10. PH to Mother, November 12, 1927, December 3, 8, 1927, Tom Mooney to Mary Donovan, July 20, 1928, PH Papers.

11. Carl Meyerhuber, *Less Than Forever: The Rise and Decline of Union Solidarity in Western Pennsylvania* (Selinsgrove, 1987), 89–90; Melvyn Dubofsky and Warren Van Tine, *John L. Lewis: A Biography* (New York, 1977), 144–46; James Mark to John L. Lewis, August 26, 1927, box 27.5a, UMWA Papers; James Mark to John L. Lewis, November 1, 1927, box 54, District 2 Papers; PH to Mother and Father, December 8, 1927,

January 16, 1928, February 6, 1928, PH to Mary, December 23, 1927, John Brophy to Norman Thomas, December 8, 1927, PH Papers.

12. Perry K. Blatz, *Democratic Miners: Work and Labor Relations in the Anthracite Coal Industry, 1875–1925* (Albany, 1994), 239–60; Clement Valetta, "'To Battle for Our Ideas': Community Ethic and Anthracite Labor, 1920–1940," *Pennsylvania History* 58, no. 4 (October 1991): 311–21; PH to Alex, February 17, 1928, "Notes of Left-Wing Conference," February 19, 1928, PH Papers; PH and Mary Donovan, "Murdered Miners," *The Nation* 126, no. 3271 (March 14, 1928): 293–94.

13. PH to Mother and Father, March 4, 1928, PH to Father, March 10, 1928, PH Papers; PH and Mary Donovan, "Murdered Miners"; *Wilkes-Barre Times Leader,* March 3, 1928.

14. Bulletin No. 2, National Save the Union Conference, April 1, 1928, Pittsburgh, Pennsylvania, box 45, District 2 Papers; Edward P. Johanningsmeier, *Forging American Communism: The Life of William Z. Foster* (Princeton, 1994), 239–44; Saul Alinsky, *John L. Lewis: An Unauthorized Biography* (New York, 1949), 58; Theodore Draper, *American Communism and Soviet Russia* (New York, 1986), 297; Alan Singer, "Communists and Coal Miners: Rank-and-File Organizing in the UMWA During the 1920s," *Science and Society* 55, no. 2 (summer 1991): 145–50.

15. PH to Mother Bloor, September 28, 1928, PH to C. H. Mayer, July 10, 1929, John Brophy to PH, June 20, 1928, July 8, 1928, August 20, 1928, Mother Bloor to PH, September 13, 1928, PH Papers; Human Relations Council Meeting Minutes, November 22, 1929, Columbia Conserve Company Papers, Lilly Library, Indiana University, Bloomington (hereafter CCC Papers).

16. PH to Mother Bloor, September 28, 1928, PH Papers.

17. PH to Tony (Minerich), June 22, 1928, PH to Mother Bloor, September 28, 1928, PH Papers.

18. PH to Mary Donovan, September 9, 1928, PH Papers.

19. Joseph Freeman, *An American Testament: A Narrative of Rebels and Romantics* (London, 1938), 252–53.

20. Frank Palmer to PH, September 5, 1928, PH to Mother and Father, January 16, 1929, John Brophy to Powers, February 3, 1929, PH Papers; *Kansas City Times,* October 2, 1931, rpt. in *Columbia Cauldron,* vol. 4, September 1931, CCC Papers; Irving Bernstein, *The Lean Years: A History of the American Worker, 1920–1933* (Baltimore, 1966), 100.

21. Mary Donovan Hapgood, "No Tears for My Youth," 5, MDH Papers; *Denver Post,* February 13, 1929, Thomas Kennedy to PH, March 9, 1929, PH Papers; *Columbia Cauldron,* vol. 4, September 1931, PH to Edward H. Buehrig, February 13, 1931, correspondence, 1931, box 1, CCC Papers; Mary Van Kleeck, *Miners and Management* (New York, 1934) 248. Columbia Conserve not only provided Rocky Mountain Fuel with moral support but even granted Josephine Roche a $20,000 interest-free loan in 1929 to assist the company through a lean period. See Minutes, Special Business Council Meeting, October 25, 1929, CCC Papers. One of the headlines in the *Denver Post* read: "Hapgood, Son of Rich Canner, Works in Mine." Try as he might, Hapgood was continually frustrated in his quest to transcend his origins.

22. PH to the Members of the International Executive Board, United Mine Workers of America, March 30, 1929, PH Papers.

23. Hutchins Hapgood, *A Victorian in the Modern World* (Seattle, 1972) 289; Robert H. Zieger, *John L. Lewis: Labor Leader* (Boston, 1988), 40–41; John L. Lewis, "The Futility of Union Democracy," in *Unions, Management, and the Public,* ed. E. Wight Bakke, Clark

Kerr, and Charles W. Anrod (New York, 1967), 178–79. A good discussion of Lewis's ideological views is contained in Dubofsky and Van Tine, *John L. Lewis,* 291–92.

24. PH to International Executive Board, John L. Lewis to PH, September 20, 1929, C. L. Rosemund to PH, November 25, 1929, Charles Ghizzoni to PH, January 20, 1930, PH to Oscar Ameringer, February 21, 1930, O. A. Nicholson to PH, March 6, 1930, PH Papers.

25. Dubofsky and Van Tine, *John L. Lewis,* 157–65.

26. David Thoreau Wieck, *Woman from Spillertown: A Memoir of Agnes Burns Wieck* (Carbondale, 1992), 119–20; Lorin Lee Carey, "Adolph Germer: From Labor Agitator to Labor Professional" (Ph.D. diss., University of Wisconsin, 1968), 55–58; Brophy, *Miner's Life,* 231–32; Dubofsky and Van Tine, *John L. Lewis,* 157–65; PH to Oscar Ameringer, February 21, 1930, PH to Mary Donovan, April 12, 1930, March 10, 13, 14, 16, 17, 30, 1930, PH Papers; John Brophy to Patrick McDermott, March 15, 1930, John Brophy to PH, March 26, 1930, Brophy Papers.

27. Roger Baldwin to PH, July 22, 1930, PH Papers.

28. Dubofsky and Van Tine, *John L. Lewis,* 157–65; Carey, "Adolph Germer," 58–65; PH to Mary Donovan, April 6, 1930, June 17, 1930, PH Papers.

29. PH to Mary Donovan, May 29, 1930, PH Papers.

30. PH to Mary Donovan, June 17, 1930, PH letter of resignation, July 16, 1930, PH Papers.

31. PH to Mary Donovan, June 17, 1930, July 8, 11, 1930, Tom Tippett to PH, undated, 1930, PH Papers.

7. Debacle at Columbia Conserve

1. Russell E. Vance, Jr., "An Unsuccessful Experiment in Industrial Democracy: The Columbia Conserve Company" (Ph.D. diss., Indiana University, 1956), 34–43, 48–53, 135–43, 170–74; William P. Hapgood, *The Columbia Conserve Company: An Experiment in Workers' Management and Ownership* (Philadelphia, 1975), 20–26, 36–38, 58, and "The High Adventures of a Cannery," *Survey* 48, no. 15 (September 1, 1922): 655–58, 682; *Labor Clarion,* October 24, 31, 1930, Scrapbooks, CCC Papers; Gerold Baumann, "Powers Hapgood: Profile of a Hoosier Radical" (master's thesis, Butler University, August 1964), 54; Sanford Jacoby, *Employing Bureaucracy: Managers, Unions, and the Transformation of Work in American Industry, 1900–1945* (New York, 1985), 193. For an extended discussion of the Columbia Conserve Company, see Robert Bussel, "'Business Without a Boss: The Columbia Conserve Company and Workers' Control, 1917–1943," *Business History Review* 71, no. 3 (autumn 1997).

2. Vance, "Unsuccessful Experiment," 52–58, 87, 95–99, 159–62; Jack Evans to William P. Hapgood, *Columbia Cauldron,* vol. 1, February 1927, CCC Papers.

3. Vance, "Unsuccessful Experiment," 170–74; John Brophy, reflection on the Columbia Conserve Company, undated, 1933, Brophy Papers; *Columbia Cauldron,* vol. 4, April 1932, CCC Papers.

4. John Brophy to PH, October 29, 1929, PH to Mother and Father, October 25, 1927, February 4, 1929, undated, September 1929, Jack to PH, September 24, 1928, PH to Jack Evans, September 27, 1928, PH Papers; Council Minutes, September 10, 1928, October 5, 1928, October 23, 1931, January 13, 1933, *Columbia Cauldron,* vol. 1, November 1927, CCC Papers.

5. PH to Mary Donovan, March 9, 1931, May 11, 1931, PH Papers; *Emporia Daily Gazette,* March 17, 1931, Council Minutes, February 20, 1921, CCC Papers.

6. PH to Mary Donovan, January 9, 10, 15, 19, 1931, March 4, 1931, PH Papers; Council Minutes, November 6, 1931, CCC Papers; PH, "Kidnapping in Council Bluffs," *The Nation* 133, no. 3467 (December 16, 1931): 669–70.

7. Council Minutes, November 6, 1931, CCC Papers.

8. Council Minutes, May 13, 17, 1932, July 15, 1932, PH to Father, April 21, 1932, box 1, correspondence, 1932, CCC Papers. On the approach of traditional American corporations to depression-inspired job insecurity, see David Brody, *Workers in Industrial America: Essays on the Twentieth Century Struggle* (New York, 1980), 66–78; Lizabeth Cohen, *Making a New Deal: Industrial Workers in Chicago, 1919–1939* (Cambridge, 1990), 238–46; and Jacoby, *Employing Bureaucracy,* 207–13.

9. PH to CCC Council, January 5, 1931, PH Papers.

10. PH to Father, April 21, 1932, box 1, correspondence, 1932, CCC Papers. Hapgood complained in this letter that "even when the Commonwealth students [referring to a left-wing labor college] who were later deported from Kentucky tried to hold a meeting at the plant in Indianapolis, the attendance was a shameful indication of the willingness of most Columbians to let some people give everything to the Columbia cause when most Columbians won't give anything to another cause."

11. Daniel Bell, *The End of Ideology: On the Exhaustion of Political Ideas in the Fifties,* rev. ed. (New York, 1962), 298; *Columbia Cauldron,* vol. 2, May 1928, vol. 4, April 1932, Lloyd Reynolds, "Industrial Experimenters, Unlimited," *Columbia Cauldron,* vol. 4, November 1931, 6, CCC Annual Meeting, 1927, H. Dorothea NordHolt to Frank Walser, May 19, 1933, box 1, correspondence, 1933, CCC Papers; William P. Hapgood, *Columbia Conserve Company,* 39.

12. CCC Annual Meetings, January 19, 1923, undated, 1927, and July 19, 1929, Human Relations Council Meeting, February 1, 1929, Council Minutes, April 13, 1931, *Columbia Cauldron,* vol. 3, January 1930, CCC Papers; Vance, "Unsuccessful Experiment," 148–52; Daniel Nelson, *Farm to Factory: Workers in the Midwest, 1880–1990* (Bloomington, 1995), 7, 11, 15, 28.

13. Hapgood brought T. N. Taylor, president of the Indiana AFL, to the April 13, 1931 Council meeting to discuss the possibility of union affiliation with Columbia employees. Notably, even such a union stalwart as Jack Evans demurred on the idea of Columbia Conserve affiliating with an AFL union, suggesting that the company's attention would be better directed to solving its problems internally. See Council Minutes, April 13, 1931, CCC Papers.

14. Norman Hapgood to James Myers, July 1933, box 11, CCC Papers.

15. William P. Hapgood to PH April 18, 1932, William P. Hapgood to Norman Hapgood, April 22, 1932, PH to Father, April 18, 1932, box 1, correspondence, 1932, CCC Papers.

16. PH to Mary Donovan, August 25, 1932, PH Papers; John Bartlow Martin, *Indiana: An Interpretation* (Bloomington, 1992), 167–68.

17. Minutes of Indiana Organization Conference, November 20, 1932, reel 12, part D, PH, "The Miners' Only Hope," *America for All,* August 27, 1932, September 12, 1932, reel 128, Socialist Party Papers, microfilm edition, Perkins Library, Duke University; Irving Howe, *Socialism and America* (New York, 1985), 52–53.

18. Boyd Gurley, "What Is Success?" *Indianapolis Times,* December 19, 1932; Norman Thomas to Mary Donovan Hapgood, December 19, 1932, PH Papers. The incident also underscored the level of estrangement between Hapgood's parents and his wife. Mary

Donovan later recalled that William Hapgood asked her not to go the hospital following the accident, explaining that her presence made Eleanor Hapgood "feel like a fifth wheel." See Mary Donovan Hapgood, "No Tears for My Youth," MDH Papers.

19. Charles to PH, January 6, 1933, PH to Andy, May 4, 1935, PH Papers; PH to Rose Pesotta, undated, 1936 and September 8, 1936, RP Papers, NYPL. In one letter, Hapgood urged Mary Donovan to send his parents a copy of Sinclair Lewis's *It Can't Happen Here* so they would understood why he might have to "kill fascists" someday. See PH to Mary Donovan, November 20, 1935, PH Papers.

20. William P. Hapgood, *Columbia Conserve Company,* 59–61; Vance, "Unsuccessful Experiment," 209; Council Minutes, November 4, 1932, January 4, 1933, William P. Hapgood to Council, February 10, 1933, CCC Papers; John Brophy, reflection on the Columbia Conserve Company, Brophy Papers.

21. Council Minutes, November 18, 27, 1932, December 8, 27, 1932, January 30, 1933, William P. Hapgood to Council, May 8, 1933, CCC Papers; Vance, "Unsuccessful Experiment," 216–17, William P. Hapgood, *Columbia Conserve Company,* 52–53, 80. The letter that the salesmen sent protesting the appointment of the new committee to oversee finances was also signed by Albert Armstrong, underscoring the extent to which even Powers's closest friends were questioning William Hapgood's stewardship. See salesmen's letter to Council, Council Minutes, December 12, 1932, CCC Papers.

22. CCC Minutes, January 6, 1933, February 3, 10, 1933, CCC Papers; William P. Hapgood, *Columbia Conserve Company,* 79.

23. Council Minutes, February 3, 1933, William P. Hapgood to Council, February 10, 1933, CCC Papers; Kim McQuaid, "Industry and the Cooperative Commonwealth: William P. Hapgood and the Columbia Conserve Company, 1917–1943," *Labor History* 17, no. 4 (fall 1976): 523; Michael Marcaccio, *The Hapgoods: Three Earnest Brothers* (Charlottesville, 1977), 175–80; Martin, *Indiana,* 168–69.

24. Council Minutes, February 26, 1923, CCC Papers; William P. Hapgood, *Columbia Conserve Company,* 88–97; Vance, "Unsuccessful Experiment," 237–45.

25. Statement by the Committee of Four (Sherwood Eddy, Jerome Davis, Paul Douglas, James Myers) July 12, 1933, PH Papers.

26. McQuaid, "Industry and the Cooperative Commonwealth," 527. For liberal reaction to the Columbia debacle, see "The Case of the Columbia Conserve Company," *Christian Century* 50, no. 51 (December 13, 1933): 1565, "Industrial Democracy Investigated," *The World Tomorrow* 16, no. 29 (December 21, 1933): 678–79, Malcolm Cowley to Hutchins Hapgood, January 4, 12, 1934, and Hutchins to Billy, February 8, 1934, in William P. Hapgood, *Columbia Conserve Company.*

27. PH to Columbia Conserve Council, March 17, 1933, PH Papers; "Industrial Democracy Investigated," 129. For an example of the shrillness that sometimes accompanied the criticism of William Hapgood, see Daniel Donovan to William Hapgood, June 1, 1933, Brophy Papers, where the former condemned the latter as a "con man whose values are no better than those of any mediocre Hoosier business shark."

28. Norman Hapgood, "The Columbia Conserve Company and the Committee of Four," February 1934, box 11, CCC Papers; John Brophy and Daniel Donovan to Messrs. Paul H. Douglas, Jerome Davis, Sherwood Eddy, and James Myers, May 8, 1933, Brophy, reflection on the Columbia Conserve Company, Brophy Papers.

8. *"Lone Wolf Crying in the Wilderness"*

1. Irving Howe, *Socialism and America* (New York, 1985), 49–86; Frank A. Warren, *An Alternative Vision: The Socialist Party in the 1930s* (Bloomington, 1974), 24–40; Bernard K. Johnpoll, *Pacifist's Progress: Norman Thomas and the Decline of American Socialism* (Westport, 1987), 77–82; Daniel Bell, "Marxian Socialism in the United States," in *Socialism and American Life*, vol. 1, ed. Donald Drew Egbert and Stow Persons (Princeton, 1967), 157–60; Bernard Karsh and Philips L. Gorman, "The Impact of the Political Left," in *Labor and the New Deal*, ed. Milton Derber and Edwin Young (Madison, 1957), 102–3; PH, "The Socialist Party and the Labor Movement," *American Socialist Quarterly* 2, no.3 (summer 1933): 37–44, in reel 128, part A, no. 2, Socialist Party Papers, microfilm edition, Perkins Library, Duke University.

2. Carl D. Oblinger, *Divided Kingdom: Work, Community, and the Mining Wars in the Central Illinois Coal Fields During the Great Depression* (Springfield, 1991), 3, 8–10; David Thoreau Wieck, *Woman from Spillertown: A Memoir of Agnes Burns Wieck* (Carbondale, 1992), 126–41; Stephane E. Booth, "Ladies in White: Female Activism in the Southern Illinois Coalfields, 1932–1938," in *The United Mine Workers of America: A Model of Industrial Solidarity?* ed. John H. M. Laslett (University Park, 1996), 381–82; Jack Battuello memoir, Oral History Office, University of Illinois at Springfield, 1982, 1–11; PH, "Socialist Party and the Labor Movement"; PH to National Executive Committee, January 16, 1933, James D. Graham to Clarence Senior, March 31, 1933, Darlington Hoopes Papers, Historical Collections and Labor Archives, Pennsylvania State University; Agnes Wieck to PH, December 24, 1932, Gerry Allard to PH, December 27, 1932, PH Papers.

3. PH to Clarence Senior, July 13, 1933, James Maurer to PH, July 18, 1933, PH to Mary Donovan, July 24, 26, 1933, PH Papers; Robert H. Zieger, *John L. Lewis: Labor Leader* (Boston, 1988), 64–65; David Brody, *In Labor's Cause: Main Themes on the History of the American Worker* (New York, 1993), 155. On the SP's attitude toward the NIRA, see "Socialists Call upon Workers to Use NIRA for Themselves," *New Leader*, July 8, 1933; "The Philosophy of the NIRA Seeks Recovery of the Wage System," *New Leader*, July 15, 1933; and "Socialists to Fight Code Violations," *New Leader*, August 12, 1933. For similar fears to Hapgood's regarding the NRA, see Roger Baldwin's statements in *"We Are All Leaders": The Alternative Unionism of the Early 1930s*, ed. Staughton Lynd (Urbana, 1996), 9–10; and Rose Pesotta Diary, January 15, 1934, box 15, RP Papers, NYPL. Pesotta worried that her union, the International Ladies' Garment Workers, would "become an appendix [*sic*] to the government and the NRA."

4. H. L. Williams to John L. Lewis, June 14, 1933, E. C. Carlson and J. Malone to John L. Lewis, July 21, 1933, box 27.5b, UMWA Papers; Mildred A. Beik, *The Miners of Windber: The Struggles of New Immigrants for Unionization, 1890s-1930s* (University Park, 1996), 332–36.

5. James Mark to John L. Lewis, June 24, 1933, box 27.5b, UMWA Papers; Elizabeth Ricketts, "'Our Battle for Industrial Freedom': Radical Politics in the Coal Fields of Central Pennsylvania" (Ph.D. diss., Emory University, 1996), 581; Robert H. Zieger, *American Workers, American Unions* (Baltimore, 1986), 29; Beik, *Miners of Windber*, 334;

6. James Feeley to Philip Murray, August 11, 1933, A5–3, Brophy Papers; Fred D. Thomas to Philip Murray, July 20, 1933, box 27.5b, UMWA Papers, Frank Rosenblum to PH, August 8, 1933, PH Papers; Mary Donovan Hapgood, "No Tears for My Youth," MDH

Papers; John Brophy, *A Miner's Life* (Madison, 1964), 236–37; Steve Fraser, *Labor Will Rule: Sidney Hillman and the Rise of America Labor* (New York, 1991) 295–96.

7. PH to Mary, August 23, 24, 1933, PH to Frank Rosenblum, August 26, 30, 1933, September 26, 1933, PH Papers.

8. PH to Mary, August 24, 1933, PH to Frank Rosenblum, August 21, 26, 1933, September 3, 1933, PH Papers.

9. PH to Frank Rosenblum, August 26, 30, 1933, September 14, 1933, Sidney Hillman to PH, August 31, 1933, "An Appeal to Intelligent Americans," 1933, PH Papers.

10. PH to Frank Rosenblum, August 26, 1933, September 14, 1933, PH Papers. On the meaning of Franklin Roosevelt's purported support for union organizing, see David Brody, *Workers in Industrial America: Essays on the Twentieth Century Struggle* (New York, 1980), 146; Steve Fraser, "The 'Labor Question,'" in *The Rise and Fall of the New Deal Order, 1930–1980,* ed. Steve Fraser and Gary Gerstle (Princeton, 1989) 68; and Howe, *Socialism and America,* 76–78, 84–86.

11. PH to Frank Rosenblum, September 26, 1933, October 11, 14, 18, 1933, Cecilia Bloomfield to PH, October 16, 1933, Frank Rosenblum to PH, October 18, 1933, Sidney Yellen to PH, September 26, 1933, PH to Clarence Senior, September 28, 1933, PH to Jacob S. Potofsky, October 8, 1933, PH Papers; "Socialists to Fight Code Violations," *New Leader,* August 12, 1933.

12. "An Appeal to the Socialists from 47 Members," *The World Tomorrow* 17, no. 8 (April 12, 1934): 183–88; Donald Meyer, *The Protestant Search for Political Realism, 1919–1941* (Middletown, 1988), 180–84; Warren, *Alternative Vision,* 12–18; Johnpoll, *Pacifist's Progress,* 118–19; Bell, "Marxian Socialism," 164–65. Some of the RPC's members were or would become labor officials, including Roy Reuther of the United Auto Workers, Franz Daniel and Elizabeth Hawes of the Amalgamated Clothing Workers, Howard Kester of the Southern Tenant Farmers Union, and Philip Van Gelder of the Shipbuilding Workers. Hapgood went on to work with Kester and Van Gelder and became quite friendly with Daniel.

13. "Proceedings of the 1934 Convention," Socialist Party Papers, microfilm edition, Perkins Library, Duke University, 399; Johnpoll, *Pacifist's Progress,* 125; Howe, *Socialism and America,* 71.

14. Howe, *Socialism and America,* 72. Hapgood also feared the political fallout from any hesitation by the Socialist Party on entering a united front with the Communists, worrying that the "Commies will have plenty of ammunition" if the SP turned them down. See PH to Maynard (Krueger), July 3, 1934, NT Papers.

15. Janet Irons, "The Challenge of National Coordination: Southern Textile Workers and the General Strike of 1934," in *"We Are All Leaders,"* ed. Staughton Lynd (Urbana, 1996), 72–101; Irving Bernstein, *Turbulent Years: A History of the American Worker, 1933–1941* (Boston, 1970), 298–306; Gertrude Weil Klein, "Well, the Debate Was Held and Here's How," *New Leader,* December 22, 1934; PH Organizing Report, September 23, 1934, PH to Mary Donovan, September 30, 1934, PH to Dr. Samuel Eliot, October 8, 1934, PH Papers; *Worcester Daily Telegram,* August 25, 1934.

16. PH to the editor of *The Nation,* unpublished letter, October 13, 1934, PH Organizing Reports, September 16, 23, 1934, PH Papers; "Observer of the Firing Line," *New Leader,* October 6, 1934.

17. PH Organizing Report, November 11, 1934, PH Papers.

18. PH Organizing Report, April 26, 1935, PH Papers.

19. Roy Rosenzweig, *Eight Hours for What We Will: Workers and Leisure in an Industrial City, 1870–1920* (Cambridge, 1983), 12–30, 191–228; Alan Brinkley, *Voices of*

Protest: Huey Long, Father Coughlin, and the Great Depression (New York, 1982), 200–202; and Lizabeth Cohen, *Making a New Deal: Industrial Workers in Chicago, 1919–1939* (Cambridge, 1990), 120–29. Rosenzweig argues that the movies in certain instances permitted workers to begin interethnic associations, leading some to find their way "from the cinema to the CIO" (228). On Father Coughlin's appeal in Worcester, see Hyman Blumberg to Mary Donovan, July 27, 1937, PH Papers.

20. H. L. Mitchell, *Mean Things Happening in This Land* (Montclair, 1979), 43–45, 64–65; PH to Howard Kester, April 17, 1935, May 21, 1935, PH Papers. Before going to Arkansas, Hapgood requested that his "defense weapons" be sent to him from Indianapolis. See PH to Andy, May 4, 1935, PH Papers.

21. PH to Mary Donovan, June 17, 20, 21, 27, 1935, PH Papers; Mitchell, *Mean Things Happening,* 74; Howe, *Socialism and America,* 75; Johnpoll, *Pacifist's Progress,* 147–51.

22. Gary L. Bailey, "The Terre Haute, Indiana General Strike, 1935," *Indiana Magazine of History* 80, no. 3 (September 1984): 193–226; I. George Blake, *Paul V. McNutt: Portrait of a Hoosier Statesman* (Indianapolis, 1966), 162–63.

23. John Bartlow Martin, *Indiana: An Interpretation* (Bloomington, 1992), 171; PH to Mary Donovan, undated, August 1935, PH to Alfred Baker Lewis, September 1, 1935, PH Papers.

24. PH to Civil Service Commission, February 25, 1935, William C. Hall to PH, March 7, 1935, PH to Mary Donovan, May 12, 1935, July 20, 1935, PH Papers. Interestingly, Roy Reuther, brother of the eventual UAW president and himself a Socialist militant, was able to obtain a post with the FERA and taught the radical Brookwood Labor College curriculum to workers in Flint, Michigan, under government auspices. See Nelson Lichtenstein, *The Most Dangerous Man in Detroit: Walter Reuther and the Fate of American Labor* ((New York, 1995), 41.

9. *"An Effectiveness That Few of Us Could Muster"*

1. Melvyn Dubofsky and Warren Van Tine, *John L. Lewis: A Biography* (New York, 1967), 200; John Brophy, *A Miner's Life* (Madison, 1964) 237–46; PH to Mary Donovan, July 16, 24, 1935, PH Papers.

2. John Brophy, interview with Ed Hall, box A5–39, reel 24, 18, Brophy Papers; Brophy, *Miner's Life,* 259; Ed (Edward Wieck) to Agnes, undated, October 1935, Edward A. Wieck Collection, Archives of Labor History and Urban Affairs, Walter P. Reuther Library, Wayne State University, Detroit, Mich. (hereafter Wieck Collection); "The Reminiscences of Gardner Jackson," Columbia University Oral History Collection, New York, 1955, 689; Saul Alinsky, *John L. Lewis* (New York, 1970), 79–80.

3. Alan Brinkley, *Voices of Protest: Huey Long, Father Coughlin, and the Great Depression* (New York, 1982), 143–65; Lizabeth Cohen, *Making a New Deal: Industrial Workers in Chicago, 1919–1939* (Cambridge, 1990), 213–38; and Christopher Lasch, *The True and Only Heaven: Progress and Its Critics* (New York, 1991), 321.

4. On the PMA, see *The Progressive Miner,* December 13, 1935, PH Papers; Jack Battuello memoir, Oral History Office, University of Illinois at Springfield, 1982, 24; David Thoreau Wieck, *Woman from Spillertown: A Memoir of Agnes Burns Wieck* (Carbondale, 1992), 149–54; and Gerry Allard, "The Dilemma of the PMA," CIO Files of John L. Lewis (microfilm edition), reel 10, series 1, ed., Robert H. Zieger, published from

the holdings of the United Mine Workers of America, Department of Archives and Manuscripts, Catholic University of America, Washington, D.C. (hereafter CIO Files of John L. Lewis). PH to Adolph Germer, December 15, 1935, reel 1, Adolph Germer Papers, microfilm edition, State Historical Society of Wisconsin; PH to Friend Jack (Jack Battuello), December 24, 1935, PH Papers.

5. PH to John L. Lewis, December 16, 1935, International Executive Board of UMWA to PH, February 6, 1936, PH Papers; "Tom T. talk to Powers Hapgood in Washington, D.C., during UMWA convention first week in February 1936," March 8, 1936, box 15, Wieck Collection. Like Hapgood, both Adolph Germer and John Brophy faced similar restrictions in having their UMWA memberships restored. See Lorin Lee Carey, "Institutionalized Conservatism in the Early CIO: Adolph Germer, A Case Study," *Labor History* 13, no. 4 (fall 1972): 480–82; John L. Lewis to John Brophy, December 12, 1933, and John Brophy to John L. Lewis, December 31, 1933, A5–3, Brophy Papers. Brophy protested the electoral restrictions imposed by Lewis not because he had a "political urge" but "as a matter of sentiment."

6. Saverio Beninato to PH, February 8, 1936, PH Papers.

7. Louis Stark, "The Crisis in the Labor Movement," *New Republic* 86, no. 1112 (March 25, 1936): 187–89; "Tom T. talk to PH," March 8, 1936, Edward A. Wieck to Oscar Ameringer, February 8, 1936, Wieck Collection; Jack Battuello to PH, December 24, 1935, PH to Mary Donovan, December 16, 1935, PH Papers.

8. PH to Friend Jack, December 31, 1935, PH Papers.

9. Ibid.; Dubofsky and Van Tine, *John L. Lewis,* 213. Expressing a view of John L. Lewis similar to Hapgood's, Saul Alinsky, who became a leading practitioner of community organizing, cited the labor leader as his greatest teacher in learning the meaning of "power and mass organization." See Alinsky, *John L. Lewis,* 388–89. For other left-wing impressions of Lewis, see Len DeCaux, *Labor Radical: From the Wobblies to the CIO: A Personal History* (Boston, 1970), 216; and Rose Pesotta, *Bread upon the Waters* (Ithaca, 1987), 180. In a reference that literally portrayed Lewis as a fighter, DeCaux described him as the "John L. Sullivan of industrial organization."

10. Daniel Nelson, *American Rubber Workers and Organized Labor, 1900–1941* (Princeton, 1988), 143–44.

11. Ibid., 57, 119–23, 188; Pesotta, *Bread upon the Waters,* 197–206; Brophy, *Miner's Life,* 263–64; PH to Mary Donovan, March 24, 1936, PH Papers. For a vivid, if not always reliable, account of the strike in Akron, see Ruth McKenney, *Industrial Valley,* rev. ed. (Ithaca, 1992).

12. PH to Mary, March 26, 1936, PH Papers.

13. Pesotta, *Bread upon the Waters,* 197–215; Nelson, *American Rubber Workers,* 175–201; McKenney, *Industrial Valley,* 334–35; McAlister Coleman, *Men and Coal* (New York, 1943), 165–66. The workers named some of their strike outposts after John L. Lewis, Franklin Roosevelt, and National Labor Relations Act author Robert Wagner, testifying to the esteem in which they held both the New Deal and the CIO as defenders of workers' rights.

14. Pesotta, *Bread upon the Waters,* 197–215; Nelson, *American Rubber Workers,* 175–201; Coleman, *Men and Coal,* 165–66.

15. PH to Mary Donovan, undated, March 1936, PH Papers; PH to Rose Pesotta, April 6, 1936, May 12, 20, 1936, RP Diary, March 19, 1936, box 15, RP Papers, NYPL.

16. Nelson, *American Rubber Workers,* 99–102; Pesotta, *Bread upon the Waters,* 199, Robert H. Zieger, *The CIO, 1935–1955* (Chapel Hill, 1995), 29–30.

17. Henry Kraus, *Heroes of Unwritten Story: The UAW, 1934–1939* (Urbana, 1993),

259; Dubofsky and Van Tine, *John L. Lewis,* 234. Further testifying to his new status, Hapgood told Rose Pesotta that upon being introduced as John L. Lewis's personal representative at a Steel Workers' Organizing Committee meeting in Ohio, he received an ovation. See PH to Rose Pesotta, June 8, 1936, RP Papers, NYPL.

18. PH to Rose Pesotta, October 1936, undated, 1936, November 18, 1936, October 1937, March 1938, July 24, 1938, Rose Pesotta to PH, May 21, 1938, July 18, 1938, RP Papers, NYPL; PH to Charles H. Veigle, January 27, 1948, PH Papers; John Brophy, interview with Ed Hall, box A5–39, reel 10, 95, Brophy Papers. Notably, when interviewed about Hapgood's drinking, his cohorts denied its adverse impact. See Gerold Baumann, "Power Hapgood: Profile of a Hoosier Radical" (masters' thesis, Butler University, August 1964), 78–79.

19. Rose Pesotta to PH, July 15, 1936, RP Papers, NYPL. For views of Pesotta's career and her relationship with Hapgood, see Elaine Leeder, *The Gentle General: Rose Pesotta, Anarchist and Labor Organizer* (Albany, 1993), esp. 129–37; Ann Schofield, *"to do and to be": Portraits of Four Women Activists, 1893–1986* (Boston, 1997), 131–36; and Robert Bussel, "'A Love of Unionism and Democracy': Rose Pesotta, Powers Hapgood, and the Industrial Union Movement, 1933–1949," *Labor History* 38, nos. 2–3 (spring/summer 1997): 202–28.

20. PH to RP, undated, September 1936, RP to PH, September 26, 1936, RP Papers, NYPL.

21. RP to Pal, September 26, 1936, October 6, 1936, PH to RP, undated, 1936, August 26, 1936, undated, September 1936, December 1, 1936, Rose Pesotta to Mary Donovan, September 22, 1936, Rose Pesotta to PH, February 24, 1937, RP Papers, NYPL.

22. PH to Rose Pesotta, November 27, 1936, May 5, 1937, two letters, undated, July 1937, Rose Pesotta to PH, September 28, 1936, RP Papers, NYPL.

23. PH to RP, undated, February 1937, RP to PH, March 31, 1937, RP Papers, NYPL; Mary Donovan to PH, August 15, 1930, PH Papers; Mary Donovan Hapgood, "Why Do Intelligent Women Marry?" undated, "No Tears for My Youth," 9, MDH Papers. In "Why Do Intelligent Women Marry?" Donovan noted that on occasions when both she and Hapgood were nominated for positions within the Socialist Party in Indiana, she was forced to withdraw. On gender, work, and the labor movement, see Mildred A. Beik, *The Miners of Windber: The Struggles of New Immigrants for Unionization, 1890s–1930s* (University Park, 1996), 103–6; Elizabeth Faue, *Community of Suffering and Struggle: Women, Men, and the Labor Movement in Minneapolis, 1915–1945* (Chapel Hill, 1991), 69–99; and Lizabeth Cohen, *Making a New Deal: Industrial Workers in Chicago, 1919–1939* (Cambridge, 1990), 346–48.

24. PH to Rose Pesotta, November 18, 1936, undated, August 1937, undated, October 1937, December 6, 1937, Rose Pesotta to PH, May 21, 1938, July 18, 1938, RP Papers, NYPL.

25. PH to Rose Pesotta, undated, June 1936, June 8, 1936, July 15, 1936, RP Papers, NYPL; PH to Mary Donovan, July 2, 7, 23, 27, 28, 31, 1936, August 3, 1936, PH Papers; *Camden Evening Post,* August 1, 1936.

26. Irving Bernstein, *Turbulent Years: A History of the American Worker, 1933–1941* (Boston, 1970), 607–10; Ronald W. Schatz, *The Electrical Workers: A History of Labor at General Electric and Westinghouse, 1923–1960* (Urbana, 1983), 95–96; Ronald L. Filippelli and Mark McColloch, *Cold War in the Working Class: The Rise and Decline of the United Electrical Workers* (Albany, 1995), 33–34; Melvyn Dubofsky "Not-so 'Turbulent Years': A New Look at the American 1930s," in *Life and Labor: Dimensions of American Working-Class History,* ed. Charles Stephenson and Robert Asher (Albany, 1986), 218–19;

David Palmer, "Organizing the Shipyards: Unionization at New York Ship, Federal Ship, and Fore River, 1898–1945" (Ph.D. diss., Brandeis University, 1989), 383; PH to Father and Mother, August 15, 1936, PH to Mary Donovan, August 6, 1936, undated, August 1936, PH Papers; PH to Rose Pesotta, July 15, 1936, RP Papers, NYPL.

27. Steve Fraser, *Labor Will Rule: Sidney Hillman and the Rise of American Labor* (New York, 1991), 352–62; Melvyn Dubofsky, *The State and Labor in Modern America* (Chapel Hill, 1994), 134–35; David Brody, *In Labor's Cause: Main Themes in the History of the American Worker* (New York, 1993), 68–69; Bernard K. Johnpoll, *Pacifist's Progress: Norman Thomas and the Decline of American Socialism* (Chicago, 1970), 172–74; and Irving Howe, *Socialism and America* (New York, 1985), 75–77.

28. PH Speech to NAACP banquet, Cleveland, Ohio, April 18, 1936, PH to Mary, August 3, 1936; PH Papers; PH to Rose Pesotta, undated, August 1936 (two letters), RP Papers, NYPL.

29. Bell, "Marxian Socialism," 171; Howe, *Socialism and America,* 79, Johnpoll, *Pacifist's Progress,* 171; Fraser, *Labor Will Rule,* 362. Hapgood noted Krzycki speaking on FDR's behalf but suspected "they are just using his name" and doubted that Leo "could do it." See PH to Mary, October 15, 1936, PH Papers.

30. Cohen, *Making a New Deal,* 314–15; John C. Boland to John L. Lewis, December 16, 1936, PH to John L. Lewis, January 18, 1936, CIO Files of John L. Lewis, series 1, reel 4; John L. Lewis to PH, March 31, 1936, February 18, 1937, PH Papers. Hapgood privately sought support from John L. Lewis for Socialist initiatives. Among his requests were help for the STFU, a list of CIO affiliates to aid imprisoned militant Tom Mooney, and assistance for the Farmer-Labor Progressive Federation in Wisconsin, an independent political effort that Socialists were spearheading. While Lewis valued Hapgood's contributions as a trade unionist, he was disinclined to assist his old foe in political endeavors and responded lukewarmly to his requests.

31. Ronald Edsforth, *Class Conflict and Cultural Consensus: The Making of a Mass Consumer Society in Flint, Michigan* (New Brunswick, 1987), 106–8; 112–13, 145, 150–51, 162, 169; Sidney Fine, *Sit-down: The General Motors Strike of 1936–37* (Ann Arbor, 1970), 217–18; PH to Mary Donovan, January 13, 27, 1937, PH to Mother and Father, January 17, 1937, February 12, 1937, PH Papers.

32. Nelson Lichtenstein, *The Most Dangerous Man in Detroit: Walter Reuther and the Fate of American Labor* (New York, 1995), 77–79; Bernstein, *Turbulent Years,* 499–551; Pesotta, *Bread upon the Waters,* 244; Brophy, *Miner's Life,* 270–71; Flint sit-down interview, February 2, 1966, Roy Reuther Collection, Archives of Labor History and Urban Affairs, Walter P. Reuther Library, Wayne State University, Detroit, Mich.; Fine, *Sit-down,* 267; PH to Mary Donovan, January 13, 1937, February 2, 6, 1937, PH Papers; PH to Rose Pesotta, two letters, undated, February 1937, RP Papers, NYPL. While Hapgood was praising Pesotta, he wrote Mary Donovan that "only the importance of the fight keeps me going at this moment" and lamented how badly he had treated her. See PH to Mary Donovan, January 18, 1937, PH Papers.

33. PH to Rose Pesotta, January 19, 1937, RP Papers, NYPL; Pesotta, *Bread upon the Waters,* 216.

34. Roy Reuther, quoted in Lichtenstein, *Most Dangerous Man in Detroit,* 79, Pesotta, *Bread upon the Waters,* 251–52; Dubofsky, *State and Labor in Modern America,* 138–43; Cohen, *Making a New Deal,* 333–49.

35. PH to Mother and Father, February 12, 1937, PH Papers; Pesotta, *Bread upon the Waters,* 248–49; Loren Baritz, *The Good Life: The Meaning of Success for the American Middle Class* (New York, 1982), 133–34.

36. PH to Mary Donovan, February 13, 1937, PH to Mother and Father, July 28, 1937, PH Papers.

10. *"The Duty of Every Patriot"*

1. John R. Commons, "American Shoemakers, 1648–1895: A Sketch of Industrial Evolution," *Quarterly Journal of Economics* 24 (November 1909): 39–83; Mary H. Blewett, *We Will Rise in Our Might: Workingwomen's Voices from Nineteenth-Century New England* (Ithaca, 1991) 1–19; John T. Cumbler, *Working-Class Community in Industrial America: Work, Leisure, and Struggle in Two Industrial Cities, 1880–1930* (Westport, 1979), 56–65; Benjamin Stolberg, *The Story of the CIO* (New York, 1938), 229–30; Frank McGrath and James J. Mitchell to Philip Murray, February 24, 1941, National and International Unions, United Shoe Workers of America, 1935–57, box 7–32, CIO Papers, Department of Archives and Manuscripts, Catholic University of America, Washington, D.C. (hereafter CIO Papers).

2. Benjamin Stolberg, "Inside the CIO," *New York World Telegram,* January 20, 1938; *Boston Globe,* March 14, 1937; Mary Donovan to PH, December 10, 1936, PH Papers.

3. John Brophy, *A Miner's Life* (Madison, 1964), 276; PH to John Brophy, December 2, 1936, Minutes of proposed Shoe Workers' Organizing Committee, December 21, 1936, Thomas F. Burns to John Brophy, February 11, 1937, box A7–32, CIO Papers; PH to Rose Pesotta, undated, October 1936, RP Papers, NYPL; Stolberg, "Inside the CIO."

4. Stolberg, "Inside the CIO"; PH to Governor of Massachusetts, December 17, 1936, George Roemer to *Ware River News,* May 25, 1937, George Roemer to Mary Donovan, June 3, 1937, PH Papers; W. J. Mackesy to Donald W. Curtis, January 1939, appendix to Donald Whitehouse Curtis, "The Lewiston-Auburn Shoe Strike of 1937: A Case Study in the Social Control of Industrial Disputes" (bachelor's thesis, Bates College, April 1939); PH to John Brophy, April 6, 1937, box A7–32, CIO Papers; Richard James, "The Committee for Industrial Organization's Effort to Organize the Shoe Shops of Lewiston and Auburn, Maine" (bachelor's thesis, Bates College, March 18, 1970), 30.

5. PH to John Brophy, April 6, 1937, box A7–32, CIO Papers; Richard H. Condon, "Bayonets at the North Bridge: The Lewiston-Auburn Shoe Strike, 1937," *Maine Historical Society Quarterly,* fall 1981, 76.

6. Interview transcripts, Mary Rice-DeFosse and Yves Frenette, used for the video "Roughing the Uppers: The Great Shoe Strike of 1937," 1992, courtesy of Professor Robert Branham, Bates College, Lewiston, Maine; Madeleine Giguere, "To Make a Living: Franco-American Work Traditions in Lewiston and Auburn," booklet accompanying exhibition "The Franco-American Work Experience," Lewiston-Auburn College, University of Southern Maine, April 24-May 31, 1994; Gary Gerstle, *Working-Class Americanism: The Politics of Labor in a Textile City, 1914–1960* (Cambridge, 1989), 19–30; Condon, "Bayonets at the North Bridge," 75; Cumbler, *Working-Class Community,* 122–24; Loren Baritz, *The Good Life: The Meaning of Success for the American Middle Class* (New York, 1982) 134; Rose Pesotta to PH, December 15, 1936, March 31, 1937, PH to Rose Pesotta, March 15, 1937, RP Papers, NYPL.

7. Edgar Allen Beeme, "Ça magnifique église gothique SS. Pierre et Paul," *Maine Times,* May 17, 1991. For accounts of the Corporation Sole Controversy and the Sentinelle Affair, disputes embodying local protest against centralized clerical authority, see

Gerard J. Brault, *The French-Canadian Heritage in New England* (Hanover, 1988), 72; Robert H. Babcock, Yves Frenette, Charles A. Scontras, and Eileen Eagan, "Work, Workers, and the Industrial Age, 1865–1930," in *Maine: The Pine Tree State from Prehistory to the Present,* ed. Richard W. Judd, Edwin A. Churchill, and Joel W. Eastman (Orono, 1995), 469; and Gerstle, *Working-Class Americanism,* 50–51. On Americanization of workers in the 1930s, see Yves Frenette, interview transcript; Lizabeth Cohen, *Making a New Deal: Industrial Workers in Chicago, 1919–1939* (Cambridge, 1990), 323–33; Steve Fraser, *Labor Will Rule: Sidney Hillman and the Rise of American Labor* (New York, 1991), 337–40; and Thomas Bell, *Out of This Furnace,* reissued ed. (Pittsburgh, 1976), 410–11. On attitudes toward the CIO, see Maurice Filteau interview, courtesy of Robert Branham; Curtis, "The Lewiston-Auburn Shoe Strike," 7; and Condon, "Bayonets at the North Bridge," 77–78.

8. Condon, "Bayonets at the North Bridge," 80; *Lewiston Evening Journal,* March 12, 27, 1937.

9. *Lewiston Evening Journal,* March 18, 27, 29, 31, 1937, April 2, 1937; Rose Pesotta to PH, December 15, 1936, RP Papers, NYPL.

10. Curtis, "Lewiston-Auburn Shoe Strike," 12; Condon, "Bayonets at the North Bridge," 81.

11. PH, et al. to John L. Lewis, April 28, 1937, CIO Files of John L. Lewis, series 1, reel 4; *Lewiston Daily Sun,* April 3, 1937, quoted in James "Committee for Industrial Organization's Effort," 47.

12. *Lewiston Evening Journal,* March 15, 16, 17, 29, 1937, April 5, 8, 10, 1937; Curtis, "Lewiston-Auburn Shoe Strike," 45; Sacred Heart Church 60th anniversary souvenir album, Diocese of Portland, Portland, Maine; James, "Committee for Industrial Organization's Effort," 49; Gerstle, *Working-Class Americanism,* 249–51; Reverend Edouard Nadeau, "Les Unions: Ce qu'en pense l'église," *Le Messager* (Lewiston, Maine), April 9, 1937.

13. Condon, "Bayonets at the North Bridge," 83–84; Curtis, "Lewiston-Auburn Shoe Strike," 21–31, *Lewiston Evening Journal,* April 20, 1937; "The Fascist Shoe Hits Maine: Findings and Facts of the National Lawyers' Guild (Boston Chapter) and the Civil Liberties Union," 1937, PH Papers.

14. Mackesy to Curtis, January 1939, appendix to Curtis, "Lewiston-Auburn Shoe Strike"; *Lewiston Evening Journal,* March 12, 1937.

15. *Lewiston Evening Journal,* March 29, 31, 1937, April 19, 1937.

16. "Angry Citizen" to editor, *Lewiston Evening Journal,* April 3, 1937, April 28, 1937. For a related argument but one that strives to infuse the language of Americanism with more radical meanings, see Gerstle, *Working-Class Americanism,* 153–95.

17. PH, et al. to John L. Lewis, April 28, 1937, PH to John Brophy, April 6, 1937, CIO Papers. In his letter to Brophy, Hapgood explained that six Jewish employers were on the verge of breaking ranks with the manufacturers' association, a defection that ultimately did not occur. On the role of women in the strike and within the CIO more generally, see *Lewiston Evening Journal,* April 7, 10, 1937; Elizabeth Faue, *Community of Suffering and Struggle: Women, Men, and the Labor Movement in Minneapolis, 1915–1945* (Chapel Hill, 1991), 100–125; and Gerstle, *Working-Class Americanism,* 204–5. Gerstle found militancy among French-Canadian women over violations of their rights on the shop floor but a reluctance to participate formally in union governance.

18. Condon, "Bayonets at the North Bridge," 84–85; James, "Committee for Industrial Organization's Effort," 6; *Lewiston Evening Journal,* April 22, 1937; PH to Mother and Father, April 19, 1937, PH Papers. Ironically, on the Lewiston side of the bridge that

linked it with Auburn stood a sign that read: "World's Highest Standard of Living—There Is No Way Like the American Way."

19. Milton Bracker, "Maine Strikers Defy Bayonets," *New York Times,* April 23, 1937; *Lewiston Evening Journal,* April 22, 1937; *Boston American,* April 24, 1937; Condon, "Bayonets at the North Bridge," 85–86.

20. PH to Mother and Father, April 28, 1937, May 6, 28, 1937, PH Papers.

21. Condon, "Bayonets at the North Bridge," 86–90; Curtis, "Lewiston-Auburn Shoe Strike," 14–15, 48; *Lewiston Evening Journal,* April 29, 1937, May 1, 12, 1937.

22. PH to Mother and Father, June 28, 1937, PH Papers; *Lewiston Evening Journal,* July 1, 1937; Condon, "Bayonets at the North Bridge," 89–90, Mackesy to Curtis, in Curtis, "Lewiston-Auburn Shoe Strike," 72.

23. PH to Rose Pesotta, June 28, 1937, RP Papers, NYPL; Mackesy to Curtis, 65; Condon, "Bayonets at the North Bridge," 92; *Lewiston Evening Journal,* March 18, 29, 1937, April 7, 14, 1937. In marked contrast to Hapgood, Rose Pesotta consciously appealed to the religiosity of French-Canadian workers in Montreal. See Pesotta, *Bread upon the Waters,* 272–76.

24. PH to Rose Pesotta, June 12, 1937, RP Papers, NYPL; PH, "Report of the Shoe Workers' Organizing Committee to CIO Convention, October 12, 1937, CIO Files of John L. Lewis, series 2, reel 2; Condon, "Bayonets at the North Bridge," 92. The union did receive some help from the Federal Works Progress Administration (WPA), which provided jobs for some three to four hundred strikers. Local officials, however, stalled further efforts to employ strikers under the aegis of the WPA, hindering the Shoe Workers' efforts to ease the burden of supporting the strikers. See Joseph Kovner to John L. Lewis, June 7, 1937, CIO Files of John L. Lewis, series 1, reel 4.

11. *"The Most Responsible Job I've Ever Had"*

1. PH to Mother and Father, July 28, 1937, PH Papers.

2. PH to Rose Pesotta, undated, July 1937, RP Papers, NYPL; Report of Shoe Workers' Organizing Committee to CIO Convention, October 12, 1937, CIO Files of John L. Lewis, series 2, reel 2; PH to Mother and Father, July 15, 28, 1937, PH to Mary Donovan, July 22, 1937, PH Papers; Frank McGrath and James J. Mitchell to Philip Murray, February 24, 1941, National and International Unions, United Shoe Workers of America, 1935–57, box 7–32, CIO Papers.

3. PH to Mother, September 28, 1937, PH to Mary Donovan, January 13, 1938, PH Papers; PH to Rose Pesotta, October 1, 1937, RP Papers, NYPL; Gerald Zahavi, *Workers, Managers, and Welfare Capitalism: The Shoeworkers and Tanners of Endicott-Johnson, 1890–1950* (Urbana, 1988), 151–52; Daniel Bell, *The End of Ideology: On the Exhaustion of Political Ideas in the Fifties,* rev. ed. (New York, 1962), 212–14.

4. PH to Rose Pesotta, undated, October 1937, RP Papers, NYPL; PH to Mary Donovan, March 6, 1938, PH Papers; Bell, *End of Ideology,* 215–16; Robert H. Zieger, *John L. Lewis: Labor Leader* (Boston, 1988), 98–99.

5. C. Wright Mills, *The New Men of Power: America's Labor Leaders* (New York, 1948), 7–10, 224–25; Warren R. Van Tine, *The Making of the Labor Bureaucrat: Labor Leadership in the United States, 1870–1920* (Amherst, 1973); A. J. Muste, "Army and

Town Meeting," in *Unions, Management and the Public,* ed. E. Wight Bakke, Clark Kerr, and Charles W. Anrod (New York, 1967), 168–72.

6. PH to Hamilton-Brown Shoe Company, January 19, 1939, PH Papers.

7. Ibid.; "Proceedings of the United Shoe Workers of America," Second Convention, October 2–6, 1939, 59; Frank McGrath and James J. Mitchell to Philip Murray, February 24, 1941, National and International Unions, United Shoe Workers of America, 1935–56, box A7–32, CIO Papers. On the NLRB and the CIO, see Melvyn Dubofsky, *The State and Labor in Modern America* (Chapel Hill, 1994), 148–58; Robert H. Zieger, *The CIO, 1935–1955* (Chapel Hill, 1995), 131–32; Christopher L. Tomlins, *The State and the Unions: Labor Relations, Law, and the Organized Labor Movement in America, 1880–1960,* (Cambridge, 1985), 188, 200–201; James A. Gross, *The Making of the National Labor Relations Board: A Study in Economics, Politics, and the Law,* vol. 1 (Albany, 1974), 237–54; and Fraser, *Labor Will Rule,* 397.

8. "Proceedings of the Second Convention," 62–63; Zahavi, *Workers, Managers, and Welfare Capitalism,* 154.

9. Zahavi, *Workers, Managers, and Welfare Capitalism,* 151.

10. Ibid., 157–61.

11. Ibid., 64, 163–67, 176.

12. Ibid., 168; "Proceedings of Second Convention," 63. On welfare capitalism and paternalism, see David Brody, *Workers in Industrial America: Essays on the Twentieth Century Struggle* (New York, 1980), 78; Lizabeth Cohen, *Making a New Deal: Industrial Workers in Chicago, 1919–1939* (Cambridge, 1990), 350–55; and Sanford M. Jacoby, *Employing Bureaucracy: Managers, Unions, and the Transformation of Work in American Industry, 1900–1945* (New York, 1985), 238–39.

13. PH to Rose Pesotta, October 13, 1939, Rose Pesotta to David Dubinsky, November 7, 1939, RP Papers, NYPL. On Pesotta's struggles with the leadership of the ILGWU, see Robert Bussel, "'A Love of Unionism and Democracy': Rose Pesotta, Powers Hapgood, and the Industrial Union Movement, 1933–1949," *Labor History* 38, nos. 2–3 (spring/summer 1997): 219–22.

14. PH to Mary Donovan, June 28, 1939, PH Papers; PH to Rose Pesotta, undated, March 1937, RP Papers, NYPL. In this letter to Pesotta, Hapgood reported that he was "too busy" with CIO business to attend the Socialist Party convention.

15. PH to Mary Donovan, July 27, 1937, September 18, 20, 1939, PH Papers; PH to Rose Pesotta, September 8, 1936, November 24, 1936, undated, 1936, undated, July 1937, undated, February 1938, RP Papers, NYPL.

16. "Memorandum for Mr. Brophy," undated, 1938, William P. Hapgood to John L. Lewis, March 15, 1938, CIO Files of John L. Lewis, reel 12; Rose Pesotta to PH, July 18, 1938, RP Papers, NYPL; PH to Norman Thomas, January 1, 1940, NT Papers.

17. PH to Rose Pesotta, December 6, 1937, RP Papers, NYPL.

18. PH to Rose Pesotta, March 6, 1939, RP Papers, NYPL; PH to Mary Donovan, October 1939, PH Papers; James J. Mitchell et al. to John L. Lewis, March 5, 1939, Frank McGrath and James J. Mitchell to Philip Murray, February 24, 1941, National and International Unions, United Shoe Workers of America, 1935–55, box A7–32, CIO Papers.

19. John Green to Allan Haywood, December 13, 1939, PH Papers; Edward Levinson, *Labor on the March* (New York, 1938), 257–58; David Palmer, "Organizing the Shipyards: Unionization at New York Ship, Federal Ship, and Fore River, 1898–1945" (Ph.D. diss., Brandeis University, 1989), 313–18, 370–71, 858, 861.

20. PH to Philip Murray, May 25, 1940, PH to John Green and Philip Van Gelder, May 25, 1940, PH to Mary Donovan, undated, May 1940, PH Papers.

21. PH to Mother and Father, July 25, 1940, PH to Mary Donovan, July 11, 1940, PH Papers; Bernard Mergen, "A History of the Industrial Union of Marine and Shipbuilding Workers of America, 1933–1951" (Ph.D. diss., University of Pennsylvania, 1968), 236; Palmer, "Organizing the Shipyards," 453, 503–4.

22. Fraser, *Labor Will Rule,* 452–70; Alan Brinkley, *The End of Reform: New Deal Liberalism in Recession and War* (New York, 1995), 220–21; Dubofsky, *State and Labor,* 176–77; Zieger, *CIO,* 72–73; "Report of Proceedings," Sixth National Convention, Industrial Union of Marine and Shipbuilding Workers of America, September 13–15, 1940, 98; Mergen, "A History of the Industrial Union," 237; Palmer, "Organizing the Shipyards," 504, 970–71.

23. PH to Mary Donovan, undated, June 1940, PH Papers; PH to Rose Pesotta, RP Papers, NYPL.

24. PH to Rose Pesotta, June 9, 10, 1940, PH Papers. On the Wobblies and intellectuals, see Michael Robert Bussel, "Hard Traveling: Powers Hapgood, Harvey Swados, Bayard Rustin and the Fate of Independent Radicalism in Twentieth-Century America" (Ph.D. diss., Cornell University, May 1993), 272–73.

25. PH to Mary Donovan, October 26, 1940, PH Papers; Edward A. Wieck, Report on CIO Convention, Atlantic City, November 18–22, 1940, Wieck Collection. On the tensions between Lewis, Murray, and Hillman, see Fraser, *Labor Will Rule,* 432–42; Zieger, *CIO,* 103–8; Melvyn Dubofsky and Warren Van Tine, *John L. Lewis: A Biography* (New York, 1997), 339–50; and John Brophy, *A Miner's Life* (Madison, 1964), 284–85.

26. PH to Mary Donovan, October 26, 1940, November 11, 1940, PH to Mother and Father, November 13, 1940, PH Papers; Irving Howe, *A Margin of Hope: An Intellectual Biography* (New York, 1982), 32–33.

27. PH to Rose Pesotta, October 24, 1940, November 9, 1940, RP Papers, NYPL; Edward A. Wieck to Agnes and Dave, November 18, 1940, Wieck Collection.

28. PH to Rose Pesotta, November 2, 1940, RP Papers, NYPL.

12. "The Fundamental Principles of the CIO"

1. PH to Rose Pesotta, December 11, 31, 1940, April 16, 1941, RP Papers, NYPL; PH to Mary Donovan, March 31, 1941, undated, April 1941, May 11, 15, 1941, PH Papers.

2. PH speech to International Harvester workers, June 8, 1941, PH to Mary Donovan, June 9, 1941, PH Papers; PH to Rose Pesotta, June 7, 9, 1941, RP Papers, NYPL; Lizabeth Cohen, *Making a New Deal: Industrial Workers in Chicago, 1919–1939* (Cambridge, 1990), 32–33.

3. PH to Rose Pesotta, August 14, 1940, December 9, 31, 1940, January 6, 1941, July 23, 1941, November 12, 1941, RP Papers, NYPL. Hapgood discussed the possibility of leaving his wife with his father, underscoring his enduring need to obtain parental approval for his actions.

4. PH to Rose Pesotta, August 28, 1941, RP Papers, NYPL; PH to Rose Pesotta, April 22, 1943, RP Papers, Kheel Center for Labor-Management Documentation and Archives, Martin P. Catherwood Library, Cornell University (hereafter Catherwood Library).

5. PH to Rose Pesotta, January 14, 1942, RP Papers, NYPL. On the development of

the new system of industrial relations during the New Deal and World War II, see David Brody, *In Labor's Cause: Main Themes on the History of the American Worker* (New York, 1993), 102–3, 175–214, 221–45; Nelson Lichtenstein, *Labor's War at Home: The CIO in World War II* (Cambridge, 1982); and *The Most Dangerous Man in Detroit: Walter Reuther and the Fate of American Labor* (New York, 1995), 194–219; Steve Fraser, *Labor Will Rule: Sidney Hillman and the Rise of American Labor* (New York, 1991), 452–94; Robert H. Zieger, *The CIO, 1935–1955* (Chapel Hill, 1995), 141–42, 163–76; Alan Brinkley, *The End of Reform: New Deal Liberalism in Recession and War* (New York, 1995), 201–26; and Howell Harris, "The Snares of Liberalism: Politicians, Bureaucrats, and the Shaping of Federal Labour Policy in the United States, ca. 1935–1947," in *Shop Floor Bargaining and the State: Historical and Comparative Perspectives,* ed. Steven Tolliday and Jonathan Zeitlin (Cambridge, 1985), 148–91.

6. PH to Mary Donovan, September 21, 1938, August 24, 1939, September 14, 18, 1939, PH to Irwin Jaffee, January 10, 1941, PH Papers; Nick Salvatore, *Eugene V. Debs: Citizen and Socialist* (Urbana, 1982), 274–75; Bernard K. Johnpoll, *Pacifist's Progress: Norman Thomas and the Decline of American Socialism* (Chicago, 1970), 205–14.

7. PH to Mary Donovan, July 10, 1939, PH to Allan Haywood, May 4, 1942, PH Papers; Fifth Annual Convention, Indiana State Industrial Union Council, September 1942, 82–83, Records of the Indiana State AFL-CIO, Indianapolis, Indiana.

8. PH to George S. Olive, April 20, 1942, PH Papers.

9. Leo Goodman to PH, June 2, 1942, PH to Heber Blankenhorn, June 5, 1942, PH to David Niles, September 1, 1942, PH to Fowler Harper, November 20, 1942, PH to Gardner Jackson, November 21, 1942, PH to Drew Pearson, April 16, 1943, PH Papers.

10. Fowler Harper to James P. Mitchell, March 5, 1943, PH FBI file, Freedom of Information and Privacy Act nos. 225, 644, September 4, 1940, April 1941, October 16, 1941, January 28, 1942, May 22, 1942, August 19, 1942, September 4, 1942, K. P. McIntire, "Memo for Mr. Mumford," October 15, 1942, J. Edgar Hoover to Wendell Burge, August 28, 1942, all in PH Papers. Hapgood was not removed from the FBI's list of suspected subversives until May 13, 1948. A report closing his case concluded that he had never been a member of the Communist Party and "does not appear to be potentially dangerous."

11. Norman Thomas to PH, July 9, 1941, PH to Russell McDermott, September 26, 1941, PH to Harry F. Schricker, November 4, 1941, Pearl Crist to PH, November 4, 1942, PH to Fred F. Bays, June 6, 1942, PH Papers; PH to Rose Pesotta, December 15, 1941, March 18, 1943, RP Papers, NYPL; Mark Levinson and Brian Morton, "The CIO, John Lewis, and the Left: An Interview with Philip Van Gelder," *Dissent* 32 no. 4 (fall 1985): 463; Dale R. Sorenson, "The Anti-Communist Consensus in Indiana, 1945–1958" (Ph.D. diss., Indiana University, 1980); "CIO Officials Wrap Politics in Rationing," *Indianapolis Star,* January 2, 1943.

12. "Organizing Labor for Collective Bargaining," Third Annual Leadership Forum, Indianapolis Chamber of Commerce, 1941, PH Papers; John Brophy, *A Miner's Life* (Madison, 1964), 299–301; David Brody, *Workers in Industrial America: Essays on the Twentieth Century Struggle* (New York, 1980), 176–77; and *In Labor's Cause,* 195; Lichtenstein, *Most Dangerous Man in Detroit,* 164; Brinkley, *End of Reform,* 204–5; Fourth Annual Convention, Indiana State Industrial Union Council, September 1941, Records of the Indiana State AFL-CIO, Indianapolis, Indiana.

13. PH to Scotty (James J. Mitchell), September 30, 1941, PH to Doris Tuller, July 21, 1942, PH to Arthur Donovan, February 19, 1943, PH to Adolph Germer, June 22, 1943, PH Papers; PH to Rose Pesotta, February 16, 1943, October 6, 8, 1943, May 12, 1944, RP

Papers, NYPL; PH to Rose Pesotta, June 29, 1943, August 25, 1943, RP Papers, Catherwood Library.

14. PH to William Mayo, April 6, 1943, PH to Mary Donovan, undated, October 1943, PH Papers; Gerold Baumann, "Powers Hapgood: Profile of a Hoosier Radical" (master's thesis, Butler University, August 1964), 78; PH to Lewis Merrill, January 18, 1944, Papers of the CIO Secretary-Treasurer, CIO Papers.

15. PH to Mary Donovan, undated, April 1941, PH Papers.

16. PH to Rose Pesotta, June 29, 1943, August 25, 1943, September 22, 1943, Rose Pesotta to PH, August 28, 1943, RP Papers, Catherwood Library; PH to Clara M. Beyer, August 20, 1943, PH to Mary Donovan, undated, October 1943, PH Papers; "Monopoly's Drive for Power," Report to Ninth Annual Convention, Indiana State Industrial Union Council, 1946, Records of the Indiana State AFL-CIO, Indianapolis, Indiana. Ever ready for combat, Hapgood told Rose Pesotta that he had his gun ready in case racist neighbors should attempt to harm the Jamaicans working on his father's farm.

An excellent account of one CIO union's approach to racial matters during World War II is August Meier and Elliott Rudwick, *Black Detroit and the Rise of the UAW* (Oxford, 1979). See esp. 175–206.

17. Proceedings, Eight Annual Convention, Indiana State Industrial Union Council, 1945, 356, Records of the Indiana State AFL-CIO, Indianapolis, Indiana; PH to John Brophy, January 7, 1947, Local Industrial Union Files, 1937–55, Indiana File, CIO Papers; PH to Rose Pesotta, September 22, 1943, RP Papers, Catherwood Library; Dallas W. Sells interview, Indiana University Oral History Project, Indiana University, 1979, 19. On the CIO and race, see Cohen, *Making a New Deal,* 333–55; Zieger, *CIO,* 83–85, 155–59, 346; Brody, *In Labor's Cause,* 123–26; and Lucy Randolph Mason, *To Win These Rights: A Personal Story of the CIO in the South* (New York, 1952).

18. PH to Peter Mallon, April 20, 1942, PH to Ray Edmondson, August 9, 1944, Faber McCloskey to PH, July 19, 26, 1945, PH Papers; Committee for Democracy within the Miners Union, Johnstown, Pennsylvania, August 26, 1942, box 54, District 2 Papers; Brody, *In Labor's Cause,* 102–3; John L. Lewis, "The Futility of Union Democracy," in *Unions, Management, and the Public,* ed. E. Wight Bakke, Clark Kerr, and Charles W. Anrod (New York, 1967), 180. Although the correspondence with McCloskey appeared subsequent to Hapgood's involvement with the autonomy movement, the earlier correspondence with Mallon, another District 2 dissident, suggests that Hapgood was probably aware of McCloskey's efforts before 1945.

19. "Our Boys at the Front Die for Democracy . . . Let's Have It in the UMWA," *The Voice,* August 18, 1944, box 367, District 2 Papers.

20. PH to Ray Edmondson, August 9, 1944, PH Papers.

21. Edward A. Wieck, Thirty-eighth Constitutional Convention of the UMWA, September 12–20, 1944, box 13, Wieck Collection. An astute account of the autonomy movement is contained in Melvyn Dubofsky and Warren Van Tine, *John L. Lewis: A Biography* (New York, 1977), 451–54.

22. Michael Walzer, *The Company of Critics: Social Criticism and Political Commitment in the Twentieth Century* (New York, 1988), 4.

23. Joseph K. Shepard to Allan Haywood, January 15, 1948, PH Papers.

24. PH to Rose Pesotta, September 22, 1943, RP Papers, Catherwood Library; PH to Rose Pesotta, October 23, 1944, RP Papers, NYPL; PH to Fowler Harper, January 9, 1943, Rae Brandstein to PH, August 31, 1944, PH Papers.

25. PH to Rose Pesotta, January 11, 1945, Rose Pesotta to PH, November 22, 1944, RP Papers, NYPL; PH to Adolph Germer, February 19, 1945, PH to Allan Haywood, March

16, 1945, January 17, 1946, February 1, 1946, Allan Haywood to PH, January 18, 1946, PH Papers; *Indianapolis Star,* January 11, 1946.

26. PH to Rose Pesotta, July 8, 1945, RP Papers, NYPL; Brinkley, *End of Reform,* 224–26.

27. *Indianapolis Star,* November 16, 1945; PH to T. Alan Goldsborough, December 5, 1946, PH Papers; Brinkley, *End of Reform,* 224–26.

28. Zieger, *CIO,* 266–70; Willy Bartels to PH, September 22, 1947, PH to Phil Murray, November 19, 1947, PH Papers; Brody, *Workers in Industrial America,* 221–27.

29. Zieger, *CIO,* 273–74; Brophy, *Miner's Life,* 288–94; Sorenson, "Anti-Communist Consensus," 27–30; Harvey A. Levenstein, *Communism, Anti-Communism, and the CIO* (Westport, 1981) 211, 225–26; Lorin Lee Cary, "Adolph Germer: From Labor Agitator to Labor Professional" (Ph.D. diss., University of Wisconsin, 1968), 165–75; Allan Haywood to PH, August 12, 1946, March 24, 1947, Delmond Garst to PH, March 28, 1947, Amanda Palmer to PH, August 29, 1946, PH FBI File, August 19, 1942, PH Papers.

30. Bert Cochran, *Labor and Communism: The Conflict That Shaped American Unions* (Princeton, 1977), 366; Harvey Klehr, *The Heyday of American Communism: The Depression Decade* (New York, 1984), 453, 455; Benjamin Gitlow, *I Confess: The Truth About American Communism* (Freeport, 1939), 383; PH to Humphrey Bogart and Lauren Bacall, November 3, 1947, PH Papers; PH to Norman Thomas, January 1, 1940, NT Papers.

31. Sorenson, "Anti-Communist Consensus," 46, 68; Joseph K. Shepard, "Communism Issue Upsets CIO Parley," *Indianapolis Star,* August 24, 1947; "Indiana CIO Throws Out McEwan, Frisbie," *Indianapolis Star,* August 25, 1947; Mary Donovan, "No Tears for My Youth," 7, MDH Papers; Zieger, *CIO,* 273–74; "Winning the Peace," Report to the Eighth Annual Convention, Indiana State Industrial Union Council, 1945, Neal Edwards Collection, Archives of Labor History and Urban Affairs, Walter P. Reuther Library, Wayne State University, Detroit, Mich. Allan Haywood was certainly aware of Hapgood's activities defending the Communist Party's political rights. He noted that the presence of Hapgood's name on a petition asking the governor of Indiana to let the CP remain on the ballot was "to the dissatisfaction" of some unionists. See Allan Haywood to PH, August 12, 1946, PH Papers.

32. Shepard, "Communism Issue"; Jep Cadou, Jr., "State CIO Heads Purged," *Indianapolis Star,* March 22, 1948; Neal Edwards and Claude Becktell to Affiliated Councils, Locals, and District and Regional Officers, March 23, 1948, Neal Edwards Collection. Edwards and Becktell, the new state CIO leaders, denied receiving orders from John Brophy to proceed with ousting the communists. Given Brophy's zeal in performing this task elsewhere, it appears likely that he condoned if not actively supported the expulsion efforts in Indiana.

33. Harry Read to James B. Carey, September 12, 1947, Papers of the CIO Secretary-Treasurer (James B. Carey), September 12, 1947, Archives of Labor History and Urban Affairs, Walter P. Reuther Library, Wayne State University, Detroit, Mich.; PH to Adolph Germer, February 19, 1945, PH to Allan Haywood, January 13, 1946, February 1, 1946, December 12, 1947, January 27, 1948, Marcus Deardorff to Allan Haywood, November 28, 1947, Allan Haywood to PH, December 3, 1947, Joseph Romer to Allan Haywood, December 8, 1947, Jim McEwan to PH, December 10, 1947, PH Papers.

34. PH to Allan Haywood, December 12, 1947, PH Papers.

35. Joseph K. Shepard to Allan S. Haywood, January 15, 1948, PH Papers.

36. Allan Haywood to Joseph K. Shepard, January 16, 1948, Allan Haywood to PH,

January 16, 1948, PH Papers; Gary Gerstle, *Working-Class Americanism: The Politics of Labor in a Textile City, 1914–1960* (Cambridge, 1989) 278–309.

37. Mary Donovan Hapgood, "No Tears for My Youth," 7–8, MDH Papers; Allan Haywood to PH, January 16, 1948, PH to John Brophy, November 14, 1948, PH to Mike Demchak, January 2, 1948, PH Papers; PH and Mary Donovan Hapgood Farm Diaries, January 19, 1947, February 20, 1948, March 1, 1948, April 18, 1948, May 6, 1948, October 6, 12, 1948, Indiana Historical Society, Indianapolis, Indiana; Harvey Swados, "The Miners: Men Without Work," *Dissent* 6, no. 4 (fall 1959): 389–401.

38. Mary to Liza and Eve, February 10, 1949, John L. Lewis to Mary Donovan Hapgood, March 19, 1949, autograph book, March 1, 1948, PH Papers; Baumann, "Profile of a Hoosier Radical," 80; *Indianapolis Star,* "A Man of Principle," February 6, 1949.

39. Rose Pesotta, "Powers Hapgood: A Tribute," February 8, 1949, RP Papers, NYPL.

40. RP Diary, February 7, 1949, RP Papers, NYPL.

41. Pesotta, "Powers Hapgood."

Epilogue

1. For a wide-ranging analysis of the prospects for a revitalized labor-intellectual alliance, see Steve Fraser and Joshua B. Freeman, eds., *Audacious Democracy: Labor, Intellectuals, and the Social Reconstruction of America* (Boston, 1997).

2. "Christmas Greetings," December 25, 1943, PH Papers.

Selected Bibliography

Manuscript Collections

Heber Blankenhorn Papers. Archives of Industrial Society, Hillman Library, University of Pittsburgh, Pittsburgh, Pennsylvania.

John Brophy Papers. Department of Archives and Manuscripts, Catholic University of America, Washington, D.C.

James B. Carey Papers. Collection of the Congress of Industrial Organizations Secretary-Treasurer. Archives of Labor History and Urban Affairs, Walter P. Reuther Library, Wayne State University, Detroit, Michigan.

Columbia Conserve Company Papers. Lilly Library, Indiana University, Bloomington, Indiana.

Congress of Industrial Organizations Files of John L. Lewis (microfilm edition). Department of Archives and Manuscripts, Catholic University of America, Washington, D.C.

Congress of Industrial Organizations Papers. Department of Archives and Manuscripts, Catholic University of America, Washington, D.C.

District 2, United Mine Workers of America Collection. Stapleton Library, Indiana University of Pennsylvania, Indiana, Pennsylvania.

Neal Edwards Collection. Archives of Labor History and Urban Affairs, Walter P. Reuther Library, Wayne State University, Detroit, Michigan.

Adolph Germer Papers (microfilm version). State Historical Society of Wisconsin, Madison, Wisconsin.

Mary Donovan Hapgood Papers. Lilly Library, Indiana University, Bloomington, Indiana.

Norman and Elizabeth Reynolds Hapgood Papers. Manuscript Division, Library of Congress, Washington, D.C.

Powers Hapgood Papers. Lilly Library, Indiana University, Bloomington, Indiana.

Powers and Mary Donovan Hapgood Farm Diaries. Indiana Historical Society, Indianapolis, Indiana.

Darlington Hoopes Papers. Historical Collections and Labor Archives, Pattee Library, Pennsylvania State University, University Park, Pennsylvania.

Indiana State CIO Industrial Union Council Files. Indiana State AFL-CIO, Indianapolis, Indiana.

Rose Pesotta Papers. Kheel Center for Labor-Management Documentation and Archives, Martin P. Catherwood Library, Cornell University, Ithaca, New York.

Rose Pesotta Papers. New York Public Library, New York, New York.

Socialist Party Papers (microfilm edition). Perkins Library, Duke University, Durham, North Carolina.

Norman Thomas Papers. New York Public Library, New York, New York.

United Mine Workers of America Papers. Historical Collections and Labor Archives, Pattee Library, Pennsylvania State University, University Park, Pennsylvania.

Edward A. Wieck Collection. Archives of Labor History and Urban Affairs, Walter P. Reuther Library, Wayne State University, Detroit, Michigan.

Secondary Works

Aitken, Hugh G. J. *Taylorism at Watertown Arsenal: Scientific Management in Action*. Cambridge: Harvard University Press, 1960.

Albright, Raymond W. *Focus on Infinity: A Life of Phillips Brooks*. New York: Macmillan, 1961.

Alinsky, Saul. *John L. Lewis: An Unauthorized Biography*. New York: Putnam, 1949. Reprint, New York: Vintage Books, 1970.

Allen, Devere. *Adventurous Americans*. New York: Farrar and Rinehart, 1932.

Babcock, Robert H., Yves Frenette, Charles A. Scontras, and Eileen Eagan. "Work, Workers, and the Industrial Age, 1865–1930." In *Maine: The Pine Tree State from Prehistory to the Present,* ed. Richard W. Judd, Edwin A. Churchill, and Joel W. Eastman. Orono: University of Maine Press, 1995.

Bailey, Gary L. "The Terre Haute, Indiana General Strike, 1935." *Indiana Magazine of History* 80, no. 3 (September 1984): 193–226.

Bakke, E. Wight, Clark Kerr, and Charles W. Anrod, eds. *Unions, Management and the Public*. New York: Harcourt, Brace, and World, 1967.

Baritz, Loren. *The Culture of the Twenties*. Indianapolis: Bobbs Merrill, 1970.

———. *The Good Life: The Meaning of Success for the American Middle Class*. New York: Perennial Library, 1989.

Baumann, Gerold. "Powers Hapgood: Profile of a Hoosier Radical." Master's thesis, Butler University, 1964.

Beik, Mildred Allen. *The Miners of Windber: The Struggles of New Immigrants for Unionization, 1890s–1930s*. University Park: The Pennsylvania State University Press, 1996.

Bell, Daniel. *The End of Ideology: On the Exhaustion of Political Ideas in the Fifties,* rev. ed. New York: Free Press, 1962.

———. "Marxian Socialism in the United States." In *Socialism and American Life,* vol. 1., ed. Donald Drew Egbert and Stow Persons. Princeton: Princeton University Press, 1967.

Bell, Thomas. *Out of This Furnace.* 1941. Reprint, Pittsburgh: University of Pittsburgh Press, 1991.

Bernstein, Irving. *The Lean Years: A History of the American Worker, 1920– 1933.* Baltimore: Penguin Books, 1966.

———. *Turbulent Years: A History of the American Worker, 1933–1941.* Boston: Houghton Mifflin, 1970.

Blake, I. George. *Paul V. McNutt: Portrait of a Hoosier Statesman.* Indianapolis: Central Publishing, 1966.

Blankenhorn, Heber. "Liberty and Union in the Coal Fields." *The Nation* 114, no. 2467 (May 17, 1922): 594–96.

———. *The Strike for Union.* 1924. Reprint, New York: Arno Press, 1969.

Blatz, Perry K. *Democratic Miners: Work and Labor Relations in the Anthracite Coal Industry, 1875–1925.* Albany: State University of New York Press, 1994.

Blewett, Mary H. *We Will Rise in Our Might: Workingwomen's Voices from Nineteenth-Century New England.* Ithaca: Cornell University Press, 1991.

Boothe, Stephane E. "Ladies in White: Female Activism in the Southern Illinois Coalfields." In *The United Mine Workers of America: A Model of Industrial Solidarity?* ed. John H. M. Laslett. University Park: The Pennsylvania State University Press, 1996.

Bracker, Milton. "Maine Strikers Defy Bayonets." *New York Times,* April 23, 1937.

Brault, Gerard J. *The French-Canadian Heritage in New England.* Hanover: University Press of New England, 1988.

Brinkley, Alan. *The End of Reform: New Deal Liberalism in Recession and War.* New York: Alfred A. Knopf, 1995.

———. *Voices of Protest: Huey Long, Father Coughlin, and the Great Depression.* New York: Vintage Books, 1982.

Brody, David. *In Labor's Cause: Main Themes on the History of the American Worker.* New York: Oxford University Press, 1993.

———. *Workers in Industrial America: Essays on the Twentieth Century Struggle.* New York: Oxford University Press, 1980.

Brophy, John. "Elements of a Progressive Union Policy." In *American Labor Dynamics,* ed. J. B. S. Hardman. New York: Harcourt, Brace, 1928.

———. *A Miner's Life.* Madison: University of Wisconsin Press, 1964.

Bussel, Robert. "'Business Without a Boss': The Columbia Conserve Company and Workers' Control, 1917–1943." *Business History Review* 71, no. 3 (autumn 1997): 417–43.

———. "'A Love of Unionism and Democracy': Rose Pesotta, Powers Hapgood, and the Industrial Union Movement, 1933–1949." *Labor History* 38, nos. 2–3 (spring/summer 1997): 203–29.

Cadou, Jep, Jr. "State CIO Heads Purged." *Indianapolis Star,* March 22, 1948.

Cantor, Milton. *The Divided Left: American Radicalism, 1900–1975.* New York: Hill and Wang, 1978.

Carew, Beatrice. "From a Miner's Wife." *New Republic* 30, no. 388 (May 10, 1922): 305–7.

Carey, Lorin Lee. "Adolph Germer: From Labor Agitator to Labor Professional." Ph.D. diss., University of Wisconsin, 1968.

———. "Institutionalized Conservatism in the Early CIO: Adolph Germer, A Case Study." *Labor History* 13, no. 4 (fall 1972): 475–504.

Chambers, Clarke A. *Seedtime of Reform: American Social Service and Social Action, 1918–1933.* Ann Arbor: University of Michigan Press, 1967.

Charney, George. *A Long Journey.* Chicago: Quadrangle Books, 1968.

Cochran, Bert. *Labor and Communism: The Conflict That Shaped American Unions.* Princeton: Princeton University Press, 1977.

Cohen, Lizabeth. *Making a New Deal: Industrial Workers in Chicago, 1919–1939.* Cambridge: Cambridge University Press, 1990.

Coleman, McAlister. *Men and Coal.* New York: Farrar and Rinehart, 1943.

Commons, John R. "American Shoemakers, 1648–1895: A Sketch of Industrial Evolution." *Quarterly Journal of Economics* 24 (November 1909): 39–84.

Condon, Richard H. "Bayonets at the North Bridge: The Lewiston-Auburn Shoe Strike, 1937." *Maine Historical Society Quarterly,* fall 1981, 75–98.

Cooper, Eileen Mountjoy. "That Magnificent Fight for Unionism." *Pennsylvania Heritage* 17, no. 4 (fall 1991): 12–17.

Cross, Gary. "Redefining Workers' Control: Rationalization, Labor Time, and Union Politics in France, 1900–1928." In *Work, Community, and Power: The Experience of Labor in Europe and America, 1900–1925,* ed. James E. Cronin and Carmen Sirianni. Philadelphia: Temple University Press, 1983.

Cumbler, John T. *Working-Class Community in Industrial America: Work, Leisure, and Struggle in Two Industrial Cities, 1880–1930.* Westport, Conn.: Greenwood Press, 1979.

Curtis, Donald Whitehouse. "The Lewiston-Auburn Shoe Strike of 1937: A Case Study in the Social Control of Industrial Disputes." Bachelor's thesis, Bates College, 1939.

Davis, Colin J. *Power at Odds: The 1922 Railroad Shopmen's Strike.* Urbana: University of Illinois Press, 1997.

DeCaux, Len. *Labor Radical, From the Wobblies to the CIO, A Personal History.* Boston: Beacon Press, 1970.

Derber, Milton. *The Idea of Industrial Democracy in America, 1865–1965.* Urbana: University of Illinois Press, 1970.

Derickson, Alan. *Workers' Health, Workers' Democracy: The Western Miners' Struggle, 1891–1925.* Ithaca: Cornell University Press, 1988.

Diggins, John P. *The American Left in the Twentieth Century.* New York: Harcourt Brace Jovanovich, 1973.

———. *The Rise and Fall of the American Left.* New York: W. W. Norton, 1992.

———. *Up from Communism: Conservative Odysseys in American Intellectual History.* New York: Harper and Row, 1975.

Draper, Theodore. *American Communism and Soviet Russia*. New York: Vintage Books, 1986.

Dubofsky, Melvyn. "'Not-so Turbulent Years': A New Look at the American 1930s." In *Life and Labor: Dimensions of American Working-Class History*, ed. Charles Stephenson and Robert Asher. Albany: State University of New York Press, 1986.

—— —. *The State and Labor in Modern America*. Chapel Hill: University of North Carolina Press, 1994.

Dubofsky, Melvyn, and Warren Van Tine. *John L. Lewis: A Biography*. New York: Quadrangle/New York Times, 1979.

Dye, Nancy Schrom. *As Equals and Sisters: Feminism, the Labor Movement, and the Women's Trade Union League of New York*. Columbia: University of Missouri Press, 1980.

Edsforth, Ronald. *Class Conflict and Cultural Consensus: The Making of a Mass Consumer Society in Flint, Michigan*. New Brunswick: Rutgers University Press, 1987.

Edwards, Richard C. *Contested Terrain: The Transformation of the Workplace in the Twentieth Century*. New York: Basic Books, 1979.

Fagge, Roger. *Power, Culture, and Conflict in the Coalfields: West Virginia and South Wales, 1900–1922*. Manchester: Manchester University Press, 1996.

Faue, Elizabeth. *Community of Suffering and Struggle: Women, Men, and the Labor Movement in Minneapolis, 1915–1945*. Chapel Hill: University of North Carolina Press, 1991.

Feuerlicht, Roberta Strauss. *Justice Crucified: The Story of Sacco and Vanzetti*. New York: McGraw-Hill, 1977.

Filene, Peter. *Him / Her / Self: Sex Roles in Modern America*. Baltimore: Johns Hopkins University Press, 1986.

Filipelli, Ronald L. and Mark McColloch. *Cold War in the Working Class: The Rise and Decline of the United Electrical Workers*. Albany: State University of New York Press, 1995.

Filler, Louis. *Vanguards and Followers: Youth in the American Tradition*. Chicago: Nelson-Hall, 1978.

Fine, Sidney. *Sit-down: The General Motors Strike of 1936–37*. Ann Arbor: University of Michigan Press, 1970.

Fishbein, Leslie. *Rebels in Bohemia: The Radicals of the Masses, 1911–1917*. Chapel Hill: University of North Carolina Press, 1982.

Fishburn, Janet. *The Fatherhood of God and the Victorian Family: The Social Gospel in America*. Philadelphia: Fortress Press, 1981.

Forgacs, David, ed. *An Antonio Gramsci Reader: Selected Writings, 1916–1935*. New York: Schocken Books, 1988.

Fox, Alan. *History and Heritage: The Social Origins of the British Industrial Relations System*. London: G. Allen and Unwin, 1985.

Francis, Hywel, and David Smith. *The Fed: A History of the South Wales Miners in the Twentieth Century*. London: Lawrence and Wishart, 1980.

Fraser, Steve. *Labor Will Rule: Sidney Hillman and the Rise of American Labor*. New York: Free Press, 1991.

Fraser, Steve, and Joshua B. Freeman, eds. *Audacious Democracy: Labor,*

Intellectuals, and the Social Reconstruction of America. Boston: Mariner Books, 1997.

Fraser, Steve, and Gary Gerstle, eds. *The Rise and Fall of the New Deal Order, 1930–1980.* Princeton: Princeton University Press, 1989.

Freeman, Joseph. *An American Testament: A Narrative of Rebels and Romantics.* London: Victor Gollancz, 1938.

Gerstle, Gary. *Working-Class Americanism: The Politics of Labor in a Textile City, 1914–1960.* Cambridge: Cambridge University Press, 1989.

Giguere, Madeleine. "To Make a Living: Franco-American Work Traditions in Lewiston and Auburn." Booklet accompanying exhibition of "The Franco-American Work Experience," Lewiston-Auburn College, University of Southern Maine, 1994.

Gillam, Richard Davis. "C. Wright Mills: An Intellectual Biography." Ph.D. diss., Stanford University, 1972.

Gitlin, Todd. *The Sixties: Years of Hope, Days of Rage.* New York: Bantam Books, 1987.

Gitlow, Benjamin. *I Confess: The Truth About American Communism.* Freeport, 1939.

Gross, James A. *The Making of the National Labor Relations Board: A Study in Economics, Politics, and the Law,* vol. 1 (1933–37). Albany: State University of New York Press, 1974.

Gurley, Boyd. "Business Without a Boss." *Indianapolis Times,* February 13, 1930.

———. "What Is Success?" *Indianapolis Times,* December 19, 1932.

Gutman, Herbert G. *Work, Culture, and Society in Industrializing America.* New York: Vintage Books, 1977.

Hapgood, Hutchins. *The Spirit of the Ghetto.* Cambridge: Harvard University Press, 1967.

———. *The Spirit of Labor.* New York: Duffield, 1907.

———. *A Victorian in the Modern World.* Seattle: University of Washington Press, 1972.

Hapgood, Norman. *The Changing Years.* New York: Farrar and Rinehart, 1930.

Hapgood, Powers. "Car Pushing in the Mines." *Survey* 46, no. 10 (June 4, 1921): 310–11.

———. "The Coal Strikes Continues." *New Republic* 32, no. 409 (October 4, 1922): 147.

———. "From College to the Ranks of Labor." *The World Tomorrow* 6, no. 2 (February 1923).

———. "Gangsterism Rules the Mines." *New Masses* 2, no. 5 (March 1927): 19–20.

———."Greenwich Number Three." *Locomotive Engineers Journal* 58 (March 1924): 173–75, 230.

———. "In a Boston Insane Asylum." *The Nation* 125, no. 324 (September 7, 1927): 226–27.

———. "In Non-Union Mines: The Diary of a Coal Digger." New York: Bureau of Industrial Research, 1922.

— — —. "Kidnapping in Council Bluffs." *The Nation* 133, no. 3467 (December 16, 1931): 669–70.

— — —. "On Being a Manual Worker (An Appeal to Young Progressives)." *New Student* 12, no. 17 (May 19, 1923): 5.

— — —. "Paternalism vs. Unionism in the Mining Camps." *The Nation* 112, no. 2913 (May 4, 1921): 661–62.

— — —. "The Socialist Party and the Labor Movement." *American Socialist Quarterly* 2, no. 3 (summer 1933).

Hapgood, Powers, and Mary Donovan. "Murdered Miners." *The Nation* 126, no. 3271 (March 14, 1928): 293–94.

Hapgood, William P. *The Columbia Conserve Company: An Experiment in Workers' Ownership and Management.* Philadelphia: Porcupine Press, 1975.

— — —. "The High Adventures of a Cannery." *Survey* 48, no. 5 (September 1, 1922): 655–58, 682.

Harris, Howell John. "The Snares of Liberalism: Politicians, Bureaucrats, and the Shaping of Federal Labour Policy in the United States, ca. 1935–1947." In *Shop Floor Bargaining and the State: Historical and Comparative Perspectives*, ed. Steven Tolliday and Jonathan Zeitlin. Cambridge: Cambridge University Press, 1985.

Hofstadter, Richard. *The Age of Reform.* New York: Vintage Books, 1955.

— — —. *The American Political Tradition.* New York: Vintage Books, 1973.

— — —. *Anti-Intellectualism in American Life.* New York: Vintage Books, 1962.

Horowitz, Daniel. *The Morality of Spending: Attitudes Towards the Consumer Society in America.* Baltimore: Johns Hopkins University Press, 1985.

Howe, Irving. *A Margin of Hope: An Intellectual Biography.* New York: Harcourt Brace Jovanovich, 1982.

— — —. *Socialism and America.* New York: Harcourt Brace Jovanovich, 1985.

Irons, Janet. "The Challenge of National Coordination: Southern Textile Workers and the General Strike of 1934." In *"We Are All Leaders": The Alternative Unionism of the Early 1930s*, ed. Staughton Lynd. Urbana: University of Illinois Press, 1996.

Jacoby, Sanford. *Employing Bureaucracy: Managers, Unions, and the Transformation of Work in American Industry, 1900–1945.* New York: Columbia University Press, 1985.

James, Richard. "The Committee for Industrial Organization's Effort to Organize the Shoe Shops of Lewiston and Auburn, Maine." Bachelor's thesis, Bates College, 1970.

Johanningsmeier, Edward P. *Forging American Communism: The Life of William Z. Foster.* Princeton: Princeton University Press, 1994.

Johnpoll, Bernard K. *The Impossible Dream: The Rise and Demise of the American Left.* Westport, Conn.: Greenwood Press, 1981.

— — —. *Pacifist's Progress: Norman Thomas and the Decline of American Socialism.* Westport, Conn.: Greenwood Press, 1987.

Kammen, Michael G. *Mystic Chords of Memory: The Transformation of American Culture.* New York: Alfred A. Knopf, 1991.

Karsh, Bernard L., and Philips L. Gorman. "The Impact of the Political Left." In

Labor and the New Deal, ed. Milton Derber and Edwin Young. Madison: University of Wisconsin Press, 1957.

Kennedy, David M. *Over Here: The First World War and American Society.* Oxford: Oxford University Press, 1980.

Klehr, Harvey. *The Heyday of American Communism: The Depression Decade.* New York: Basic Books, 1984.

Klein, Gertrude Weil. "Well, the Debate Was Held and Here's How." *New Leader,* December 22, 1934.

Kornbluh, Joyce L., ed. *Rebel Voices: An IWW Anthology.* Ann Arbor: University of Michigan Press, 1964.

Kraus, Henry. *Heroes of Unwritten Story: The UAW, 1934–1939.* Urbana: University of Illinois Press, 1993.

Lamson, Peggy. *Roger Baldwin: Founder of the American Civil Liberties Union.* Boston: Houghton Mifflin, 1976.

Lasch, Christopher. *The New Radicalism in America, 1889–1963: The Intellectual as a Social Type.* New York: Vintage Books, 1965.

———. *The True and Only Heaven: Progress and Its Critics.* New York: W. W. Norton and Company, 1991.

Lears, T. J. Jackson. *No Place of Grace: Anti-Modernism and the Transformation of American Culture, 1880–1920.* New York: Pantheon Books, 1981.

Leary, Edward A. *Indianapolis: The Story of a City.* Indianapolis: Bobbs-Merrill, 1971.

Leeder, Elaine. *The Gentle General: Rose Pesotta, Anarchist and Labor Organizer.* Albany: State University of New York Press, 1993.

Leuchtenburg, William E. *The Perils of Prosperity, 1914–1932.* Chicago: University of Chicago Press, 1958.

Levenstein, Harvey A. *Communism, Anti-Communism, and the CIO.* Westport, Conn.: Greenwood Press, 1981.

Levine, Lawrence W. "Progress and Nostalgia: The Self-Image of the Nineteen Twenties." In *The American Novel in the Twentieth Century,* ed. Malcolm Bradbury and David Palmer. London: 1971.

Levinson, Edward. *Labor on the March.* New York: Harper and Brothers, 1938.

Levinson, Mark, and Brian Morton. "The CIO, John Lewis, and the Left: An Interview with Philip Van Gelder." *Dissent* 32, no. 4 (fall 1985): 460–63.

Lichtenstein, Nelson. *Labor's War at Home: The CIO in World War II.* Cambridge: Cambridge University Press, 1982.

———. *The Most Dangerous Man in Detroit: Walter Reuther and the Fate of American Labor.* New York: Basic Books, 1995.

Lutz, Tom. *American Nervousness, 1903: An Anecdotal History.* Ithaca: Cornell University Press, 1991.

Lynd, Staughton, ed. *"We Are All Leaders": The Alternative Unionism of the Early 1930s.* Urbana: University of Illinois Press, 1996.

Madison, James H. *The Indiana Way.* Bloomington: Indiana University Press, 1986.

Magraw, Roger. *A History of the French Working Class,* vol. 2. Oxford: Blackwell, 1992.

Maier, Joseph, and Richard W. Weatherhead. *Frank Tannenbaum: A Bio-*

graphical Essay. New York: University Seminars, Columbia University, 1974.

Marcaccio, Michael. *The Hapgoods: Three Earnest Brothers*. Charlottesville: University of Virginia Press, 1971.

Martin, John Bartlow. *Indiana: An Interpretation*. Bloomington: Indiana University Press, 1992.

Mason, Lucy Randolph. *To Win These Rights: A Personal Story of the CIO in the South*. New York: Harper, 1952.

May, Henry. *The End of American Innocence*. New York: Alfred A. Knopf, 1959.

McCartin, Joseph A. "'An American Feeling': Workers, Managers, and the Struggle over Industrial Democracy in World War I." In *Industrial Democracy in America: The Ambiguous Promise*, ed. Nelson Lichtenstein and Howell John Harris. Cambridge: Cambridge University Press, 1993.

McKenney, Ruth. *Industrial Valley*. Ithaca: ILR Press, 1992.

McQuaid, Kim. "Industry and the Cooperative Commonwealth: William P. Hapgood and the Columbia Conserve Company." *Labor History* 17, no. 4 (fall 1976): 510–29.

McWilliams, Wilson Carey. *The Idea of Fraternity in America*. Berkeley: University of California Press, 1973.

Meacham, Standish. *A Life Apart: The English Working Class, 1890–1914*. Cambridge: Harvard University Press, 1977.

Meier, August, and Elliott Rudwick. *Black Detroit and the Rise of the UAW*. Oxford: Oxford University Press, 1979.

Mergen, Bernard. "A History of the Industrial Union of Marine and Shipbuilding Workers of America, 1933–1951." Ph.D. diss., University of Pennsylvania, 1968.

Meyer, Donald. *The Protestant Search for Political Realism, 1919–1941*, 2d ed. Middletown, Conn.: Wesleyan University Press, 1988.

Meyerhuber, Carl. *Less Than Forever: The Rise and Decline of Union Solidarity in Western Pennsylvania, 1914–1948*. Selinsgrove: Susquehanna Press, 1987.

Mills, C. Wright. *The New Men of Power: America's Labor Leaders*. New York: A. M. Kelley, 1948.

Mink, Gwendolyn. *Old Labor and New Immigrants in American Political Development: Union, Party, and State, 1875–1920*. Ithaca: Cornell University Press, 1986.

Mitchell, H. L. *Mean Things Happening in This Land*. Montclair: Allanhold, Osmun, 1979.

Montgomery, David. *The Fall of the House of Labor: The Workplace, the State, and American Labor Activism: 1865–1925*. Cambridge: Cambridge University Press, 1987.

Moore, R. Laurence. *Religious Outsiders and the Making of Americans*. New York: Oxford University Press, 1986.

Morawska, Ewa. "'For Bread with Butter': Life Worlds of Peasant Immigrants from East Central Europe." *Journal of Social History* 117, no. 3 (spring 1984): 387–404.

Mortimer, Wyndham. *Organize! My Life as a Union Man*. Boston: Beacon Press, 1971.

Nelson, Daniel. *American Rubber Workers and Organized Labor, 1900–1941*. Princeton: Princeton University Press, 1988.

———. *From Farm to Factory: Workers in the Midwest, 1880–1990*. Bloomington, Indiana University Press, 1995.

Nelson, Steve, James R. Barrett, and Rob Ruck. *Steve Nelson: American Radical*. Pittsburgh: University of Pittsburgh Press, 1981.

Oblinger, Carl D. *Divided Kingdom: Work, Community, and the Mining Wars in the Central Illinois Coal Fields During the Great Depression*. Springfield: Illinois State Historical Society, 1991.

O'Donnell, L. A. *Irish Voice and Organized Labor in America: A Biographical Study*. Westport, Conn.: Greenwood Press, 1997.

Palmer, David. "Organizing the Shipyards: Unionization at New York Ship, Federal Ship, and Fore River, 1898–1945." Ph.D. diss., Brandeis University, 1989.

Parker, Carleton H. *The Casual Laborer and Other Essays*. Seattle: University of Washington Press, 1982.

Parker, Cornelia Stratton. *An American Idyll: The Life of Carleton H. Parker*. Boston: Little, Brown, 1919.

Pesotta, Rose. *Bread upon the Waters*. Ithaca: ILR Press, 1987.

Phillips, Clifton J. *Indiana in Transition*. Bloomington: Indiana University Press, 1968.

Polenberg, Richard. *War and Society: The United States, 1941–1945*. Philadelphia: Lippincott, 1972.

"Questions for Coal Barons." *New Republic* 31, no. 340 (May 24, 1922): 360–61.

Ricketts, Elizabeth Cocke. "'Our Battle for Industrial Freedom': Radical Politics in the Coal Fields of Central Pennsylvania, 1916–1920." Ph.D. diss., Emory University, 1996.

Robinson, Jo Ann. *Abraham Went Out, A Biography of A. J. Muste*. Philadelphia: Temple University Press, 1981.

Rodgers, Daniel T. *The Work Ethic in Industrial America, 1850–1920*. Chicago: University of Chicago Press, 1978.

Rosenzweig, Roy. *Eight Hours for What We Will: Workers and Leisure in an Industrial City, 1870–1920*. Cambridge: Cambridge University Press, 1983.

Rotundo, E. Anthony. *American Manhood: Transformations in Masculinity from the Revolution to the Modern Era*. New York: Basic Books, 1993.

Saltmarsh, John A. *Scott Nearing: An Intellectual Biography*. Philadelphia: Temple University Press, 1991.

Salvatore, Nick. *Eugene V. Debs: Citizen and Socialist*. Urbana: University of Illinois Press, 1982.

Salvatore, Nick, ed. *Seventy Years of Life and Labor: An Autobiography of Samuel Gompers*. Ithaca: ILR Press, 1984.

Saxton, Alexander. *The Indispensable Enemy: Labor and the Anti-Chinese Movement in California*. Berkeley: University of California Press, 1971.

Scales, Junius, and Richard Nickson. *Cause at Heart: A Former Communist Remembers.* Athens: University of Georgia Press, 1987.

Schatz, Ronald W. *The Electrical Workers: A History of Labor at General Electric and Westinghouse, 1923–1960.* Urbana: University of Illinois Press, 1983.

Schofield, Ann. *"to do and to be": Portraits of Four Women Activists, 1893–1986.* Boston: Northeastern University Press, 1997.

Shepard, Joseph K. "Communism Issue Upsets CIO Parley." *Indianapolis Star,* August 24, 1947.

Singer, Alan J. "Class-Conscious Coal Miners: Nanty Glo Versus the Open Shop in the Post World War I Era." *Labor History* 29, no. 1 (winter 1988): 56–65.

———. "Communists and Coal Miners: Rank-and-File Organizing in the UMWA During the 1920s." *Science and Society* 55, no. 2 (summer 1991): 132–57.

———. "John Brophy's 'Miners' Program': Workers' Education in UMWA District 2 During the 1920s." *Labor Studies Journal* 13, no. 4, (winter 1988): 50–64.

———. " 'Something of a Man': John L. Lewis, the UMWA, and the CIO, 1919–1943." In *The United Mine Workers of America: A Model of Industrial Solidarity?* ed. John H. M. Laslett. University Park: The Pennsylvania State University Press, 1996.

Smillie, Robert. *My Life for Labour.* London: Mills and Boon, 1924.

Smith, Bruce James. *Politics and Remembrance: Republican Themes in Machiavelli, Burke, and Tocqueville.* Princeton: Princeton University Press, 1985.

Smith, Timothy L. *Revivalism and Social Reform: American Protestantism on the Eve of the Civil War.* Gloucester, Mass.: Harper Torchbooks, 1976.

Sorenson, Dale R. "The Anti-Communist Consensus in Indiana, 1945–1958." Ph.D. diss., Indiana University, 1980.

Stark, Louis. "The Crisis in the Labor Movement." *New Republic* 86, no. 1112 (March 25, 1936): 187–89.

Stolberg, Benjamin. "Inside the CIO." *New York World Telegram,* January 20, 1938.

———. *The Story of the CIO.* New York: Viking Press, 1938.

Susman, Warren I. *Culture as History: The Transformation of American Society in the Twentieth Century.* New York: Pantheon Books, 1984.

Swados, Harvey. "The Miners: Men Without Work." *Dissent* 6, no. 4 (autumn, 1959): 389–401.

Thomas, John L. *Alternative America: Henry George, Edward Bellamy, Henry Demarest Lloyd and the Adversary Tradition.* Cambridge: Harvard University Press, 1983.

Tomlins, Christopher L. *The State and the Unions: Labor Relations, Law and the Organized Labor Movement in America, 1880–1960.* Cambridge: Cambridge University Press, 1985.

Valetta, Clement. " 'To Battle for Our Ideas': Community Ethic and Anthracite Labor, 1920–1940." *Pennsylvania History* 58, no. 4 (October 1991): 311–29.

Vance, Russell E., Jr. "An Unsuccessful Experiment in Workers Management and Ownership: The Columbia Conserve Company." Ph.D. diss., Indiana University, 1956.

Van Kleeck, Mary. *Miners and Management.* New York: Russell Sage Foundation, 1934.

Van Tine, Warren R. *The Making of the Labor Bureaucrat: Labor Leadership in the United States, 1870–1920.* Amherst: University of Massachusetts Press, 1973.

Vonnegut, Kurt. *Jailbird.* New York: Dell, 1979.

Walzer, Michael. *The Company of Critics: Social Criticism and Political Commitment in the Twentieth Century.* New York: Basic Books, 1988.

Warren, Frank A. *An Alternative Vision: The Socialist Party in the 1930s.* Bloomington: Indiana University Press, 1974.

Wieck, David Thoreau. *Woman from Spillertown: A Memoir of Agnes Burns Wieck.* Carbondale: University of Southern Illinois Press, 1992.

Williams, Whiting. *What's on the Worker's Mind.* New York: Scribner's Sons, 1920.

Zahavi, Gerald. *The Shoeworkers and Tanners of Endicott-Johnson, 1890–1950.* Urbana: University of Illinois Press, 1988.

Zieger, Robert H. *American Workers, American Unions, 1920–1985.* Baltimore: John Hopkins University Press, 1986.

———. *The CIO: 1935–1955.* Chapel Hill: University of North Carolina Press, 1995.

———. *John L. Lewis: Labor Leader.* Boston: Twayne, 1988.

Oral Histories

Jack Battuello Memoir. Oral History Office, University of Illinois at Springfield. 1982.

The Reminiscences of John Brophy. Oral History Collection, Columbia University, New York. 1972.

The Reminiscences of Gardner Jackson. Oral History Collection, Columbia University, New York. 1955.

Roy Reuther sit-down interview. Archives of Labor and Urban Affairs, Walter P. Reuther Library, Wayne State University, Detroit, Michigan. February 2, 1966.

Dallas W. Sells interview. Indiana Oral History Project, Indiana University, Bloomington. 1979.

Index